THE CANTERBURY TALES
A Reading

An Approach to Shakespeare
Shakespeare: From Richard II to Henry V
Shakespeare: The Last Phase
Shakespeare: The Roman Plays
T. S. Eliot: The Longer Poems

THE CANTERBURY TALES

A Reading

DEREK TRAVERSI

'. . . we been pilgrymes, passynge to and fro . . .'
The Knight's Tale, 1. 2848

THE BODLEY HEAD
LONDON   SYDNEY
TORONTO

British Library Cataloguing
in Publication Data
Traversi, Derek
The Canterbury tales.
1. Chaucer, Geoffrey. Canterbury Tales
I. Title
821'.1   PR1874

ISBN 0-370-30546-9
0-370-30547-7 paperback

© Derek Traversi 1983
Printed in Great Britain for
The Bodley Head Ltd
9 Bow Street, London WC2E 7AL
by Redwood Burn Ltd, Trowbridge
Typeset by Wyvern Typesetting Ltd, Bristol
*First published as a paperback and
simultaneously as a hard-cover edition 1983*

CONTENTS

AUTHOR'S NOTE

The author of one more book on a work as frequented as *The Canterbury Tales* will do well to begin by stating the nature and the limits of his enterprise. The study which follows is not the work of a professional 'medievalist'. It makes no claim to be a contribution to Chaucer 'scholarship' in the strictest sense of the term, although its author hopes to have shown a proper appreciation for what has been so impressively achieved in the field and to have assimilated as much of it as one man can reasonably be expected to cover without overwhelming the possibility of his own response to the poem. What is offered is an exercise in literary criticism. It is addressed primarily to the interested but non-specialist reader who is willing to consider the proposition that Chaucer's work is the product of a humane and highly civilized intelligence; and that it constitutes, together with Dante's *Commedia*, the greatest literary achievement of the Middle Ages and one of the highest expressions of the English genius in any age.

A growing acquaintance with the *Tales* leads to the conclusion that none of its parts, including those which are often dismissed as arid or artistically inferior, is without meaning for our sense of the whole. The length of an acceptable book makes it impossible to cover the ground in its completeness, and I have chosen to build my argument round the tales and episodes which seem to serve as focal points gathering round themselves the constantly shifting and developing concerns which animate the entire work.

The resulting study falls into three parts. The first covers the continuous opening fragment, from the General Prologue to the abortive intervention of the Cook. It traces the process by which the design inspired by the conception of human life as a 'pilgrimage' is at once diversified and, in the process, subjected to increasing strains which threaten to qualify, if not to subvert, the values of ordered chivalry so impressively advanced by the Knight in his tale. The second part, covering the so-called 'marriage group' of tales, is built round the more than life-size intervention of the Wife of Bath. It raises the question of marriage and of the part played by the urge to 'maistrie', or domination, in the relationship between the sexes. It prompts a series of tales offering partial reflections of a central human problem which is increasingly seen to qualify the efforts at 'final' solutions offered by human partiality. A third series of tales, initiated by the uniquely challenging contribution of the Pardoner, introduces disquieting aspects of human nature. In the process, it challenges both the moral assumptions which are assumed to govern 'right-thinking' society and the validity of 'tale-telling' in its claim to reflect a 'truth' which, if it exists – as a deeply rooted instinct prompts men and women to believe – appears to be inevitably outside the limits of human experience. Finally, in the tale told by the Nun's Priest, the comic spirit triumphs in the act of accepting the necessary relativity of all human insights, and produces an invention which may be as close to the poet's own elusive standpoint as any of the tales offers.

The exposition developed in support of the plan thus outlined is in certain respects incomplete. Two episodes in particular – those connected with *The Franklin's Tale* and *The Manciple's Tale* – which have been omitted to comply with limitations of space, offer insights essential to the argument. I have included studies of both in my collection of essays on *The Literary Imagination*, published by the University of Delaware Press in 1982, and hope that these can be considered as forming an inseparable part of my thesis. Consideration of the remaining episodes, and more particularly of the tales told by the Friar and the Summoner, *The Man of Law's Tale*, and the easily neglected 'tales' in prose, would no doubt have contributed to a fuller understanding of Chaucer's conception in its breadth and complexity. Practical considerations have dictated their exclusion, but I hope that enough is said in the course of the argument to give some indication of the part played by them in the whole.

Quotations from Chaucer's work follow F. N. Robinson's text, *The Works of Geoffrey Chaucer*, available in paperback from Oxford University Press, and published in the United States by Houghton Mifflin Company, Second Edition (Boston, 1957).

DEREK TRAVERSI

I
THE
ORDER OF
PILGRIMAGE

I

THE
'FRAME' OF THE TALES

Critical readings of Chaucer's *Canterbury Tales* have generally envisaged one of two possibilities. One view represents the work as a collection of essentially separate tales, designed to entertain and loosely held together in the framework provided by an ongoing journey. The alternative reading centres on the conception of 'pilgrimage' as an image for man's journey in time, and sees the tales as contributing, each in its own way, to a firmly conceived and dominating plan. Each view has its defenders, who can point to elements in the text which support their contention; and each tends, in advancing its thesis, to do less than justice to the creative ambivalence which emerges from a balanced reading of Chaucer's text.

The declared subject of the *Tales* is a pilgrimage to the shrine of St. Thomas Becket at Canterbury: a pilgrimage set at a definite moment in time and in which the poet is said to have participated. The account of the journey is *framed* by an introduction and a conclusion, the twin pillars, as it were, within which the unfolding fresco of the action is contained. Chaucer did not complete his design, and it would be rash to impose upon it any unduly restrictive unity; but the 'pillars' were evidently intended to remain constant and to mark the limits within which the free, open plan operated.

The opening 'pillar' – which, so to speak, limits the composition on what is, from the point of view of the observer of a continuing action depicted in a fresco painting, the 'left' – is the passage of eighteen lines which introduces the General Prologue:

> Whan that Aprill with his shoures soote
> The droghte of March hath perced to the roote,
> And bathed every veyne in swich licour
> Of which vertu engendred is the flour;
> Whan Zephirus eek with his sweete breeth

Inspired hath in every holt and heeth
The tendre croppes, and the yonge sonne
Hath in the Ram his halve cours yronne,
And smale foweles maken melodye,
That slepen al the nyght with open ye
(So priketh hem nature in hir corages);
Thanne longen folk to goon on pilgrimages,
And palmeres for to seken straunge strondes,
To ferne halwes, kowthe in sondry londes;
And specially from every shires ende
Of Engelond to Caunterbury they wende,
The hooly blisful martir for to seke,
That hem hath holpen whan that they were seeke.

(I. 1–18)

It will be helpful, in considering this familiar passage, to begin by observing that the lines are by no means the naïve, artless expression that they are sometimes assumed to be. The fact that the speaking or reciting voice moves with deceptive ease across the constraining limits of the couplets, that the rhymes point the essential meanings without in any way stressing the skill that has gone to their disposition, is not a sign of naïvety, but of the poet's consummate, if deliberately unemphatic art. The passage is steeped in literary and rhetorical convention. Numerous parallels for some of the chief ideas and images have been suggested from both classical and medieval sources,[1] and it is likely that some at least were in the poet's mind as he wrote. More importantly, the passage can be shown to be an elaborate construction based on rhetorical principles familiar to Chaucer's age. It is divided into two clearly distinguished sections at the beginning of the twelfth line. The structure is intended to establish a relationship of cause and effect, to assert that *when* certain natural phenomena are to be observed ('Whan that Aprill . . .'), *then* certain consequences – or concurrent features – in the human order are to be expected: 'Thanne longen folk to goon on pilgrimages'.

Expanding this general statement, the first part of the 'paragraph' is built up in the form of an accumulation of particular instances: 'Whan . . . and . . . whan . . . and . . . and' – which tends to expand progressively to take in a widening range of illustrating phenomena. After the first two rhyming couplets (those beginning respectively 'Whan that Aprill' and 'bathed every veyne') have given a self-contained instance of the renewed life of the spring season, the third ('Whan Zephirus eek . . .') expands to carry over beyond the containing rhyme into the first half ('The tendre croppes . . .') of the line which follows. This correspondingly reduces the next instance (that of 'the yonge sonne') to a line and a half, and paves the way for the last three verses, which are broken into a single-line statement – 'And smale foweles maken melodye' – to which is added a qualification ('That slepen . . .') and a parenthesis ('So priketh hem . . .') that serves to bind the examples given to the living processes of nature and so to bring this first period to a conclusion that underlines the prevailing intention.

The second part, in the process of developing a sense of the universal normative urge of *all* men to follow the specific and 'natural' impulse to become 'pilgrims', concentrates attention on *one*, particular manifestation of this instinct: that which is typical of *England* and which leads those who dwell in every part of that country – 'every shires ende' – to seek the goal of *their* journey in the shrine of the saint at Canterbury. Once again the poet makes effective use of the rhyming scheme to underline his meanings. The emphasis in this second part of the introductory unit, beginning at 'Thanne', falls on the second rhyme of its couplet in such a way as to lay stress on the governing conception of 'pilgrimage'. After examples illustrating this conception ('And palmeres . . .') attention is focussed on a particular country – 'Engelond' – and a specific place, 'Caunterbury': a place which is to be the end of the common journey, and where – as the last couplet tells us – the travellers are to come into the presence of the 'hooly blisful martir' to be healed of their infirmity.

The deeper sense of the passage in relation to the design of the *Tales* rests firmly on this logical structure. The initial key to an understanding of it lies in the emphasis on the renewed life of spring. This is much more than a piece of sentimental nature worship. The imagery which dominates the passage answers to a sense of life reborn from the deadness, the 'draught', of winter, seeking outlet in a variety of natural fulfilments which affect man, beast, and bird as parts of a continuous order. The showers of April are 'sweet', and penetrate to the roots of the preceding deadness with a 'virtue', a vivifying power, that engenders the new manifestations of the flower. The breath of the wind from the South – the Zephyr, most literary of winds – is also 'sweet' and 'inspires' – breathes life into – the *tender* crops that spring up in the places (the 'holts' and 'heaths') that winter left barren. The sun, too, is 'young' as it follows its spring-time course, rousing the birds that sing in the morning hour after having slept through the night 'with open eye' in anticipation of their daily restoration to life: for they are so 'inspired' by 'nature' which stimulates ('priketh') them to the revival of their vital energies.

There is, however, more than this in the passage. Man, too, with whom the poet is more especially concerned, responds to the life around him. Among the impulses reborn in the new season is the urge, which answers to his specific nature, to engage in a quest, a *pilgrimage*: 'Thanne longen folk to goon on pilgrimages'. This impulse can be seen on various distinct, though not finally unrelated levels. There is the natural urge which impels 'palmers' to seek the adventure of new experiences in 'straunge strondes', moved by a *natural* impulse not dissimilar to that which inspires the birds through the 'pricking' of their instinctive 'corages': but there is also a more distinctively human desire to seek out the 'hooly blisful martir' that 'hem hath holpen' when they were, both physically and spiritually, 'sick'. Moved in the first instance by a *natural* impulse which unites him to the rest of the creation, it is *man*'s nature to be moved to complete this, more or less consciously, by reference to a distinctively *supernatural* end. The final effect is to join the two orders of *nature* and *grace* in a unity of vision that will lend to the entire enterprise its wealth of interdependent and contrasted meanings.

If this is the opening 'pillar' of the construction of Chaucer's poem, there corresponds to it another, not less germane to the complete conception, at the end. In this connection, we have to remember that there is evidence, contained in the poem, that Chaucer's project changed notably in the course of the writing, possibly under the pressure of old age and a sense of lack of time. The original *four* tales foreseen in the Prologue[2] were first reduced to two, and finally to one. The change of plan, which may have had purely contingent causes, may also answer to one of the most distinctive features of all Chaucer's work: the sense developed in it that the course of life is not easily confined within pre-established limits, that the best-laid plans for its seemly conduct are always liable to be broken into, interrupted, by the irrepressible force of instinctive self-assertion. The Host's failure to direct the project to its foreseen conclusion and his tendency to define it in different ways during the course of its unfolding may be not a sign of inconsistency on the author's part but an indication of the way in which he conceived it.

However this may be, it seems clear from the words spoken by the Host to introduce *The Parson's Tale* – 'Now lakketh us no tales mo than oon' (X. 16) – that this discourse, which is not a tale in the ordinary sense, but a long sermon on penitence, was intended to round off the whole work, or at least that part of it which actually exists and which is concerned, as it stands, with a *one-way* journey between Southwark and Canterbury.[3] The Host challenges the Parson in the rough terms that are habitual with him – 'Telle us a fable anon, for cokkes bones!' (X. 29) – and receives from him a refusal to join the others on this worldly level. The Parson does agree to tell what he calls, using what may seem to us a curious adjective[4] in view of what follows,

> a myrie tale in prose
> To knytte up al this feeste, and make an ende: (X. 46–7)

a 'tale' which is to show the way which will make of their common 'voyage' a *simulacrum*, a shadow of

> thilke parfit glorious pilgrymage
> That highte Jerusalem celestial.   (X. 50–1)

Like everything else in human life, according to the view which animates the project at this point, a work of 'literature' has *an end*, a purpose, which lies in the nature of things outside and beyond itself. In recognition of this reality, we are now asked to join the pilgrims in stepping outside 'literature', the incidental lightening of the journey, as they prepare themselves, through personal repentance and public confession, to participate in the social and religious act of reconciliation – the Eucharistic 'atonement'[5] which will bring them together in the 'figure' of a redeemed and justified society.

It is important that we should see exactly where we stand in this matter: because, otherwise, we run some risk of simplifying, or even falsifying the sense which the work actually conveys. There is significance in the fact that the *end* of the pilgrimage is not shown in correspondence to its *beginning*. We leave the pilgrims, not in Canterbury nor in the presence of the shrine which is the declared goal of the journey, but 'at a thropes ende' (X. 12), an indeterminate village from which, at most, it may be presumed that they have a first distant sight of the city and its cathedral before them. Still less is the Parson's admonition to penance followed by any act of reconciliation or communion. What we have been shown in the course of the pilgrimage is not the 'end', but the 'way' in all its human waywardness and indirection; and what we are given at the last is less a 'tale' or even a sermon – though the text suggests both, as it were, in passing – than a 'treatise' which seems to take us, as *readers*, out of the 'pilgrimage' and to stand in relation to it as 'truth' does to 'fiction', or sober prose 'doctrine' to imaginative 'creation'.

It should be noted, in this connection, that the Parson, in acceding on his own terms to the Host's request, rejects fiction in the name of 'truth', appealing in the process to the highest authority. 'Thou getest fable noon ytoold for me' (X. 31), he says brusquely enough; for

> Paul, that writeth unto Thymothee,
> Repreveth hem that weyven soothfastnesse,
> And tellen fables and swich wrecchednesse.
> Why sholde I sowen draf out of my fest,
> Whan I may sowen whete, if that me lest?   (X. 32–6)

In thus expressing himself, he is giving voice to a theme which has run for the most part submergedly but occasionally surfacing, through the entire series of tales:[6] that of the relation of fiction to 'truth', and of 'art' to 'morality'. The Host, as master of ceremonies in the order of tale-telling, has called upon the Parson to tell his tale under the sign of 'merriment', jovial conviviality, which has been almost obsessively his concern throughout. He has backed his request with one of those oaths which have been repeatedly in his mouth, and in those of not a few of his fellow-pilgrims. The Parson rejects the oath as blasphemous, and takes up the idea of a 'merry' tale in his own way, which is not devoid of irony: he will point the way to 'merriment', but of a kind which does not lie within the Host's contemplation. Beyond that, he will move the entire project out of the order of 'tale-telling' in a way which Chaucer, in his own 'retraction' at the end of the sermon seems finally to accept. Art has its limitation, is at best but an imperfect shadow of the truth which lies necessarily beyond it, *outside* the pilgrimage itself; but the 'pilgrimage' has been 'real' too, and the poet, having created it with such force and conviction, is likely to have felt that he could not reject it without experiencing the deep and disturbing tension involved.

In this respect the undoubted note of testiness in the Parson's reaction points to the intractability of the issues involved. It is significant that *The Canterbury Tales* contains *two* moral exhortations, the Pardoner's and the Parson's, and that the function of the former in his preaching can be seen as a kind of parody, an upside-down reflection of the other. The parody, moreover, carries with it implications for the realm of art. Whereas the Parson's devotion to 'truth' moves him to renounce fiction, and to produce a sermon which most of the pilgrims, like Chaucer himself, would recognize to be 'true', but which they can hardly have found 'merry' or entertaining,[7] the Pardoner – a self-confessed rogue who preaches for gain – is given a 'tale' – a sermon, indeed – which shows all the conviction of art and which carries a moral which, in one way or another, affects all his hearers.[8] Art, and morality, in other words, can serve the Pardoner's ends of *cupidity* and, in the process, appeal to us in ways that the Parson's *truthful* discourse, spoken by a man whose life answers to his teachings, cannot rival. Chaucer, in his final retraction, proposes to solve the problem by setting aside his art and by implicating his audience, as believing Christians, in the abdication; but, to get to this point, he has developed his art and followed its 'truths' to their logical conclusion in a way that leaves us less with a sense of resolution than one of creative tension. If there is Chaucer in the Parson, he has been disturbingly present in the Pardoner too; and to try to impose a one-sided resolution upon the issues raised in the course of the tales is to be less than true to the final humanity and inclusiveness of the conception.

The Parson's discourse, accordingly, is not quite the end of the project. The author is called upon at the last to step out of his creation and to accept his responsibility for what he has done and been in the course of a life dedicated to the creation of fictions, 'shadows' of what now imposes itself as reality. It is noteworthy that the Parson's sermon has been delivered at a time when the first shadows of evening begin to fall across the assembled company:[9] not so much, it may be, with a sense of menace as one of fulfilment, of the gathering of the day's activities into the time of rest, of natural, appropriate release. There is between the early setting out of the pilgrims in the General Prologue and this final reference to evening the sense of a day's complete passage which imposes a second time-scheme, based on the passage of the sun during a single day, upon that of the various 'days', themselves imprecisely defined, into which the pilgrim journey is divided.[10] The sermon is followed by a 'retraction' in which the end of the pilgrimage is left open and by which the poet, who has brought it into being, unburdens himself of his 'lewder' work. In the course of it he asks forgiveness for his 'translacions and enditynges of worldly vanitees', including 'the tales of Caunterbury, thilke that sownen into synne', and 'many a song and many a leccherous lay', and begs to be granted for these things

> grace of verray penitence, confessioun and satisfaccioun to doon in this present lyf, thurgh the benigne grace of hym that is kyng of kynges and preest over alle preestes, that boghte us with the precious blood of his herte; so that I may been oon of hem at the day of doom that shulle be saved.   (X. 1089–92)

The rejection on the part of the poet of no small portion of his work, including a great deal of what we most admire in it, has been much disputed, and it has even been questioned whether it belongs in any proper sense to the general conception of the *Tales*. This is clearly a problem which has some relation to that presented by the so-called 'epilogue' to *Troilus and Criseyde*,[11] and the answer in one case is likely to affect our conclusion about the other. Here, I would confine myself to two points. In the first place, it would seem that the 'retraction' comes appropriately after the Parson's long discourse on penance. We have not been shown the reaction of the pilgrims to his exhortation, for the simple reason that this is a matter that lies essentially outside, beyond anything that we can properly think of as 'fiction'; but we *are* shown the author's own response, for it is part of his obligation as a human being to accept his responsibility and to face the wider consequences of his actions.

In the second place we might find it true to Chaucer's intuition of life, as we see it reflected in his work, that he should express himself as sincerely repentant, but not (as a moralist of more limited vision might urge) on that account propose to renounce what he had written. Speaking generally, we can hardly fail to be struck by the fact that a great deal of the explicitly 'moral' matter of the *Tales* is concentrated into *prose* treatises which stand in a certain sense apart from the verse narratives which are, on any reasonable estimate, Chaucer's principal concern as a 'maker'. To think of the tales as designed simply in illustration of the 'morality' set forth in *The Tale of Melibeus* and in *The Parson's Tale* would clearly be as insensitive as to assume that the prose treatises have no importance for the complete design. Both tales and treatises, rather, have their part to play and Chaucer's very distinctive irony serves as a bridge to hold them together in the creative tension that constitutes the heart of his conception.

If this argument is valid, we shall neither be disposed to deny the seriousness of the final 'retraction' nor to take it at quite its face value. The truth surely lies, elusively enough but not on that account confusedly or sentimentally, somewhere between these extremes. As always, Chaucer is being true to his most considered intuition of life, which – as we shall have repeated occasion to see – precludes both facile didactic moralizing and any assumption of convenient amorality. Life – we may reflect on Chaucer's terms – is what it is, and censorship or suppression will not alter its course. His undertaking in the *Tales* has been nothing less than the creation of a *simulacrum*, a reflection of life, to which the Miller belongs not less than the Parson, the Wife of Bath not less than the Clerk who tells the story of the patient Griselda. The poet has given imaginative life to all his characters, and in so doing has been true to the nature of his vocation as he has to come to see it in the process of working out its full implications. The same regard for truth, however, impels him to recognize that poetical experience has its limits, and that what is – on its own terms – valid and satisfying is necessarily the *shadow*, the incomplete and partial reflection of a greater reality to which it points but which it cannot, in its time-conditioned and transient humanity, hope to compass.

In accordance with this general principle renunciation, the recognition of ultimate insufficiency, is not a sign of failure of nerve or purpose, but a built-in necessity of all human experience which rests finally on a recognition of *incompleteness*: and what the poet has consistently defended as belonging to the nature of his art, his *making*, needs at the last – but *only* there – to be consciously and deliberately renounced in the interest of what lies *beyond* art, and which art can, at best, only dimly and imperfectly figure. The tales therefore stand, though not all of them – it may be – are equally approved; but repentance, the *realistic* rejection by a man of what his actions may have produced, and of what his attitudes towards them may imply for his moral and human fulfilment, is also a part of life and Chaucer, speaking from his old age and with perhaps death consciously on his mind, may have been ready to accept this reality too. The fact that these seemingly contrasted attitudes are allowed to stand together in the complete conception of the *Tales* would be on this reading a proof not of inconsistency or failing confidence on Chaucer's part, but of his clear-sighted readiness to see reality as it is: a proof, in other words, of his greatness as man and as poet.

II

THE
GENERAL PROLOGUE

Between the two 'pillars' that frame the main body of *The Canterbury Tales* there lie the tales and interludes that add up between them to a poetic reflection of 'reality', individual and social, worldly and spiritual. But before the design can be set in motion, the pilgrims are introduced in what is, beyond the value of each individual portrait, a picture of English society, or of that part of it which was most open to the poet's inspection: for the higher aristocracy and the top ranks of the clergy – bishops and other representatives of ecclesiastical authority – are excluded at one end of the scale as are the very poor, those beneath the Ploughman in social standing, at the other. Within these limits, it is Chaucer's aim to bring together a *society* on its various levels, and to engage its members in a common enterprise which is a specific journey of pilgrimage, but also – and without detracting from the particularity of the presentation – a *figure* of that from unregenerate *nature*, through penitence, to spiritual *grace*.

The General Prologue contains some twenty-five portraits of persons of varied occupation and social standing. Some aspects of the art revealed in these sketches call for consideration, in as much as it is governed by presuppositions which are in certain respects notably different from those which might govern a modern writer in the same situation. Such a writer would seek to impart a dynamic, forward-moving quality to his account by showing his pilgrims interacting with one another and revealing themselves progressively *in action*. He would also be concerned to provide them with a setting, a living and changing background answering to the successive stages of a developing and organic conception. He would be concerned above all to avoid giving a static quality to his account by imparting to it a sense of *process*, of each separate part and character as contributing to a whole in motion.

The medieval approach to this problem was somewhat different. In the first place the pilgrims are presented in the General Prologue as almost entirely without relationship to any recognizable background. We are scarcely aware, as they proceed on their journey, of the places and scenes through which they must presumably pass.[1] Rather they stand, after the manner of a Sienese altar-piece or a painting by Orcagna, against a setting deprived of perspective, a uniform background of gold, as it were, and only occasionally do we hear anything of their position in relation to a place on the route. We know that the point from which they set out – the *Tabard*, in Southwark – is an inn, but no attempt is made to tell us what it was like or to distinguish it from any other hostelry of its kind.

> The chambres and the stables weren wyde,
> And wel we weren esed atte beste,   (I. 28–9)

not because the Tabard was necessarily so spacious, but because these attributes are fitting for a place in which men gather to give expression to the sociability which confers meaning upon their otherwise random and indeterminate actions. This absence of particularity answers to the very nature of the 'pilgrimage' conception, which sees human life in time as an evanescent reality, a passage through a world of 'shadows' which is indeed, humanly speaking, the only world we have; it is a world, though, which points beyond itself, and in confirmation of its final, and therefore 'real' meaning, to the *end* which lies beyond time, but by which time itself is finally justified. Chaucer's acceptance of this view of life, and his reservations in its regard, amount between them to the moving force in his conception.

Secondly, Chaucer's treatment of his theme – or his preliminary announcement of what he intends to do – answers to this difference. Having completed the introduction we have just considered,[2] he goes on to incorporate himself into the 'felaweshipe' of those who are to be his companions on the journey. The way seems to be clear for a description of the group as a whole, and this – no doubt – is what would have come next had Chaucer been a modern writer dealing with the same theme. What actually follows is in certain respects notably different:

> But nathelees, whil I have tyme and space,
> Er that I ferther in this tale pace,
> Me thynketh it acordaunt to resoun
> To telle yow al the condicioun
> Of ech of hem, so as it semed me,
> And whiche they weren, and of what degree,
> And eek in what array that they were inne;
> And at a knyght than wol I first bigynne.   (I. 35–42)

The effect is to establish a long 'parenthesis', which runs for some seven hundred lines, in the development of the Prologue.[3] At the end of it Chaucer, as though recalling the lines we have just quoted, closes the 'parenthesis' by informing us that he has done what he set out to do:

> Now have I toold you soothly, in a clause,
> Th'estaat, th'array, the nombre, and eek the cause
> Why that assembled was this compaignye. (I. 715–17)

'Me thynketh it acordaunt to resoun / To telle yow': 'Now have I toold you soothly': between these two phrases, which evidently echo one another, Chaucer has developed his 'clause'. He has set out his material methodically and is ready to return to the development of his theme.

What is of interest here is that a reading of the portraits will show Chaucer departing frequently from the rigid procedure that his statement of 'method' seems to imply. Such departures from the stated norm – departures which assume its existence in the process of violating it – are an essential part of his procedure. The details of the descriptions are not, on the whole, methodically presented, but seem to answer to impressions set down at random and in no logical order. It is only once we have become accustomed to the apparent 'disorder', the lack of obvious logical connection, that we can appreciate the way in which details are cunningly set in juxtaposition so as to illustrate, not only the characters themselves, but the attitude towards them of a narrator who is both like and unlike his creator, who is himself in fact one of the poem's most subtle and distinctive presentations.

Chaucer, in other words, shows himself in these portraits both attached to and free from the limitations of medieval convention. At the end of the 'clause' in which his long line of characters is presented he seems to find it necessary to apologize for his failure to follow the prescribed method:

> Also I prey yow to foryeve it me,
> Al have I nat set folk in hir degree
> Heere in this tale, as that they sholde stonde.
> (I. 743–5)

He ascribes this failure to his own lack of skill and intelligence in applying the rules – 'My wit is short, ye may wel understonde' – but, even at this early stage, we may have grasped enough of his method not to take him at his word. The fact is that Chaucer is both recognizing convention and turning his declared incapacity to follow its dictates to his own ends. Close enough to the assumptions of his age to be able to use them to give universality, a sense of transcending the merely personal and particular in his descriptions, he is yet free to see them in detachment, to adapt them to purposes which no mere inherited convention could exhaust. Each of his more developed 'portraits', whilst answering to a familiar type, is also fully and triumphantly the evocation of an individual; and the result is to present a series of persons, bound together by common presuppositions and (above all) engaged in a common undertaking, who exhibit at the same time that sense of wayward and enriching individuality, that refusal to be bound by abstract or limiting moral and social schemes, which is one of the signs of being genuinely and compellingly alive.

These observations can find ready application in the Prologue. As an example of Chaucer's art in this respect, we can single out one of the most familiar of his portraits:

> Ther was also a Nonne, a Prioresse,
> That of hir smylyng was ful symple and coy;
> Hire gretteste ooth was but by Seinte Loy;
> And she was cleped madame Eglentyne.
> Ful weel she soong the service dyvyne,
> Entuned in hir nose ful semely,
> And Frenssh she spak ful faire and fetisly,
> After the scole of Stratford atte Bowe,
> For Frenssh of Parys was to hire unknowe.
> At mete well ytaught was she with alle:
> She leet no morsel from hir lippes falle,
> Ne wette hir fyngres in hir sauce depe;
> Wel koude she carie a morsel and wel kepe
> That no drope ne fille upon hire brest.
> In curteisie was set ful muchel hir lest.
> Hir over-lippe wyped she so clene
> That in hir coppe ther was no ferthyng sene
> Of grece, whan she dronken hadde hir draughte.
> Ful semely after hir mete she raughte.
> And sikerly she was of greet desport,
> And ful plesaunt, and amyable of port,
> And peyned hire to countrefete cheere
> Of court, and to been estatlich of manere,
> And to ben holden digne of reverence.
> But, for to speken of hire conscience,
> She was so charitable and so pitous
> She wolde wepe, if that she saugh a mous
> Kaught in a trappe, if it were deed or bledde.
> Of smale houndes hadde she that she fedde
> With rosted flessh, or milk and wastel-breed.
> But soore wepte she if oon of hem were deed,
> Or if men smoot it with a yerde smerte;

And al was conscience and tendre herte.
Ful semyly hir wympul pynched was,
Hir nose tretys, hir eyen greye as glas,
Hir mouth ful smal, and therto softe and reed;
But sikerly she hadde a fair forheed;
It was almoost a spanne brood, I trowe;
For, hardily, she was nat undergrowe.
Ful fetys was hir cloke, as I was war.
Of smal coral aboute hire arm she bar
A peire of bedes, gauded al with grene,
And theron heng a brooch of gold ful sheene,
On which ther was first write a crowned A,
And after *Amor vincit omnia*.   (I. 118–62)

The special, and very distinctively Chaucerian art of this passage is of the kind that achieves its affects through a deliberate impression of artlessness. The details, physical and 'psychological', appear on a first reading to be put together with little or no sense of significant order, and there seems to be no attempt to arrive at any degree of 'psychological' penetration. A little further consideration will show that there are important things to be said on the other side of the question. In the first place, the appearance of a 'disorderly' set of impressions contrasts so obviously with the claim, only just advanced, to be following a specific 'method' that the departure from it can hardly be accidental. It also contributes effectively to our sense of an object directly and actually *seen*. When the narrator gives us his first impression of his subject through her smile – 'ful symple and coy' – he is reflecting the way in which observation tends to fasten on an apparently insignificant trait which turns out to concentrate on itself the full value of what we come, later and more logically, to understand. The whole character of the Prioress can be said to be concentrated on the 'simplicity', the innocent artlessness as it presents itself, of her smile.

In the second place, the details given are seen with complete objectivity. Once again, the comparison with what a modern writer might be expected to do with similar material is revealing. Nearly all portraiture in literature subsequent to Chaucer involves a certain blurring of the distinction between what is seen as *given*, proper to the person contemplated, and what the interpreter's viewpoint leads him to see, often to the exclusion of much else and, more importantly, with a tendency to blur the difference between the 'subjective' and the 'objective' vision. Chaucer may have been the last great writer in English – perhaps, indeed, the only one? – of whom it may be said that he was able to see the object as existing in itself, as standing *per se* in its own right. This is a way of seeing people and things, and – like all such ways – it rests upon assumptions as to the nature of 'seeing' which are conditioned by the mental structure of the perceiver: but it produced, in Chaucer, results which answer to the nature of his genius and which have hardly been equalled in their kind since he wrote.

This does not mean that we are to refrain from drawing certain conclusions from this apparently naive catalogue of attributes. The 'naivety', if it exists, is the narrator's, and we are meant to see it for what it is.[4] The judgements are *there*, not less unerringly made for their lack of emphatic assertion, and the appearance of 'artlessness' is compatible with a considerable exercise of 'art'. It is useful to know that the physical features of the Prioress – her straight, 'tretys' nose, her grey eyes, her small, soft, and red mouth, and even her 'fair', broad forehead – are all, like her name 'Eglentyne', characteristic of the heroines of courtly and sentimental romance: useful, too, to be reminded that the description of her table manners which evidently captivate the narrator and which we need not find other than attractive, is in fact based on a passage in the *Roman de la Rose*[5] which establishes the standard appropriate in these matters for a lady of good breeding.

Above all, we are induced to respond to the deceptively easy flow of the rhyming couplets, which serves both to knit the seemingly haphazard disposition of detail into a unity and, where appropriate, to underline the unobtrusively ironic intention. At times, the second rhyme of the couplet seems to reinforce the effect of the first; at others it serves almost imperceptibly to qualify it. At others, again, the opening of a new couplet, superficially unconnected with what has gone before, introduces a point of view implicitly critical, even destructive – if that were not too violent a word – of the preceding effect. The Prioress speaks French, according to her own conception of herself, to which the narrator enthusiastically responds, with sophisticated elegance, 'faire and fetisly'. She speaks it, however, and here we pass to the unobtrusive comment of an objective observer, after the fashion of Stratford-at-Bow, for the French of 'Parys' is to her (and the rhyme ties up the effect unerringly by stressing the significant point) 'unknowe'. The Prioress' pretension to speak French, and her manner of doing it, answer to the impulse that leads her to cultivate a certain affectation in her singing of the Office in choir, 'Entuned in hir nose ful semely'. These foibles are part of her concern with aristocratic appearance, the preoccupation with 'curteisie' which is both her attraction and her weakness and which finds expression in her continual effort (it 'peyned hire') to 'countrefete'[6] the 'cheere of court' which was, as we may think, an absorbing preoccupation of her life. 'To ben estatlich of manere' and to be held 'digne of reverence' is no doubt a proper condition for a lady who has been placed at the head of a religious community and is called upon to represent its dignity; but it can hardly exhaust the full implications of the vocation to which she has devoted herself and this portrait is at least as revealing for what it leaves out as for what it so disarmingly presents.

A similar conclusion can be drawn from Madame Eglantine's attitude to her domestic animals: the pets which her rule in all probability forbade her to keep, but on which her motherly attentions were concentrated.[7] The Prioress was 'charitable' and 'pitous', as indeed a nun vowed to the service of Christ in Holy Poverty should be; but her pity expended itself on the 'mouse' caught in a trap and on the domestic pets – 'smale houndes' and such-like – for which she wept 'sorely' when they died and which she fed, during their life-time, on luxuries certainly unavailable to the poor. The effect is not to destroy the nun, or to make a crudely moralizing or 'reforming' point of the kind from which Chaucer, more perhaps than almost any other writer, is mercifully free. There is at least a suggestion that he was attracted, and meant his readers to be attracted, by the character he had drawn, that he was ready to exercise a human indulgence in her regard and to respond positively to the implications of the comment that 'al was conscience and tendre herte'; but he also, and at the same time, requires us to see the limits within which this 'conscience' operates and to qualify his narrator's gentle, even affectionate complacency with a firmly drawn sense of the underlying moral reality.

This, perhaps, is what is conveyed by the inscription on the Prioress' brooch which rounds off the description. *Amor vincit omnia* is a phrase which derives ultimately from classical Latin poetry,[8] and which has behind it a long history of medieval associations, both religious and secular. In all probability it came to Chaucer through the *Roman de la Rose*, where it finds its place in the argument by which 'Curteisie' persuades 'Bel Aceuil' to grant the lover access to the 'rose' of his desire.[9] It is certainly none the worse for this origin. There is no reason why the motto should be found incongruous for a nun. Christianity is 'about' love, if it is 'about' anything at all; and so, indeed, is the 'pilgrimage' which Chaucer is presenting as an image of the human journey in time. A medieval theologian would have distinguished between 'charity' – 'the motion of the soul toward the enjoyment of God for his own sake, and the enjoyment of one's self and one's neighbour for the sake of God' – and 'cupidity', 'a motion of the soul towards the enjoyment of one's self, one's neighbour, or any corporal thing for the sake of something other than God',[10] and might have presented human life in terms of a conflict between these opposed principles. Chaucer, neither a theologian nor a moralist (though aware of the concerns of both), no doubt preferred to avoid these extremes and to find his theme in the infinite variety of human attitudes and decisions which occupy the ground between them; but he was certainly aware of these opposing principles and ready, in his own way, to recognize them as centrally important in the exercise of human choice. The question, in the case of each human being, is what *kind* of love finally moves him; and, in the particular case of the Prioress, we may be allowed to wonder whether her conception of 'love' is adequate to sustain the claim which her vocation may be thought to imply.

The example of the Prioress gives a clear idea of Chaucer's ability to compass a human portrait in depth and penetration. It does not, perhaps, illustrate as well as some of the other portraits that sense of being in the presence not merely of individual characters, but of representative *types* answering to unchanging aspects of human nature. The explanation of this effect lies in great part in a generalizing habit of the medieval mind which tended, in philosophical terms, to proceed from the *species* to the *individual*, to see individuality as the particularizing, separating element which the presence of *matter* imposed upon what would otherwise be the uniform perfection of each *species* as conceived in the original creative design.[11] This is associated in important ways with the ability to see allegory not as an imposition of abstract categories upon the actual but as a natural and living form, resting firmly on the perception of the particular and passing from this to infer the presence of an underlying universal.

This habit of mind, so much more deeply engrained than any intellectual formulation of it can be, illuminates not a few of the figures of the Prologue. Typical, for example, is another of Chaucer's most vivid creations, the Wife of Bath (I. 445–76), the effect of whose portrayal rests once again on a sure grasp of individual idiosyncracies. In this respect the Wife is not at all like *La Vieille* (the Duenna), the character in Jean de Meun's part of the *Roman de la Rose* from whom she derived some of her characteristics. *La Vieille* is a figure conceived as a vehicle for the exposition of certain ideas – realities, as her creator conceived them, opposed to the unreal and dishonest idealization of *amour courtois* – concerning the 'love' which is the theme of his poem.[12] The 'character' exists, finally, to carry the ideas, which concern 'love' as a universal human attribute rather than any particular lover. It is lively in as much as the ideas are lively, because they carry a criticism which is not the less valid for being carried to the point of cynicism; but, though *La Vieille* may seem at times to be on the point of realization as an individual person, the step beyond allegorical presentation is never consistently taken. With Alice of Bath the opposite is true. Whatever she may turn out to be by the time we have finished with her she is, first and above all, one particular woman, seen and realized in relation to an appropriate setting. She was 'deaf', as the narrator solicitously reports (and the prologue to her own tale will tell us, in due course, how she became so), and 'gat-tothed', unmistakable in her aggressive style of dress and in her flaunted social assertiveness. She has her own way of behaving in church, which has little to do with 'charity', and she has made a life-long habit of pilgrimage to satisfy her restless desire for unfamiliar sights and new contacts; once again, the needs and dissatisfactions which underlie her restlessness will be clarified in the course of her own prologue and story.

There is, however, more than this to the Wife. Even the details we have picked out as individualizing features bear implications that were, to a medieval reader, more than merely personal. If she was 'deaf', her inability to hear extended further than the physical defect; and if she was 'gat-tothed', Chaucer's readers would have shared with him the knowledge that this was a feature associated with the presence of powerful, even imperious sexual appetites. It is the Wife's nature to affect us as a presence larger than life, sitting 'easily', like the experienced wayfarer she is, upon her mount, with her conspicuous hat, 'As brood as is a bokeler or a targe' (I. 471), and her 'hipes large' (I. 472): whom the narrator sees as 'a worthy womman al hire lyve' (I. 459), but who is revealed, in one of those seemingly artless but devastating juxtapositions by which Chaucer, in the process of identifying himself with his 'pilgrim' personality, so effectively distances himself from his creation, as one of whom we are told in the line which immediately follows: 'Housbondes at chirche dore she hadde fyve' (I. 460). Again, we shall learn a great deal about these husbands before the pilgrimage ends; but, for the moment, the narrator expresses himself in their regard with typical delicacy – 'But therof nedeth nat to speke as nowthe' (I. 462) – and is content to see his formidable subject as an attractive, indeed a 'forward' participant in the 'fellowship' in which all the pilgrims are united.

Above all, the Wife 'koude muchel of wandrynge by the weye' (I. 467): a statement which has moral as well as geographical implications. As the prologue to her tale will abundantly show, she is by moral descent a natural devotee of the old pagan gods and goddesses: of Venus, or Aphrodite, the deity of sensual desire, and of Mars, the god of war and domination.[13] Already, indeed, we are told,

> Of remedies of love she knew per chaunce,
> For she koude of that art the olde daunce: (I. 475–6)

the 'old dance', which Pandarus, in *Troilus and Criseyde*, had also understood,[14] the unchanging order of sensuality which shadows that of Christian love as socially confirmed in the sacrament of matrimony. Here are *two* realities universally present in human nature, inextricably related to one another as passion to reason, 'nature' to 'grace', or night to day: two aspects of life, neither of which is to be repressed or censored in the name of the other, as though it did not exist or could safely be ignored. The Wife, in short, derives her vitality from many interrelated or contrasted sources, and above all, perhaps, from the universalizing tendencies of medieval

allegory as well as from her creator's gift of conferring individuality upon
the characters of his creation. We need to respond to *both* these aspects,
and to hold them continually in balance, if we are to give full value to his
achievement.

Something of the same kind can be said of the most disquieting of
Chaucer's creations, the only pilgrim from whom his gift for tolerant
sympathy seems to be largely (though even here not entirely) withdrawn.
This is the Pardoner, who sells for gain the divine gift of forgiveness which
the Parson is to make the theme of his concluding sermon. The Pardoner is
the most sinister of the pilgrims: less because we can think of him as a
diabolic figure, a manifestation of evil, than because in his person the
corruption of holy things, the reversal of spirituality, is rendered at once
grotesque and humanly plausible. It is no accident that he and the
Summoner, the man who called pleaders before the ecclesiastical courts
and who was always ready to allow his 'clients' to buy their immunity
from his attention, are the last figures to appear in Chaucer's review. The
Pardoner exploits God's mercy, the Summoner prostitutes his justice for
ends of gain; between them, they misappropriate the two attributes which
in God – and in God alone – are perfectly balanced, and which human
beings are called upon to reconcile as best they may. The implications of
their presence in the pilgrimage are disturbing, and rendered rather more
than less so by the sense, which pervades the passage, of a powerful note
of broadly based human comedy. The effect is that of a sardonic *coda*
attached to the main group of pilgrims, who – as we shall see – are led out
of town by the almost equally grotesque figure of the Miller playing on the
bag-pipe which, in so much art of popular medieval inspiration,[15]
symbolizes sensuality and the reversal of reasonable order.

By the time this pair appears, we have already been shown the Parson,
also in his own way something of an 'archetypal' figure: the embodiment
of Christian virtue, personal and social alike, who taught, like many
others, 'Cristes loore and his apostles twelve', but who – unlike not a few
professing teachers, some of them in high places – 'first folwed it
hymselve' (I. 528). In the Pardoner, we are shown the exact opposite, a
divorce between ostensible function and visible reality to which the
portrait, without in any way diminishing the comic effect, gives concrete
and sinister form:

> With hym ther rood a gentil Pardoner
> Of Rouncivale, his freend and his compeer,
> That streight was comen fro the court of Rome.
> Ful loude he soong 'Com hider, love, to me!'
> This Somonour bar to hym a stif burdoun;
> Was nevere trompe of half so greet a soun.

This Pardoner hadde heer as yelow as wex,
But smothe it heeng as dooth a strike of flex;
By ounces henge his lokkes that he hadde,
And therwith he his shuldres overspradde;
But thynne it lay, by colpons oon and oon.
But hood, for jolitee, wered he noon,
For it was trussed up in his walet.
Hym thoughte he rood al of the newe jet;
Dischevelee, save his cappe, he rood al bare.
Swiche glarynge eyen hadde he as an hare.
A vernycle hadde he sowed upon his cappe.
His walet lay biform hym in his lappe,
Bretful of pardoun, comen from Rome al hoot.
A voys he hadde as smal as hath a goot.
No berd hadde he, ne nevere sholde have;
As smothe it was as it were late shave.
I trowe he were a geldyng or a mare.
But of his craft, fro Berwyk into Ware,
Ne was ther swich another pardoner
For in his male he hadde a pilwe-beer,
Which that he seyde was Oure Lady veyl:
He seyde he hadde a gobet of the seyl
That Seint Peter hadde, whan that he wente
Upon the see, til Jhesu Crist hym hente.
He hadde a croys of latoun ful of stones,
And in a glas he hadde pigges bones.
But with thise relikes, whan that he fond
A povre person dwellynge upon lond,
Upon a day he gat hym moore moneye
Than that the person gat in monthes tweye;
And thus, with feyned flaterye and japes,
He made the person and the peple his apes.
But trewely to tellen atte laste,
He was in chirche a noble ecclesiaste.
Wel koude he rede a lessoun or a storie,
But alderbest he song an offertorie;
For wel he wiste, whan that song was songe,
He moste preche and wel affile his tonge
To wynne silver, as he ful wel koude;
Therefore he song the murierly and loude.   (I. 669–714)

To prepare the ground for the effect at which he aims, Chaucer begins by
assuming the 'naive', narrator personality which is one of his most telling

devices. In calling the Pardoner 'gentil', he is using a word which, throughout the *Tales*, carries implications of urbanity and social acceptance. When he comes to tell his tale, the more respectable pilgrims – those who are explicitly called the 'gentils'[16] – show themselves both shocked and apprehensive about the contribution they think this outlandish figure is likely to make. The Pardoner strikes them as an uncomfortable companion, from whom anything may be expected: both on account of his nature, as his grotesque appearance presents it, and of the dubious 'profession' he exercises. It is also stressed that he is newly arrived from the centre of Christian spirituality, 'streight was comen fro the court of Rome'. There follows, in immediate juxtaposition, the brilliantly effective stroke: 'Ful loude he soong "Com hider, love, to me!" ', with the grotesque accompaniment provided by his companion the Summoner as, joined in the repudiation which separates them from the rest of the group, they bring up the rear of the party.

On this foundation, and with the implications of 'gentil' ringing in our minds, Chaucer proceeds to build up his portrait, qualifying rich comedy with a subtly modulated sense of underlying unease. The full sense of the ditty which he puts into the mouth of his character is more significant than may at once appear, as we shall see when we come to consider the circumstances in which the Pardoner will, when the time comes, take the centre of the stage.[17] Meanwhile, as his equivocal appearance emerges in the course of the description – his hair 'yellow as wax', smoothly hanging, abundant but thin, his sense of living up to what he likes to think of as 'the newe jet', the latest elegance of fashion – we begin to qualify the narrator's enthusiasm, to respond to the note of falsity, half comic and half sinister, in his strained 'jolitee' and 'discheveled' appearance. Chaucer is engaged in building up a uniquely grotesque picture, which is brought increasingly into evidence in the later stages of the physical presentation, and most notably in the phrase 'Swiche glarynge eyen hadde he as an hare'. There is a definite element of lunacy, a suggestion of mental aberration, which the Pardoner – lucid as he is in his estimate of his standing in relation to his fellow-pilgrims – will consistently leave with us and which will emerge in the tale he is to tell.

It would be wrong, however, to concentrate on the sinister implications of this portrait to the exclusion of the equally essential note of humour. The two effects stand together in a way which is very Chaucerian, and to stress one element at the expense of the other is to falsify the total impression. The Pardoner *is* a sinister figure; he is also very funny, and to react to him *only* by giving vent to righteous indignation is to run the risk of identifying ourselves with some of the more self-righteous attitudes current among the pilgrims. The comic element emerges in the highly effective juxtaposition of incompatible features: in the image of the

suffering face of Christ on the 'Veronica', or 'vernicle', sewn on the
Pardoner's cap, and in the wallet, 'bretful of pardoun' come, like the
newly-baked cakes in a baker's shop, 'from Rome al hoot'. No doubt the
contrast *is*, and is intended to be, shocking; but it is also incongruous and,
as such, apt to appeal to inescapable needs of human nature. The humour
is still more evident in the list of pitiful objects which constitute the
Pardoner's stock in trade: the rubbish he will offer to the unwary and
which perhaps, just because it *is* rubbish and as such familiar to them, will
appeal to their instinctive craving for salvation. The effect is – we must
repeat – essentially *comic*, with the kind of comedy that belongs to a
familiar, even an irrepressible part of everyday life. There will be
Pardoners in every age and in every society, though the objects they sell
may vary – holy relics or life insurance policies, according to the
preoccupations of each time – and there will always be those ready to buy.
The ultimate reality is the same, though it may manifest itself in different
ways; and though the blasphemy of one age is replaced by the more
'respectable' and covert rapacity of the next, it is by no means certain
which does more harm, or constitutes the greater outrage to human life.

Comedy, then, of an essentially *un*-moralizing, *non*- 'denunciatory'
kind, is of the essence of this portrait. It is combined with keen insight into
a human predicament. Before the build-up of the Pardoner's character has
been completed, it emerges that he is sexually deficient and, as such,
twisted from human normality in a way that helps to explain the gap that
separates him from his fellow pilgrims. The implications of this situation,
again, will only be fully revealed at a later stage in the journey.[18] For the
moment, we only see what is visible to the narrator's relatively superficial,
even self-satisfied understanding: though even here, and in the light of
the details given, we must sense a qualifying irony in the continued
expressions of ingenuous admiration:

> But of his craft, fro Berwyk into Ware,
> Ne was ther swich another pardoner.

'Trewely', Chaucer concludes, still wearing his naive personality, this was
'in chirche a noble ecclesiaste': one grotesquely skilful in preaching or
singing for gain, ready at all times to 'affile his tonge' with full professional
confidence for the winning, not of souls, but of 'silver'. In a company each
member of which is presented as an exemplar, an outstandingly complete
instance of his kind, there is also a place for the Pardoner's particular type
of 'excellence'. No doubt there are many like him in circulation – if only
because he too represents, in his special way, a permanent aspect of
human nature – but none, we are assured, so perfectly incarnates in his
stressed individuality the qualities of the type, the species, to which he
belongs.

At the end of the long 'clause' in which he has given us his series of pilgrim portraits, Chaucer is ready to set his project in motion. Before he does so, the poem pauses to introduce a matter of some importance to our understanding of the undertaking as a whole. This concerns the *truth* which a work of literature may be expected to convey, and the relationship of that special kind of verisimilitude to the more general conception of *truth* which is the end towards which every human activity must be oriented and by relation to which it is finally – even if it is not conscious of the fact – justified:

> But first I pray yow, of youre curteisye,
> That ye n'arette it nat my vileynye,
> Thogh that I pleynly speke in this mateere,
> To telle yow hir wordes and hir cheere,
> Ne thogh I speke hir wordes proprely.
> For this ye knowen al so wel as I,
> Whoso shal telle a tale after a man,
> He moot reherce as ny as evere he kan
> Everich a word, if it be in his charge,
> Al speke he never so rudeliche and large,
> Or ellis he moot telle his tale untrewe,
> Or feyne thyng, or fynde wordes newe.
> He may nat spare, althogh he were his brother;
> He moot as wel seye o word as another.
> Crist spak hymself ful brode in hooly writ,
> And wel ye woot no vileynye is it.
> Eek Plato seith, whoso that kan hym rede,
> The wordes moote be cosyn to the dede.
> Also I prey yow to foryeve it me,
> Al have I nat set folk in hir degree
> Heere in this tale, as that they sholde stonde.
> My wit is short, ye may wel understonde.   (I. 725–46)

The narrator's words seem to be raising a relatively minor – and, perhaps, to a modern mind a rather trivial – problem: the problem of excusing the 'realistic' interventions of some of the pilgrims and the crudity which, in some of the tales, might offend a morally sensitive ear. More than this, however, is at stake. The question raised concerns the entire concept of art as 'imitation' on which medieval thinking in these matters was founded. For most 'authoritative' opinion, literature would at best only be concerned with doubtful and ambiguous kinds of 'truth'. 'Truth', in its serious forms, was to be looked for elsewhere. Even Dante, whose sense of his poetic vocation is not in doubt, refers to poetry in his *Convivio* as 'a beautiful lie',[19] and Aquinas only recognized grudgingly that poetry might be allowed, in recognition of human weakness, a function in making accessible to men certain aspects of reality which the sensibly conditioned terms of their experience, and their incapacity to remain consistently on the level of pure intellectual speculation, would place otherwise beyond their grasp.[20]

Art, therefore, as an 'imitation', proper to man, of the universal creative design, has at best a precarious relation to the truth which lies, logically and necessarily on this view, beyond it, in 'infinite excess'.[21] Chaucer, aware of the problem which this represents for the project on which he is embarking, prefers to approach it cautiously and very typically uses the narrower, more literal approach which we have learned to expect of his narrator to explore this issue. The narrator addresses himself to the 'courtesy', the tolerant understanding of his audience, and begs them not to ascribe to 'vileynye', coarseness of understanding, or moral insensitivity, what *truth* obliges him to set down. As a reporter he feels obliged to record 'proprely', faithfully, the words which he is supposed to have heard spoken, the actions which he witnessed. Otherwise his 'imitation' would be inaccurate and he would be obliged 'to telle his tale untrewe', to 'feyne thyng', or to assume the responsibility of inventing 'new words' and so of falling into *untruth*.

Thus far, the narrator's sense of his problem seems to raise no particular difficulty. It does, however, provoke questions concerning the nature and the limits of 'imitation' in art which, probed far enough, can become more perplexing. The obligation to report faithfully is not always easy to reconcile to an author's sense of his moral responsibility; a medieval writer, unlike a modern one, could not justify himself by appealing to an autonomous view of his calling. We shall not underestimate the reality of this preoccupation, which is echoed at significant points in the course of the pilgrimage,[22] if we look forward to the retraction which rounds off the entire work;[23] but we shall also understand that the view which leads a writer to see his work as an 'imitation' of reality will present itself to him as an obligation which he cannot – if he is a *serious* artist – evade if he is to remain true to the spirit of his design. The Miller made his presence felt among the pilgrims, as did the Cook and – in a more fundamental way – the Pardoner and the Summoner. To leave them out because their interventions might seem gross or inappropriate to refined or morally sensitive understandings would be to falsify the 'imitation', to betray the purpose by which the entire work is animated.

The narrator, therefore, in spite of his apparently naive concern with surface respectability, is expressing preoccupations more serious than he altogether understands. He is still, however, the essentially naive, simple-minded and gullible reporter whom Chaucer has chosen to give us, and so it is not surprising that his expression of these issues becomes confused when he looks for 'authorities' to back his arguments. For the 'authorities' do not seem to support his contentions, not at least in the form in which he has advanced them. Christ may well have spoken on occasions 'ful brode in hooly writ', but this hardly seems to justify the tale shortly to be told by the Miller or the Host's crushingly brutal retort to the Pardoner at the end of his tale.[24] In Plato's *Timaeus*, too, as echoed by Boethius or otherwise reported,[25] the narrator would have found something to the effect that 'The wordes moote be cosyn to the dede'; but how far this is really relevant to the matter under immediate consideration is at best doubtful. To claim that there can be no evil, no danger, in imitating the truth of reality as he sees it, is to raise a large question; and to support the claim by referring to Christ's example and Plato's teaching is both to underline the importance of the question and to suggest, subtly and unobtrusively, the difficulty of giving it a final answer.

The fact is that these 'authorities' are raising, beyond the narrator's immediate understanding – 'My wit is short, ye may wel understonde' – the question of what kind of 'truth' is represented in the artist's creation, where it stands in respect of other, more explicit and more binding affirmations of man's moral nature, and what the relation is between that creation and *truth* itself. That such questions were worth asking, were indeed bound to be asked by any poet possessed of a serious view of his art, the very nature of medieval thought implied. There is, according to the terms of that thought, a real, existent 'truth', beyond all human approximations to it; and the 'pilgrimage' in which all human beings are engaged in the fulfilment of their very creatureliness, is a movement either towards or away from it. A writer who was engaged, as Chaucer was, in elaborating the image of such a journey was bound to ask himself questions concerning the sense of his analogy, the limits of his 'imitation'. The question raised here is one which cannot – given the sense of Chaucer's art – receive an immediate or categorical reply. The reply, if indeed there is to be one, can only be given at the *end* of the pilgrimage, and even then in the process of recognizing that it lies essentially beyond and *outside* the limits which the nature of the artistic 'imitation' presupposes: but there *is* a 'truth' of art too, which answers a real human need, and the question concerning its nature and limitation is one to which the *Tales* will persistently if still undidactically and undogmatically address themselves.

Returning after this apparent digression to his main theme, and on the point of placing his company of pilgrims on the road to Canterbury, Chaucer introduces the second of the two participants in the journey – the first was the poet-narrator – who stand in some sense apart from the rest. This is the Host who is to preside over the whole project, and who is conveyed to us as at once bluff and authoritative, of whom we catch glimpses in terms of assertive common-sense and ordinary (sometimes brutal and even gross) human sensuality, but who imposes himself as an embodiment of the life, rough at times but imperious, pressing in its demand for recognition, which is being directed into the forms of pilgrimage. In the course of the journey Harry Bailey will deliver himself of a variety of opinions on matters concerning marriage, personal and social morality, literary taste, and the common man's religion. His attitude towards all these things is one which he is confident that he shares with the right-thinking majority. It is far from certain that his are always right opinions; but they are expressive of the down-to-earth humanity which he shares, in varying degrees, with most of the company and with which the alternative readings of life which the tales successively present have finally to come to terms.

As the project takes shape at the initiative of this confident master of ceremonies the emphasis is on 'merriment' and spontaneous conviviality. The Host announces his plan over a supper, with the travellers grouped round a table full of the good things which it has been his not altogether disinterested care to provide:

> He served us with vitaille at the beste,
> Strong was the wyn, and wel to drynke us leste.
>
> (I. 749–50)

The strength of the wine, and the readiness of the pilgrims to indulge themselves in drinking it, will be repeatedly referred to in the course of the journey. It can be, and often is, one of the diversions that most insistently lead the pilgrims away from a respect for their human dignity and from a proper sense of the end towards which their journey is directed; but there is also another, and more positive, way of understanding this conviviality. Eating and drinking in common are the visible signs of being bound together in a *society*, dedicated in 'fellowship' to a common purpose, a sacrament of community in the world's order, much as the Eucharist (which will follow confession at the end of the pilgrimage, at the 'blisful' martyr's shrine) is the *figure*, the living symbol of the life of the spirit.

Thus joined in conviviality the characteristic quality of the Host – 'Eek therto he was right a myrie man' – extends to the entire band, and the narrator is moved to enthusiastic comment: 'I saugh nat this yeer so *myrie* a compaignye' (I. 764). The pilgrim proposal is ready to be broached and it is, of course, the Host who broaches it:

> Ye goon to Caunterbury – God yow speede,
> The blisful martir quite yow youre meede!   (I. 769–70)

The *end* is 'blissful', indeed, because it is the goal of the pilgrimage, the Heavenly City of Jerusalem; but the *way* to it is long, and the end itself variously perceived. For this reason the *way* needs to be lightened by human entertainment:

> And wel I woot, as ye goon by the weye,
> Ye shapen yow to talen and to pleye;
> For trewely, confort ne myrthe is noon
> To ride by the weye doumb as a stoon.   (I. 771–4)

There follows the 'merry' proposal backed by the Host's firm assertion that the pilgrims are to accept his judgement: for he is to be the presiding genius in terms of the world, as the Parson will be in that of the spirit. Each pilgrim is to lighten the way by telling four tales, two on the way out and two more on the return; and, at the end, there shall be 'a soper at oure aller cost', a final act of shared conviviality to round off and express the companionship achieved on the way.

The plan thus put forward is accepted by all the pilgrims who unanimously, 'by oon assent', express themselves 'acorded' to the Host's judgement; and the agreement is confirmed in the most fitting manner:

> And therupon the wyn was fet anon;
> We dronken, and to reste wente echon.   (I. 819–20)

A 'bond' has been drawn up and, as it were, sacramentally confirmed in the sharing of wine before the pilgrims retire to enjoy their natural rest in anticipation of the morrow.

It only remains, early the next morning, for the Host – 'oure aller cok'[26] – to rouse them, gathering the group together 'in a flok' – the image has a universalizing quality – and setting them off on their journey. Once again he asserts his power of judgement – 'As evere mote I drynke wyn or ale' (I. 832) – stresses the need to maintain the agreement of the night before – 'If even-song and morwe-song accorde' (I. 830) – and prepares the lots which are to be drawn for the first tale. In this process he is careful to observe the social proprieties, addressing the Knight as 'my mayster and my lord' and the Prioress as 'my lady'; and finally, whether through what may have been either blind chance ('aventure' or 'cas') or the operation of a purposeful if obscure design ('sort': I. 844), the 'cut' fell appropriately to the Knight. The seemingly artless presentation of these alternative possibilities raises a question which affects our understanding of the very nature of the pilgrimage: raises it whilst refusing, in a very Chaucerian fashion, to point to any certain resolution. By whatever means, and under whatever auspices, the social decorum prized by the Host and by most of the company has been maintained and the Knight, as one who 'wys was and obedient' (I. 851), prepares to keep the agreement into which he has entered 'by his *free* assent' and to embark on his tale 'with right a *myrie* cheere'. The great undertaking of the pilgrimage is finally on its way.

III

THE
KNIGHT'S TALE

It is no accident that Chaucer, in embarking upon his pilgrimage project, should have chosen to give the first tale (which is also, and by a considerable margin, the longest in verse) to the Knight: fitting also that the tale should reflect, in its deliberately patterned and formal art, the conception of a universe interdependent in all its parts and aspiring to a state of inclusive harmony. It is as though he chose, through this tale, to establish as a kind of touchstone for what is to follow the image of an idealized reality: to establish it, not as in any sense final or inclusive (for the tale raises more questions than it answers, and much of what follows is an implied qualification of what it seems to assert), but as an example of what one individual vision might be capable of attaining in the shape of a coherent image of the world and of man's place within it.

Set against these large affirmations an initial reading of the tale may come as something of a disappointment. What we seem to be given is a story based on Boccaccio's *Teseida* and in all probability given its original form by Chaucer at a relatively early date and only later reworked for inclusion in *The Canterbury Tales*.[1] It concerns two young men engaged in an impossible and finally unreal rivalry in love, for which they declare their readiness to make every sacrifice. One of the pair dies when he seems to have attained his goal, and the survivor (who is hardly distinguished from his rival by any notable superiority or merit) succeeds in marrying a heroine who has already declared that she would prefer to remain single. Seen from this point of view the tale may strike a modern reader as the product of one man's old-fashioned and somewhat remote vision. We may respond to the art shown in the telling, admire the pervasive symmetry of the design, and – at the end of it all – remain substantially unaffected.

To read the tale in this way, however, is seriously to limit Chaucer's intention. Its 'hero', as far as there is one, is certainly neither of these two obsessively parallel young men, but 'Duke' Theseus: a man of reason and Stoic integrity who is called upon to exercise the high vocation of *rule*, and who tries to play a distinctively human role in the face of an obscure and difficult reality – a reality which man needs must recognize as governed by a real if inscrutable order. To further that order to the best of his capacities, and to reflect his own sense of it in his actions and choices, is the distinctive vocation of Theseus in this story. In his pursuit of it, he is in part successful and in part a failure; for he is after all a man, and the weapons which he wields in the unending struggle – those of reason and responsibility, tolerance and moderation – are limited by the very facts of his human condition. Throughout the story he is seen making the best of the situations in which he finds himself and striving, as far as lies within his power, to direct them to ends which he regards as reasonable and positive. As a man conscious of his humanity, he knows that he cannot do less; but we need not expect him to attain final success in a struggle which is constantly renewed and which cannot, of its very nature, be brought to any satisfying temporal conclusion.

As the tale, which the Knight at once defines as belonging to the category of 'olde stories', opens Theseus is presented as 'lord' and 'governor' of Athens. He is also, we are told, the greatest 'conqueror' of his time, so that he combines in his person the supreme human vocations of *warrior* and *ruler*. To be alive is to be involved in conflict and to exercise control. In the former capacity Theseus has overcome the Amazons, 'the regne of Femenye' and, by so doing, has – as the Knight and his age would believe – reasserted the proper, 'reasonable' view of the natural relationship between men and women. This view he has confirmed to ends of peace by proposing to take his defeated enemy, 'the queene Ypolita', to himself in the creative and socially validated relationship of marriage. The story, therefore, begins by stressing what the Knight regards as a proper assertion of humane and responsible civility over the forces of barbarism,[2] an affirmation of natural and ordered relationship as the indispensable foundation of human society.

Human triumphs of this kind have their equally human cost, and this the Knight – who, as we know from the General Prologue, has spent a large part of his life on fields of battle[3] – well knows. The victory won by Theseus has a dark side, which it is no part of his intention to conceal. On his way home to celebrate his triumph and his marriage, Theseus is confronted with grief and unreason, in the form of the wailing women of Thebes who so uneasily 'perturb' his 'feste' with their laments. The speaker for the mourning ladies salutes him as one who has enjoyed the favours of Fortune; by so doing she introduces one of the guiding themes of the tale. Theseus has achieved his ends, and is returning in peace to enjoy the fruits of his victory; those whom he sees before him are the helpless victims of the same violent forces in man and nature that have given him his triumph. 'Fortune' is, in man's limited understanding of her operations, a double-edged power, which seems to operate beyond human control or comprehension. The 'reasonable' Theseus is her instrument, but so equally – as far as these mourners are concerned – is the bloody Theban tyrant Creon, 'Fulfild of ire and of iniquitee' (I. 940): the man who is ready to trample on compassion and decorum by refusing the bodies of his dead foes the grace of decent burial.

Faced by this challenge Theseus postpones the celebration of his victory to restore essential civility to Thebes. The advance of his redeeming hosts is given with a splendid sense of the values of war and chivalry, which are very close to the spirit of the story and – no doubt – to the imagination of the teller:

> The rede statue of Mars, with spere and targe,
> So shyneth in his white baner large,
> That alle the feeldes glyteren up and doun;
> And by his baner born is his penoun
> Of golde ful riche, in which ther was ybete
> The Mynotaur, which that he slough in Crete,
> Thus rit this duc, thus rit this conquerour,
> And in his hoost of chivalrie the flour. (I. 975–82)

The quickening of the imaginative tempo is unmistakable: so is the fact that Theseus is presented, and presents himself on his banner, as victor over the forces of darkness and bestial unreason represented by the Minotaur. These splendours of aristocratic pageantry, however, are not allowed to stand alone. Side by side with them we are given in full measure the grim realities of war. Theseus succeeds in asserting the order of civility in Thebes; but he does so at the price which victory in this order of things entails. The city is ruthlessly destroyed – we are told that he 'rente adoun bothe wall and sparre and rafter' (I. 990) – before the ladies are able to carry out their seemly rites over their husbands' remains.

The aftermath of battle is shown again with a realism that no chivalrous idealism is allowed to disguise. The 'pilours' – the marauding human scavengers who played so large a part on ancient and medieval battlefields – were much in evidence, 'diden bisynesse and cure',

> To ransake in the taas of bodyes dede,
> Hem for to strepe of harneys and of wede. (I. 1005–6)

Against this background we are introduced to the 'heroes' of our 'romantic' story. In the bloody processes of pillage, the seemingly lifeless bodies of Palamon and Arcite are discovered: not dead, though grievously wounded, but with signs of life still in them. Their fate follows the inexorable laws of war, from which not even Theseus can separate himself. 'He nolde no raunsoun' we are told, and the pair are sent into what is envisaged as life-long imprisonment. The reality is, in essence, as we have already met it on Theseus' road to Athens. The victor's fate is to live

in joye and in honour

Terme of his lyf;   (I. 1028–9)

theirs is to languish in a tower,

in angwissh and in wo, . . .
For everemoore; ther may no gold hem quite.
(I. 1030, 1032)

'What nedeth wordes mo?', to echo one of Chaucer's favourite rhetorical questions, which makes its appearance at this point. To believe that matters might, on this level, have worked themselves out to a different end is to fall into sentimental delusion.

All this is the necessary prelude to a story that introduces the central theme of love: not 'love' in the 'romantic' sense, source of alternating ecstasy and misery (though this too finds its place in the larger design), but rather as a fundamental ruling principle in all life. For Chaucer, as for every writer of his time, man *is* in a very real sense what he loves. Created to love, and to respond to the love which fulfilled itself in making him,[4] he achieves the full range of his possibilities in the quality and the right direction of the love which moves him. *Pondus meum amor meus* ('My love is the weight that moves me', as St. Augustine classically puts it.[5] Of that universal principle, the attraction that brings together men and women is one particular instance, at once central to life and peculiarly, dangerously ambivalent.

The treatment of this force in literature was governed by conventions, and so at this point in the elaborate formal pattern which constitutes the tale, Emelye, 'the shene',[6] the fair, is introduced: less as a living woman than as a *symbol*, the season of May rendered through the consecrated devices of love poetry and walking in the enclosed garden of Love:

This passeth yeer by yeer and day by day,
Till it fil ones, in a morwe of May,
That Emelye, that fairer was to sene
Than is the lylie upon his stalke grene,
And fressher than the May with floures newe –
For with the rose colour stroof hire hewe,
I noot which was the fyner of hem two –
Er it were day, as was hir wone to do,

She was arisen and al redy dight;
For May wole have no slogardie a-nyght.
The sesoun priketh every gentil herte,
And maketh hym out of his slep to sterte,
And seith 'Arys, and do thyn observaunce.'
This maked Emelye have remembraunce
To doon honour to May, and for to ryse.
Yclothed was she fressh, for to devyse:
Hir yelow heer was broyded in a tresse
Bihynde hir bak, a yerde long, I gesse.
And in the gardyn, at the sonne upriste,
She walketh up and doun, and as hire liste
She gadereth floures, party white and rede,
To make a subtil gerland for hire hede;
And as an aungel hevenysshly she soong.   (I. 1033–55)

It is not an accident that the passage echoes themes touched upon in the opening lines of the General Prologue: here too the time of restored life 'priketh', stimulates the instinctive reactions of every 'gentil', properly disposed heart, doing away with the 'slogardie' of the dead season and prompting due recognition of human life as bound up with, essentially responsive to, the reborn energies of nature. The remoteness of the picture is appropriate to the nature of the tale. A greater degree of realism would destroy the intended effect, inducing us to fix our attention on issues of purely personal fulfilment rather than on the place of love as a universal human compulsion in the world where Theseus, as a responsible human being coping with his inescapable destiny and – within human limitation – shaping that of others, makes his choices and suffers their consequences.

The reaction of the two young men to the vision so unexpectedly, and so tantalizingly offered them, is as patterned as the presentation of Emelye itself. Palamon first catches a glimpse of her through his prison bars and is forthwith and irresistibly struck. 'He bleynte and cride, "A!"', we are told, not without a touch of unobtrusive humour. Arcite, when he hears this exclamation, assumes that it is an expression of pain at the plight in which his friend, like himself, finds himself without reasonable hope of relief. In this belief he offers Palamon consolation in the 'reasonable', Stoic attitude which prevails in so much of the tale. Palamon, he argues, should be *patient* – this is the first introduction of a word which will play an increasing part in the development of the tales – since it is clear that their situation has no remedy that lies in their hands, and since it must be presumed that some kind of providence is in fact obscurely responsible for their plight. 'We moste endure it; this is the short and playn' (I. 1091):

words, we may assume which in their laconic finality would appeal to the Knight's outlook, and which the 'reasonable' Theseus might well have made his own.

They do not, however, appeal to Palamon in his new-found love. His glimpse of Emelye has introduced into the tale a new factor which has to be reckoned with, which is indeed no small part of human life:

> The fairnesse of that lady that I see
> Yond in the gardyn romen to and fro
> Is cause of al my criyng and my wo.
> I noot wher she be womman or goddesse,
> But Venus is it soothly, as I gesse.   (I. 1098–1102)

The power of Venus – that ambivalent compound of creative life and irrational desire – provoking the confusion in Palamon's mind between a 'goddess' and a 'woman', expresses itself in pain and frustration – 'crying' and 'woe' – and compels something very like an act of worship. Arcite himself, for all his recent assertion of philosophical resignation, is soon found to be helpless in the face of this challenge. Struck with the irresistible power of Emelye's beauty, he sets aside his own advice and becomes his friend's mortal rival for her love.

Here we are required to be faithful to the central values of the tale. What is common to *both* these young men, and unites them in an excess of unreason, is that each sees nothing incongruous in asserting that he must *die* if he is not vouchsafed possession of the object of his love. The stress lies where it so often lies when medieval thought rises to the level of the great issues of human life: on the fundamental, though natural human error which leads men to assert *a part of life* – even a part in itself good and necessary – at the expense of what this story, in its delicate and patterned unity, takes to be the *whole*. Indeed, to give some measure of expression to a conception of the 'whole', to explore its nature and its relation to the varied 'parts' of life as man actually lives it, could be seen as the real aim of the tale and of *The Canterbury Tales* as a whole.

The immediate result of Emelye's entry into the story is to cause a senseless quarrel between the two friends. Here, again, we touch upon the wider presuppositions of the story, which concern the relationship of the reality represented by 'love' to the more ample human bond of 'friendship'. 'Friendship', it would seem, is a force making for unity and realism, of the kind which Palamon and Arcite have so far shown in prison: *love*, in the guise of the desire prompted by 'Venus', can reasonably be seen as a source of division leading to the extremity which Palamon evoked when he explained his feelings to his friend. The solution might lie in recognizing 'friendship' as the more inclusive reality of which 'desire' is, at best, no more than a particularly urgent aspect; and, beyond this, in seeing both as aspects of life to be reconciled in relation to a higher and more inclusive conception of *love*.

It is not a solution which is available at this moment to the two young men. The quarrel which breaks out between them is conducted in terms of *priority* and *possession* that exclude any reasonable determination. Palamon accuses his friend of the supremely divisive sin of treachery. He thereby undermines the reasonable basis of their friendship (for reason sees in *trust* an indispensable foundation for *all* human relationships) and bases his claim to Emelye quite simply on the fact that he was the first to see her. Arcite carries the story even further into unreason when he asserts that love (by which he means, in effect, desire) is an irresistible force which bends *positive law* and *degree* – those twin pillars of Theseus' conception of an ordered and humane society – to its obsessive ends:

> Love is a gretter lawe, by my pan,
> Than may be yeve to any erthely man;
> And therfore positif lawe and swich decree
> Is broken al day for love in ech degree.
> A man moot nedes love, maugree his heed.
> He may nat fleen it, thogh he sholde be deed.
>
> (I. 1165–70)

The results of Arcite's agitated squeezing of his 'pan' are perverse and absurd. A man, he rashly asserts, is *driven* to follow the impulse of what he chooses to call 'love' in despite of reason, 'maugree his heed'. He 'moot nedes love', even when the consequence of so doing is to 'be dead' and so beyond the possibility of satisfying what ought to be, by right, a craving for enhanced life. In all this it is apparent that we are meant not so much to establish differences of a psychological or moral kind as to understand that *both* these rivals are giving up the birth-right of reason and self-control which Theseus values as the distinctive heritage of man.

The immediate consequence of their quarrel is to turn the relationship between the two young men upside-down, making them less tragic than absurd. As Arcite recognizes, in what amounts to a comment on their irrational and absurd obstinacy:

> We stryve as dide the houndes for the boon;
> They foughte al day, and yet hir part was noon.
> Ther cam a kyte, whil that they were so wrothe,
> And baar awey the boon bitwixe hem bothe.
>
> (I. 1177–80)

True to the nature of his genius Chaucer allows the Knight to deflate the excessive pretensions of his heroes and to keep well on this side of romantic tragedy. Not only has neither of these two young men the least hope in reason of succeeding in his love, but its object is not even aware of the passions she has aroused. The 'law' of desire is, or so it seems, the entirely irrational one put forward by Arcite immediately after his rueful recognition of their real situation. 'Ech man for hymself, ther is noon oother' (I. 1182). It would be hard to put more strongly the point that what is called 'love', followed in this way, is not a source of life but an irrational drive inimical to the bonds of friendship and finally hostile to the very concept of society. It remains, nevertheless, a force which imposes itself in the lives of men – they 'moot nedes love' – and which no abstract resolution of the 'head' can convincingly resolve.

The story, however, is still only at its beginning, and the full development has much further to go. Both lovers share with the rest of men the situation of being subject to the laws of Fortune, considered as the instrument of an inscrutable destinal force which governs human affairs. It is Fortune which, quite unexpectedly, opens the way to freedom for Arcite. The immediate consequence is to bring out even more clearly the upside-down nature of the situation of the two lovers in terms of wry comedy. Arcite, having been given his freedom, goes so far as to envy his companion for being able to remain, in prison, close to the common object of their devotion; whilst Palamon, still behind bars, envies Arcite for the freedom which, he thinks, may yet make it possible for him to approach and win Emelye. Both men see Fortune as operating exclusively in relation to their own concerns and desires. Both, in long and patterned utterances, rail bitterly against her, because it seems that she will not do what they require of her; and *both*, of course, are unreasonable in their complaints.

The complaints, however, perverse as they are, are not without relation to the larger ends of the tale. For these it is not without meaning that Arcite is brought, however unconsciously, to a true vision of the behaviour of human beings (himself not excluded) in their subjection to Fortune:

> We witen nat what thing we preyen heere:
> We faren as he that dronke is as a mous.
> A dronke man woot wel he hath an hous,
> But he noot which the righte way is thider,
> And to a dronke man the wey is slider.   (I. 1260–4)

The comparison of man, in his erratic progress through life, to a mouse or a drunkard is proverbial in much medieval writing and preaching.[7] Chaucer uses it elsewhere in the *Tales*,[8] and not a few of the pilgrims proceed drunkenly or erratically upon their way: so much so, indeed, that the condition, and its consequences, may be thought of as one of the underlying *motifs* that bind the pilgrimage together. In this instance Arcite's words amount to an unwitting comment on his own situation: that, and a good deal more. Men do not understand 'what thyng (they) preyen heere', for the simple reason that they are moved to pray for what they see as exclusively and immediately desirable. They recognize that they have a 'house', a destination towards which, as 'pilgrims', they are bound; but they are mistaken in believing that the 'way' there can lie in the pursuit of the goals that present themselves to them as uniquely and exclusively attractive. The irony lies, as ever, in Arcite's inability to draw a true lesson from his own recognition of the truth; and much the same is true of Palamon who goes so far as to envy his companion for the happy chance, as he sees it, which has been given him to wage war against Theseus himself.

Beyond these excesses, Palamon raises in the course of his complaint valid questions which Chaucer, by the very fact of posing them, intends to introduce into his design for the *Tales*. The terms in which they are put forward owe much to his reading of Boethius and belong, no doubt, to his refashioning of the original tale:

> Thanne seyde he, 'O crueel goddes that governe
> This world with byndyng of youre word eterne,
> And writen in the table of atthamaunt
> Youre parlement and youre eterne graunt,
> What is mankynde moore unto you holde
> Than is the sheep that rouketh in the folde?
> For slayn is man right as another beest,
> And dwelleth eek in prison and arreest,
> And hath siknesse and greet adversitee,
> And ofte tymes giltelees, pardee.
>   What governance is in this prescience,
> That giltelees tormenteth innocence?
> And yet encresseth this al my penaunce,
> That man is bounden to his observaunce,
> For Goddes sake, to letten of his wille,
> Ther as a beest may al his lust fulfille.
> And whan a beest is deed he hath no peyne;
> But man after his deeth moot wepe and pleyne,
> Though in this world he have care and wo.   (I. 1303–21)

Our reaction to this 'compleynt' will not be a simple one. Like the situation which produced it, it clearly contains elements of unreason, on which the Knight reflects his own brand of detached, tolerant humour; but – we must add – in arraigning the 'cruel' divinities whom he makes responsible for what are in fact the results of his own blindness, Palamon raises questions which must affect any 'providential' philosophy of the kind which this story is designed to propose. How is the suffering of the innocent to be reconciled to a supposedly 'providential' governing of the world? How is it that the beasts, lacking foresight or freedom to choose, are able to fulfil their instinctive needs whereas man, possessed of these gifts, seems condemned to be discontented in this life and, if what we are told on the best 'authority' is true, to suffer in the next? These large questions cannot have an immediate or abstractedly conclusive 'answer'. An attitude towards them will be worked out, tentatively and without finality, in the course of the tale.

The second part of the tale opens with Arcite enjoying his unexpected freedom in Thebes. 'Enjoyment' can hardly describe his condition; he shows all the signs of a 'woeful' lover, and his state is said to be 'upso doun', an inversion of normal and responsible humanity. Advised to return to Athens through the medium of one of those capricious divine interventions which so abound in this tale, he determines to go there in disguise – defying Theseus' express decree in giving him his freedom – and enter the Duke's service.

What follows moves on strictly parallel lines from Arcite to Palamon and back again. With Arcite freed, Palamon contrives to escape from his prison and plans in his unreason to wage war on Theseus. By so doing he contemplates the possibility of sinning against what both he and the Knight would normally consider a man's deepest obligations of loyalty and civilized trust. Arcite, for his part, is shown doing his lover's 'observaunce' to May, blissfully unaware

> how ny that was his care,
> Til that Fortune had broght him in the snare.
> (I. 1489–90)

Palamon, in hiding, overhears him complaining bitterly against his adverse fate. He makes himself known and accuses his friend of having betrayed him. That the compulsive force of 'love' has destroyed the foundations of their relationship is apparent in his bitter and self-assertive challenge:

> Thou shalt nat love my lady Emelye,
> But I wol love hire oonly and namo;
> For I am Palamon, thy mortal foo. (I. 1588–90)

'Oonly and namo': the words stress the willed exclusiveness, the dedication to unreasonable and isolating self, which passion of this kind imposes on its victims. Arcite accepts the challenge of the friend who has become his enemy unto death, and they proceed to fight in obedience to the laws of chivalry as they understand them. The combat is fought out in a typical ironic balance of the chivalrous and the absurd: 'Up to the ancle foghte they in hir blood' (I. 1660).

Both lovers are by now seen to be operating beyond common sense and without any recognition of the realities which govern their destinies. These reassert themselves when the narrator restores Theseus to the centre of the action. Engaged in his favourite 'royal' sport of hunting, and following the natural impulse of the season –

> *Cleer* was the day, as I have toold er this,
> And Theseus *with alle joye and blis*,
> With his Ypolita the faire queene,
> And Emelye, *clothed al in grene*,
> On huntyng be they riden *roially* –   (I. 1683–7)

he comes upon the two young men engaged in their desperate and absurd conflict. He reproves them for carrying on their quarrel in defiance of decorum and true valour: 'Withouten juge or oother officere' (I. 1712). It is essential to his view of life that even the passionate conflicts which inevitably arise between men should be formalized, made tolerable by being conducted in the recognition of inalienable social obligations.

Caught in the act, the two young men can only admit their guilt. Palamon recognizes that he deserves to die, but asks that Arcite should share his fate. Even with his own death in prospect it is a measure of his blindness that he cannot tolerate the thought that his rival should be left in possession of Emelye. Evidently there can be no resolution on these terms. The ladies in Theseus' train fulfil their function by praying Theseus to exercise clemency. After all, as they put it, at once disarmingly and with a touch of irony,

> *gentil men* they were of greet estaat,
> And *no thyng but for love* was this debaat: (I. 1753–4)

values which may be held at this point to serve the ends of the tale, but which are scarcely adequate – however attractive they may be to the teller – to answer to its final ends. Theseus, as befits the kind of ruler he is, accedes to these requests; for, in one of Chaucer's favourite phrases, used of him at this point: 'pitee renneth soone in gentil herte' (I. 1761).

His following reflections take us rather more deeply into the substance of the tale. He states that the responsibility which rests upon his shoulders is best exercised when justice is tempered with mercy:

> And in his gentil herte he thoughte anon,
> And softe unto hymself he seyde, 'Fy
> Upon a lord that wol have no mercy,
> But been a leon, bothe in word and dede,
> To hem that been in repentaunce and drede.'
> (I. 1772–6)

The emphasis upon the values of 'gentility' – '*gentil* man', '*gentil* herte' –

points to the source of the teller's values and to their limitation. The word, it need hardly be said, covers a range of humane and civilizing values that extends beyond any association it can readily command to-day. To be *gentil* is to aspire to tolerance and graciousness in a certain context, at once social and ideal, which can be summed up in the word 'chivalry': and therein lies both its attractiveness and finally, when faced with the reality of a complex and ungovernable world, its inadequacy. A full realization of this, however, will only come later in the tale. For the moment Theseus goes on to comment with wryly dispassionate tolerance on the strange phenomenon of love – or passion – itself:

> The god of love, a, *benedicite!*
> How myghty and how greet a lord is he!
> Ayeyns his myght ther gayneth none obstacles.
> (I. 1785–7)

The proof lies before him, in the shape of two young men who were vouchsafed the good fortune to be freed from perpetual imprisonment and who have used their freedom to enter into durance of another kind, only to deliver themselves into the power of the man whose decree they have broken and who must, perforce, be their judge.

This line of reflection leads Theseus to comment, with the kind of detachment that only experience can give, on the absurd spectacle of two noble young men engaged in asserting melodramatically their rival claims upon a young woman who is his own daughter and who is not even aware that either of them loves her:

> Bihoold, for Goddes sake that sit above,
> Se how they blede! be they noght well arrayed?
> Thus hath hir lord, the god of love, ypayed
> Hir wages and hir fees for hir servyse!
> And yet they wenen for to been ful wyse
> That serven love, for aught that may bifalle.
> But this is yet the beste game of alle,
> That she for whom they han this jolitee
> Kan hem therfore as muche thank as me.
> She woot namoore of al this hoote fare,
> By God, than woot a cokkow or an hare!   (I. 1800–10)

The implications of 'jolitee' as a word to describe the murderous results of 'al this hoote fare' are exquisitely ironic. Theseus' last word, however, does not rest there. The god of love is a 'great' and 'mighty' lord whose power, as he knows from his own past experience, no man can ignore with impunity: 'I woot it by myself ful yore agon' (I. 1813). *Desire* is of its nature divisive, where true *friendship* unites. Recognition of this truth is a first step towards the resolution of this story. What cannot be denied or set aside can be controlled, directed into channels of civil humanity, and this Theseus now proposes to accomplish. He announces his decision, which is to leave the entire matter to *destiny* – upon which, however, he will impose the form of a chivalrous tournament – and promises that the winner shall receive the object of his love in marriage. Of this tournament he himself will be the moderator, 'evene juge and trewe'; for man, although he cannot create his destiny or finally shape its ends, is given the capacity to channel it into forms of reason and so make it humanly acceptable. On this assertion by Theseus of his civilizing, humanizing function the second part of the story closes.

In the third section the organization of the tournament becomes in Theseus' conception the symbol of a chivalrous and ordered conception of human life. The lists are set up in measured formality. The scene is to constitute 'a *noble* theatre' (I. 1885) in which vital, and sometimes sombre issues are to be decided. In it are to be reflected, under the eyes of the obscure 'gods' who sway the affairs of men by working upon their thoughts and passions, the conflicting issues of life and death which it is man's distinctive vocation – and his problem – to seek to bring into harmony.

With this general plan in mind, various points concerning the lists emerge with a new significance. It forms a perfect circle, so constructed that from any point within it each spectator is in full view of the whole. It is also, by virtue of constituting a 'perfect' shape, an ideal example of the art, or 'craft', of man.[9] In this perfect circle, three entrances symmetrically placed are dedicated to appropriate 'deities', who are given a presiding function over the human proceedings: Venus to the East, Mars to the West, and to the North Diana, goddess of chastity. The three 'gates' are placed at equal distance from one another, and Palamon, Arcite, and Emelye place themselves under their respective patronage. Each of their temples is decorated with the finest art, and a good deal of space is given to their description. It should be noted that roughly the same number of lines is given to each, as though in support of the sense of intricately balanced contraries at which the episode aims: also that each of the presiding 'deities', far from being simple or immediately comprehensible, answers to a sense of the sinister, or at least of the ambiguous. There is a strong suggestion that they represent forces of darkness in human nature itself: forces which seek passionately to evade the exercise of distinctively human, and civilized, control.

The details of the descriptions include some of the most powerful writing in the poem. None of these 'divinities' is identified to any marked degree with happy, or fortunate elements in human experience. They are the old pagan gods superseded – in the mind of the Knight and his audience, if not in that of the human actors in the tale – by the Christian dispensation; and they also, by exercising the 'influence' that belongs to them as planets, shape the destiny which men, in their imperfect, time-conditioned view of the ways of Providence, see as their dark and inscrutable Fate.[10] Venus, the first to be described, is associated almost exclusively with the woes of unhappy lovers. She bears in her hand the cuckoo, symbol of deception, and her description is focussed on the ambiguous pleasures of love, interwoven with grief and disappointment:

> The broken slepes, and the sikes colde,
> The sacred teeris, and the waymentynge,
> The firy strokes of the desirynge
> That loves servantz in this lyf enduren.   (I. 1920–3)

The doors of the temple are guarded by the porter 'Ydelnesse',[11] and on its walls appear the heroic figures of classical and Biblical antiquity – Hercules, Medea, Turnus, and Croesus – side by side with Solomon: nearly all of them destroyed or in some way diminished by the force of their passion. At the end of this list of unhappy 'examples' we are given the sensual, enticing image of the goddess – 'naked, fletynge in the large see', as a long tradition envisaged her[12] – and of her wayward son, Cupid, blind and dangerous in the wielding of his bow.

The account of the second presiding 'deity' – Mars, god of war – is more unequivocally sinister. His habitation is a 'grisly' place, as befits a power dedicated to death and destruction. It is decorated by the picture of a savage and uncouth forest,

> In which ther dwelleth neither man ne best,   (I. 1976)

deprived of all the comforting amenities of life. Here, appropriately, at the centre of this desolation is the temple of 'Mars armypotent'. The shrine is dark and windowless, built of iron and steel, enclosed by doors of 'adamant eterne'. All this is the background for a passage of great force, which conveys the graphic personification of 'Felonye' and of the other sinister manifestations that accompany the god of war:

> Ther saugh I first the derke ymaginyng
> Of Felonye, and al the compassyng;
> The crueel Ire, reed as any gleede;
> The pykepurs, and eek the pale Drede;
> The smylere with the knyf under the cloke;
> The shepne brennynge with the blake smoke;
> The tresoun of the mordrynge in the bedde;
> The open werre, with woundes al bibledde;
> Contek, with blody knyf and sharp manace.

Al ful of chirkyng was that sory place.
The sleere of hymself yet saugh I ther, –
His herte-blood hath bathed al his heer;
The nayl ydryven in the shode a-nyght;
The colde deeth, with mouth gapyng upright.
Amyddes of the temple sat Meschaunce,
With disconfort and sory contenaunce.
Yet saugh I Woodnesse, laughynge in his rage,
Armed Compleint, Outhees, and fiers Outrage;
The careyne in the busk, with throte ycorve;
A thousand slayn, and nat of qualm ystorve.
The tiraunt, with the pray by force yraft;
The toun destroyed, ther was no thyng laft.
Yet saugh I brent the shippes hoppesteres;
The hunte strangled with the wilde beres;
The sowe freten the child right in the cradel;
The cook yscalded, for al his longe ladel.
Noght was foryeten by the infortune of Marte
The cartere overryden with his carte:
Under the wheel ful lowe he lay adoun. (I. 1995–2023)

Many of the elements that make up this catalogue of the war-god's operation go notably beyond what is normally thought of as his province. They extend the picture to cover all forms of violent insecurity in human life, realities of which the men of Chaucer's age – and, indeed, of most periods in human history – have been intensely aware: we might do well, perhaps, to think of Mars not only as the promoter of armed conflict but as the 'deity' who presides over, or personifies, all the elements of strife and violent adversity to which man is subject. Man may hope to control these forces and so to render them tolerable; but his effort to do so will be an unending struggle, and there is no certainty of final success. The picture is rounded off by the figure of 'Conquest' (I. 2028–30), enthroned in 'grete honour', universally applauded in the midst of the ruin and desolation he has caused, and by that of the war-god himself, 'armed' and 'grim', 'as he were wood', with the wolf threateningly couched at his feet.

The third 'deity' – Diana – is given less space and makes less impression: no doubt because her devotee, Emelye, is less an active than a passive presence in this story. None the less, she too is a notably ambiguous figure. It is stressed that she is a *jealous* goddess, whose influence is shown in tales of sorrow and destruction. We are told that her gaze is directed *downward*, towards Pluto and the regions of darkness: and that she is associated with the pains of childbirth, the suffering that accompanies the hard, unwilling birth of new life.

By the end of these elaborate descriptions it is apparent that the vision of life which this tale conveys, and which is set at the outset of the pilgrimage, is far from being merely decorative or chivalrously remote. Its world is the plaything of obscure destinal forces to which the Knight seems to oppose a kind of fatalistic Stoicism and which Theseus, supported by the best human resources of reasonable understanding (but, we must add, by no more than these), is attempting to control and order by bringing them into the lists in the name of his own conception of a positive and harmonious life.

Against this background we are shown the Knight's chivalrous imagination expanding to take in the pageant of the contenders on either side. The verse notably quickens, becomes suffused with new imaginative energy, as the picture grows into actuality in his mind:

> And sikerly ther trowed many a man
> That nevere, sithen that the world bigan,
> As for to speke of knyghthod of hir hond,
> As fer as God hath maked see or lond,
> Nas of so fewe so noble a compaignye.
> For every wight that lovede chivalrye,
> And wolde, his thankes, han a passant name,
> Hath preyed that he myghte been of that game;
> And wel was hym that therto chosen was.
> For if ther fille tomorwe swich a cas,
> Ye knowen wel that every lusty knyght
> That loveth paramours and hath his myght,
> Were it in Engelond or elleswhere,
> They wolde, hir thankes, wilnen to be there, –
> To fighte for a lady, *benedicitee!*
> It were a lusty sighte for to see.   (I. 2101–16)

It is here, if anywhere, that the teller's sense of what *he* sees as the good life is most eloquently conveyed. We shall, if we are to respond adequately to the sense of the tale, give his enthusiasm its full value; but we shall *not*, equally, be tempted to identify ourselves unreservedly with it. We have been shown, after all, and in no uncertain terms, what the love of 'paramours' – which is the service of Venus – can imply, what subjection to the rule of Mars can really mean. Though it is true that Theseus aims to reduce these blind forces to a human and ordered conception of life, in which the values of 'noble' fellowship and chivalrous emulation have a distinctive part to play, we shall not be inclined to over-estimate man's ability to dominate his circumstance, or to shape it to his civilizing will. There is even in the Knight's quickened enthusiasm a sense of something that lies between the touching and the absurd, a note which the author

allows these words to insinuate without permitting his consummate tact
to fall into caricature or condescension.

The presentation of the opposing champions, to which this leads, is
conducted on a note of high formality. Theseus, as president of the lists,
opens the proceedings as dispenser of the supremely social, civilizing
obligation of hospitality:

> This Theseus, this duc, this worthy knyght,
> Whan he had broght hem into his citee,
> And inned hem, everich at his degree,
> He festeth hem, and dooth so greet labour
> To esen hem and doon hem al honour,
> That yet men wenen that no mannes wit
> Of noon estaat ne koude amenden it.
>   The mynstralcye, the service at the feeste,
> The grete yiftes to the meeste and leeste,
> The riche array of Theseus paleys,
> Ne who sat first ne last upon the deys,
> What ladyes fairest been or best daunsynge,
> Or which of hem kan dauncen best and synge,
> Ne who moost felyngly speketh of love;
> What haukes sitten on the perche above,
> What houndes liggen on the floor adoun, –
> Of al this make I now no mencioun.   (I. 2190–2206)

Once again we sense the Knight's imaginative response to scenes that
reflect his deepest sense of what is precious and distinctive in the life of
men. The values he celebrates are those of formal and ordered chivalry;
and it is significant that they allow a place, side by side with aristocratic
grace and decorum, to the sentiment of those who speak *'felyngly'* of their
emotions in love. This, or so the Knight evidently feels, is the kind of life
which man can shape for himself, setting it up, as it were, in his own
defence against the present and ever-menacing forces of chaos which
surround him and threaten an endless relapse into barbarism. Here, in
short, epitomized in terms of a convention accepted and at the same time
placed within its inescapable bounds, we are shown the possibilities, and
the limitations, of one imaginative reading of the *reasonable* and chivalrous
life.

At the height of these elaborate proceedings each contendant dedicates
himself to the 'deity' he has chosen to serve. Once again the respective
vows are given in patterned contrast. First Palamon makes his
'pilgrimage' to the goddess whom he addresses as 'Citherea benigne'. His
prayer opens with a lover's plea for 'pity'; but it is significant that he
confesses that his 'service' has brought him, not to happiness, but to a

condition which he describes as being in 'hell' and into a 'confused' state. His only remedy, as he sees it, is that of the lover of literary convention. He will beg for 'mercy' at the hands of the ambivalent goddess who bears life and death in her hands. It is important that in the name of this devotion he is ready to renounce what is – again in terms of the story and its values, as the Knight is concerned to advance them – an essential part of his true humanity. He declares his readiness to forgo martial glory and asks only to obtain possession of Emelye, either in victory or in defeat. A similar excess governs his final statement that, in the absence of the object of his desire, life itself is indifferent to him. To these confused and pathetic prayers the goddess responds, as is her wont, with an ambiguous sign.

After Palamon, it is Emelye's turn to express her devotion. She makes her sacrifice to Diana, the 'goddesse of maydens' who dwells in the 'regne of Pluto derk and lowe' (I. 2299). She has no desire to accept her natural destiny of marriage, fears the pains of childbirth, and begs to be allowed to remain a maid for the term of her life. What she most desires, disarmingly enough, is that Palamon and Arcite should live 'in love and pees'; and – for the rest – as far as marriage goes, let them look elsewhere. She fears their 'hot love', in which she sees the 'torment' of 'desire'; but, in spite of her instinctive reaction, she senses that her destiny lies in submission to her womanly condition and goes on to pray – not without pathos – that if it is indeed her fate to marry, she may be given to whichever of her suitors most loves her. To this essentially pathetic prayer the response of the goddess is ambiguous, even sinister. The fires on the altar are seen to be quenched, 'blody dropes' appear, and Emelye is plunged in fear and foreboding. Finally Diana appears in person and utters her decree. She confirms that it is indeed her subject's destiny to be given in marriage, but does not reveal which of her suitors is to prevail.

It only remains for Arcite to sacrifice to 'fierce Mars'. He reminds the god of his legendary services to Venus and stresses his unequalled sorrow and the cruelty of his beloved. His prayer is a simple one for the *victory* which it is in the god's power to give: 'I aske thee namoore'. Mars, appearing in response to his devotee, grants this prayer and leaves Arcite full of joy: a joy to which the approaching resolution will give a deeply ironic twist.

Throughout these prayers there has been an element of dark obscurity which indicates that a potentially tragic design is being worked out beneath the decorative symmetries appropriate to the tale. Now, as the lists are about to open under Theseus' watchful and benevolent eye, Venus and Mars take up their eternal dispute and look to the 'colde' Saturn to intervene in their favour. Saturn is the most deeply ambivalent of all the gods. As the oldest among them, he represents a sinister power, essentially amoral and indifferent to human aspirations. His nature is conveyed in one of the most powerfully concentrated passages in the tale:

'My deere doghter Venus,' quod Saturne,
'My cours, that hath so wyde for to turne,
Hath moore power than woot any man.
Myn is the drenchyng in the see so wan;
Myn is the prison in the derke cote;
Myn is the stranglyng and hangyng by the throte,
The murmure and the cherles rebellyng,
The groynynge, and the pryvee empoysonyng;
I do vengeance and pleyn correccioun,
Whil I dwelle in the signe of the leoun.
Myn is the ruyne of the hye halles,
The fallynge of the toures and of the walles
Upon the mynour or the carpenter.
I slow Sampsoun, shakynge the piler;
And myne be the maladyes colde,
The derke tresons, and the castes olde;
My lookyng is the fader of pestilence.   (I. 2453–69)

At the end of this menacing self-revelation, Saturn promises Venus that
she shall have her will in spite of Mars' intervention in favour of Arcite.
The whole passage is governed by a profound sense of the dark forces that
influence the behaviour of men by working through their passions: forces
which tend to the destruction of all the efforts made by mere human
beings to keep them under reasonable control. The lists which have been
set up in the name of humane chivalry are about to become the arena in
which a greater contest, involving man's inescapable tragic destiny, is to
be worked out to its conclusion.

   With this weight of destiny overshadowing the human action we pass to
the fourth and last section of the tale. Against the precarious and
foreboding background which the poem has so powerfully presented the
intimations of life stand out with increased poignancy. It is, once again,
the season of May, of love, of dancing and rejoicing, all placed under the
patronage of Venus:

> Greet was the feeste in Atthenes that day,
> And eek the lusty seson of that May
> Made every wight to been in swich plesaunce
> That al that Mondy justen they and daunce,
> And spenden it in Venus heigh servyse.   (I. 2483–7)

Presiding over the vivid scene, with its bright and colourful sense of
human life asserting itself in endless bustle and stir (I. 2491–2515), we are
given Theseus set in a window above the press, 'as he were a god in trone'
(I. 2529), making ready to receive the contending champions. In

accordance with his obligations, he declares his intention of saving 'gentil bloud'. In the combat about to take place no one is to die: for the simple reason that this is, in his conception (and in the teller's) a feast, a celebration of life. The wisdom of this benevolent decision is acclaimed by the spectators, who raise their approving voices in 'murie stevene'.

Against this background of ceaseless, living activity the formal procession is drawn up to enter the arena. No sooner have the heralds proclaimed the joust, and been echoed by the popular acclaim – 'Do now youre devoir, yonge knyghtes proude' (I. 2598) – than the combat begins:

> Ther is namoore to seyn, but west and est
> In goon the speres ful sadly in arrest;
> In gooth the sharpe spore into the syde.
> Ther seen men who kan juste and who kan ryde;
> Ther shyveren shaftes upon sheeldes thikke;
> He feeleth thurgh the herte-spoon the prikke.
> Up spryngen speres twenty foot on highte;
> Out goon the swerdes as the silver brighte;
> The helmes they tohewen and toshrede;
> Out brest the blood with stierne stremes rede;
> With myghty maces the bones they tobreste.
> He thurgh the thikkeste of the throng gan threste;
> Ther stomblen steedes stronge, and doun gooth al;
> He rolleth under foot as dooth a bal;
> He foyneth on his feet with his tronchoun,
> And he hym hurtleth with his hors adoun.   (I. 2601–16)

The scene could be said to remind us of certain battle paintings by such artists as Paolo Uccello.[13] The blood and the wounds, we feel, belong to a decorative, almost fantastic world. It is interesting to note that as his enthusiasm rises, the Knight falls very noticeably into the old, alliterative models of English verse, to a degree perhaps unparalleled in Chaucer.[14] We may feel that this not only contributes to rendering the scene more lively, but to distancing it, making it clear that we are being asked to respond imaginatively to a world not only more colourful and humanly attractive, but definitely situated in an imaginatively recreated, even 'romanticized' past.

Thus far, all has proceeded in accordance with Theseus' design; and, for a time, this continues. As the conflict reaches its resolution Palamon is wounded and Theseus, as befits an impartial judge, awards the victory to Arcite. Mars' *protégé* seems to have won the day, and Venus is correspondingly, and very humanly, mortified: 'I am ashamed, doutelees'. The last word, however, remains with Saturn, who has already promised his intervention. In the moment of his triumph Arcite

suffers a fall, a stern reminder that in the world of time no man's state is
finally secure. Mortally wounded, and beyond the best efforts of
medicine, he is left to lament the universal fate of mortal man:

> What is this world? what asketh men to have?
> Now with his love, now in his colde grave
> Allone, withouten any compaignye.   (I. 2777–9)

'What asketh men to have?' Just – or so it seems – what they cannot in the
nature of things obtain: the overcoming of their inescapable final solitude.
Faced with his end, which is that of all men, Arcite urges Emelye, his
'sweete foo', to take his former friend for a husband, recognizing in the
light of his new situation the vanity of the quarrel that divided them:

> I have heer with my cosyn Palamon
> Had strif and rancour many a day agon
> For love of yow, and for my jalousye.   (I. 2783–5)

To make such restitution as is open to him, he pleads the cause of his
friend, the 'gentil' man whose virtues he failed to respect in life, but whom
he now recognizes for what he has always been. It may be worth noting, as
typical of the spirit of the story, which points to no easy or simply
orthodox resolution, that the Knight expresses himself at this point as
puzzled to determine the final destination of the dying man's soul:

> His spirit chaunged hous and wente ther,
> As I cam nevere, I kan nat tellen wher.   (I. 2809–10)

Perhaps appropriate in relation to this 'pagan' story, the Knight's
admission seems also to indicate, in the deliberately off-hand, gently
deprecating fashion so characteristic of Chaucer's art, a deeper, more
fundamental sense of the relativity of all human certainty.

Faced by the bitter outcome of this rivalry, the survivors are left to
'shriek' and 'howl' in expression of their grief:

> 'Why woldestow be deed,' thise wommen crye,
> 'And haddest gold ynough, and Emelye?'   (I. 2835–6)

Absurd though their expression of it may be, the grief is real enough, and
Theseus makes it his own. As he gives expression to it, he receives from
his father Egeus the typical consolation of 'experience', expressed with a
certain banality:

> 'Right as ther dyed nevere man,' quod he,
> 'That he ne lyvede in erthe in some degree,
> Right so ther lyvede never man,' he seyde,
> 'In al this world, that som tyme he ne deyde'.
> (I. 2843–6)

We may think that neither the statement of this indubitable fact, nor Egeus' expression of it, are calculated to bring much comfort or to throw much light on the situation. It would seem that Chaucer, through the Knight, is having recourse to the kind of dead-pan elusiveness which so often indicates his unwillingness to take comforting or solemn generalizations at their supposed value; but it is fair to add, lest we be induced to see in this passage nothing more than a rather facile jibe, that the metaphor which at once follows, comparing the course of human life to a journey of pilgrimage –

> This world nys but a thurghfare ful of wo,
> And we been pilgrymes, passynge to and fro –
>
> (I. 2847–8)

carries a greater measure of conviction, when taken with the nostalgic reference to death as release which follows – 'Deeth is an ende of every worldly soore' (I. 2849) – and points to a relevant, if by no means exclusive theme of the *Tales* as a whole.

Mourning, though appropriate and necessary, cannot be the last word. The business of life must be carried on, a 'parliament' is summoned, and before it Theseus makes his final summing-up. Eloquently and persuasively, he relates the events we have witnessed to a providential, 'Boethian' view of the universe and of man's place within its order. The statement is sober and realistic, as befits the orator: no excessive claims are made, and no assertion of pride or overweening confidence emerges. It is recognized that man, being what he is, cannot hope to dominate his circumstance. What he *can* do, is live within it in a spirit of sober faith regarding its final end, making for himself a tolerable and humane island of life in what must appear, where such faith is lacking, a sea of chaos and malign confusion. To do just this – to recognize his limitation and, at the same time, to entertain the faith which looks, however obscurely, beyond it – is man's distinctively human vocation as this tale presents it.

The argument which leads to this conclusion is, substantially, the argument which sustained Boethius in prison. It assumes the existence of a 'First Mover' who brought into being an ordered and comprehensive 'chain of being'[15] to establish a significant and purposive pattern throughout the universe which has emerged from his creative act:

> The Firste Moevere of the cause above,
> Whan he first made the faire cheyne of love,
> Greet was th'effect, and heigh was his entente,
> Wel wiste he why, and what thereof he mente;
> For with that faire cheyne of love he bond
> The fyr, the eyr, the water, and the lond
> In certeyn boundes, that they may nat flee.   (I. 2987–93)

Such is the picture – the reality rather – of the universe as it must appear to the understanding of the Creator who alone can know 'why' he brought it into existence. Seen from any lesser point of view this order presents itself, at least in part, as 'wrecched': for that death and change – 'Certeyne dayes and duracioun' (I. 2996) – are part of its nature is abundantly 'preeved by experience'. To a pagan view, such as that of Theseus, the contradiction between man's necessary submission to Fortune and his possession, or illusion, of free choice is not finally capable of resolution. At best, men may believe that a plan exists and that the apparently capricious ways of Fortune must be a part of it; but, beyond this, the Christian assertion that these ways are beneficent, to be seen in relation to a loving and creative purpose which governs the whole is beyond the limits of Theseus' essentially Stoic philosophy.

In what follows Theseus proceeds to consider how 'philosophy' can account for this apparent anomaly. He tells his audience that the 'First Mover' is of his nature 'stable' and 'eterne'; for it is an axiom that 'every part dirreyveth from his hool', and no partial thing can be conceived as having being except in relation to a complete and stable reality. The providential wisdom – the 'purveiaunce' – of the original Mover has so established the creation

> That speces of thynges and progressiouns
> Shullen enduren by successiouns,
> And nat eterne.   (I. 3013–15)

This much may be understood by observing the facts as they present themselves to men involved in time, and examples are available to show that all created things – the oak, the stone, the river, and the city – are destined to pass away: 'al this thynge hath ende' (I. 3026).

What is true of all created things is also valid for man, who is himself created and who shares the impermanence of the world of which, at least in his body, he forms a part:

> Of man and womman seen we wel also
> That nedes, in oon of thise termes two,
> This is to seyn, in youthe or elles age,
> He moot be deed, the kyng as shal a page;
> Som in his bed, som in the depe see,
> Som in the large feeld, as men may see;
> Ther helpeth noght, al goth that ilke weye.
> Thanne may I seyn that al this thyng moot deye.
>   (I. 3027–34)

Here, of course, as indeed through the whole of Theseus' discourse, we are concerned less with a supposedly 'philosophical' profundity than with some of the great moral commonplaces that governed medieval life. Chaucer is not giving us, through Theseus, an 'explanation', an answer to the problem which a recognition of his mortality presents to man. He is rather introducing a theme which will receive its variations, be considered from a succession of different standpoints, accepting and rejecting, in the course of the pilgrimage. Hard though it may be to recognize this truth, to rebel against it is vain:

> heer-agayns no creature on lyve,
> Of no degree, availleth for to stryve. (I. 3039–40)

It should be stressed – as we have already said – that all this represents a 'pagan' philosophy of Stoicism rather than a specifically Christian outlook. It is, after all, a tale of pagan times that we have been following. There exists also a distinctively Christian approach to these same problems which rests on an affirmation of man's nature as essentially spiritual, outside the order and the limitation of time to which, in the changing body, he is bound; but though Chaucer will elsewhere introduce this point of view he refrains from doing so at this stage in the pilgrimage. Theseus' reflections involve no leap of faith, no final conviction of the necessary beneficence of the creative purpose, at least as far as man can perceive it. They lead to a sober recognition of the inevitability of death as inseparable from human life: a fact, perhaps, which needs to be recognized because without it life, in any distinctively human sense, would be inconceivable. We value what we know we are bound, in time, to lose; indeed, if we did not know that we should lose it, it seems that the very idea of value would be inconceivable to us.

Wisdom, for this tale, consists in making 'Vertu of necessitee' (I. 3042), in accepting incontrovertible facts and in building, soberly and without vain self-assertion, on the recognition. Man, indeed, 'moot deye'; but he can at least reach some measure of fulfilment, as the Knight sees it, by dying *in honour*, in deference to the most deeply human values available to him, and it is right that we should be *glad* for those who so die. The contrary is 'wilfulness', a useless attempt to affirm the self in the face of reality. Better is it to consider that Arcite, by dying, has escaped the 'foule prisoun of this lyf': the 'prison' to which all forms of passionate self-assertion finally lead, and that – this being so – there is no *reason* why we whose lives are so fraught with mortal instability, should in the last resort grieve for him.

After these appropriate, if sombre reflections – which are, let us remember, the product of *this* tale and its teller, not the author's own considered vision, whatever that may have been – the ways of life resume their course. If Arcite has emerged victorious, and died, in the pursuit of his ideal, Palamon is left alive, to transform his romantic devotion into something more down to earth and more responsive to the realities of human life: to become, in other words, not a 'servaunt' of love but a responsible husband. Theseus, making the best of things as they are, prepares to make one joy out of two sorrows in the process of marrying Emelye to her surviving lover. By so doing, he shows himself true to his human vocation, which consists in bringing life out of death, in affirming man's instinct to *create*, to assert the specifically *social* nature of his commitment to life, in the face of forces which seem continually to threaten it with destruction. His final words to the successful, but – we must suppose – suitably chastened Palamon are expressed in terms of a characteristically humane wit which achieves its effect against the dark solemnity of what has gone before:

> 'I trowe ther nedeth litel sermonyng
> To make yow assente to this thyng'; (I. 3091–2)

the implied qualifying comment on his own preceding discourse, or 'sermon', is as evident as it is unobtrusive. The pair are joined together in the social bond of matrimony, itself seen as a reflection of the universal order previously declared.[16] Love is a function of Nature, and only when it is related to a positive and 'generative' purpose beyond, but including, individual satisfaction can it escape the final disenchantment which is the inevitable end of 'romantic' fantasy. The tale ends on a note of fulfilled if sober happiness as the Knight invokes the blessing of the assembled pilgrims in the form of a solemn and appropriate final 'Amen'.

IV

THE MILLER'S TALE
AND
THE REEVE'S TALE

The opening segment of *The Canterbury Tales* which starts with the General Prologue and ends with the abortive tale begun but not finished by the Cook is the longest connective sequence in the entire project. As such, it affords an important glimpse into the author's deeper purposes for the whole. What emerges, surely not by accident, is an initial proposal of ordered tale-telling which descends progressively into something like total chaos. The Knight's opening contribution has been an impressive expression of chivalry, the reflection of ideals of *order*, *gentility*, and *propriety* that meant a great deal to the medieval mind, and evidently to Chaucer himself. As such, it stands as a point of reference in relation to which we might reasonably expect the following tales to be judged. Its beauties, however, are compatible with a certain remoteness, and it is after all not Chaucer but the Knight who delivers it. What follows in this opening section is not an orderly progression, but a deliberate descent into disorder. The Miller's insistence on telling his tale represents a challenge to the standards of decorum represented by the Host as master of ceremonies and dear to the hearts of the 'gentils' who constitute the respectable part of the pilgrim company; and, as if this outrageous intervention were not sufficient, it is followed by the Reeve's resentful attack upon the Miller and, finally, by the barely coherent intervention of the Cook. By the end of this descending series of tales the original intention of ordered development and purpose has been subjected to something very like a complete reversal.

Considered in this light the brief prologue to *The Miller's Tale* is variously significant. The Knight's tale has been saluted by those who have heard it – or at least by some of them: 'And namely the gentils everichon' (I. 3113) – as a 'noble story'. The adjective answers very adequately to the values of the tale, and the Host greets this expression of enthusiasm with typical bluffness, laughing and swearing heartily before he calls on the Monk to follow with his contribution.

By making this proposal, the Host doubtless intends to preserve the appearance of hierarchical order. The Monk, by virtue of his vocation and his standing in the monastery, could be thought of as a learned man who might suitably follow the Knight in maintaining the dignity and moral tone of the enterprise. For the first of many occasions, however, the element of *disorder* inherent in *real* human life erupts into the pilgrimage. The Miller, already far gone in drink, thrusts aside all considerations of politeness – we are told that he would 'abyde no man for his curteisie' (I. 3123) – and cries out, in a grotesque parody of the central drama of Christian belief, 'in Pilates voys'. Interjecting his words with popular oaths which are themselves an echo of more 'serious' things – 'By armes, and by blood and bones'[1] – he takes up the Host's phrase and inserts an adjective which has an explicit bearing on what the company has just heard:

> I kan a *noble* tale for the nones,
> With which I *wol* now quite the Knyghtes tale.
> (I. 3126–7)

'I wol': the assertion of *will*, which will be echoed by other pilgrims of perverse or unseemly intention,[2] represents the entry of a new and challenging force into the ideal harmony of the pilgrimage. The Miller's is to be a tale which will set out to rival that of the Knight and to advance a disruptive comment upon the 'noble' aspirations which it embodied.

The Host, in his presiding capacity, sees where this will lead in terms of subverted decorum. He hastens to head off the Miller, addressing him as befits a fellow-pilgrim, as 'my leeve brother', and calling upon him to recognize his inferiority to others in the group: 'Som bettre man shal telle us first another' (I. 3130). The Miller, however, is in no mood to defer to a 'better' man, whomsoever he may be. 'By Goddes soule', he rejoins, 'that wol nat I', and threatens to abandon the company if his demand to speak is not met; and the Host, faced with this threat to the very spirit of the pilgrimage, gives him leave to proceed. For the first of many occasions, self-will asserts itself at the expense of ordered propriety, demanding to be inserted on its own terms in the design which the pilgrimage, as a reflection of human life, is intended to foster.

Having got his way the Miller is ready to admit that he is drunk, and that this may lead him to 'mysspeke'; but, having conceded this, he goes on to state his real purpose, which is to tell a tale at the expense of the carpenter-Reeve, who is his enemy by virtue of character and profession. A shadow of personal rivalry is for the first time openly thrown over the pilgrim brotherhood, declaring itself in the blunt, clipped malevolence of the Reeve's retort: 'Stynt thy clappe!', he says, and continues with his old man's ungenerous expression of moral resentment and contempt:

> Lat be thy lewed dronken harlotrye.
> It is a synne and eek a greet folye
> To apeyren any man, or hym defame,
> And eek to bryngen wyves in swich fame.
>
> (I. 3145–8)

The Miller's reply is a laughing evasion of this accusation of immorality. It is not Chaucer's voice in this matter, but we may think it does contain something of the author's instinct for recognizing human realities as they are. 'Leve brother Osewold', he says ironically echoing the Host's recent emphasis upon brotherhood: and then he goes on to make his point with what amounts to a repudiation, poised between cynicism and human tolerance, of the concentrated venom contained in the Reeve's 'moral' reproof. 'Who hath no wyf, he is no cokewold'; the position of those who are married is apt, in his 'realistic' view, to be less secure than they would like to think, but this will not, as he affirms with scarcely disguised irony, lead him to assert as much of his enemy: 'I sey nat therfore that thou art oon' (I. 3153).

All this points a good deal further than the immediate clash of personalities. The Miller is advancing the view that *all* men, himself included –

> Why artow angry with my tale now?
> I have a wyf, pardee, as wel as thow –
>
> (I. 3157–8)

are liable to undergo deception, and that the more prudent part may be to cling to illusion without seeking to look too closely into a truth that may prove to be anything but comforting. As to being a cuckold he says, 'I wol bileve wel that I am noon' (I. 3162); and 'you', he implies, with reference to his rival, might do well to set aside your old man's suspicions in case they should lead to the discovery of an inconvenient truth, of the kind which most men spend their lives evading. We are all, according to this 'philosophy', as well off as we think we are; and, for himself, the Miller affirms,

> Yet nolde I, for the oxen in my plogh,
> Take upon me moore than ynogh,
> As demen of myself that I were oon.
>
> (I. 3159–61)

To refrain from stirring up the likely unpalatable truth is, to the Miller's way of thinking, a condition of living tolerably, in reasonable comfort

within our circumstance. This is the attitude which he urges, in the name
of a finally specious but very human cynicism, upon the rival who, as he
well knows, is quite incapable of adopting it.[3]

The observation leads, still in the Miller's train of thought, to a typically
double-edged comment on the reality of marriage:

> An housbonde shal nat been inquisityf
> Of Goddes pryvetee, nor of his wyf.
> So he may fynde Goddes foyson there,
> Of the remenant nedeth nat enquere.
>
> (I. 3163–6)

These lines have reverberations which echo through the following tale
and indeed, in a larger sense, through the whole pilgrimage. The
carpenter of *The Miller's Tale* follows this advice quite literally, congratulat-
ing himself on being a man of simple belief, who has no desire to enquire
into 'Goddes pryvetee';[4] and certainly his happiness, while it lasts,
depends upon his willingness to remain blind to the conduct of his young
wife in whom he believes, with an old man's capacity for self-deception
where his comfort is concerned, that he has found nothing less than
'Goddes foyson'.[5] As to the 'remenant' – the reality which lies beyond this
illusion of beatitude – a married man 'nedeth nat enquere'; because,
though he may fail to recognize the fact, and would no doubt refuse to do
so if it were pressed upon him, the effect might be to disturb the state of
blissful ignorance which is, for most men, a condition of tolerable living.
The weakness of this 'philosophy' is double. It rests, in the first place, on
an attitude which blasphemously parallels God's 'privety' with that of a
woman's sensual attractions; and, in the second place, it answers to man's
invincible tendency to seek comfort at the price of willing his own
deception. The echo of these lines will extend far beyond the Miller's tale
to reflect on the Wife of Bath's story and on the tale to be told, in due
course, by the Merchant.[6] A main theme has been introduced into the
general plan of a pilgrimage which will repeatedly turn out to be
refractory to the designs of those who would like to impose upon it their
own sense of solid, ordered 'reality'.

At this point Chaucer chooses to intervene in his character as narrator to
raise once again the problem posed by the writer's obligation to adhere to
the truth of his matter. The Miller has advanced cynical attitudes, with
more than a touch of blasphemy in them. His tale will be crude, even
repellent in the ears of the 'gentils' to whom it was addressed and of those
who will now hear Chaucer's reading of it. The poet accordingly addresses
himself in excuse to every 'gentil wight', asserting – as he has already done
in the General Prologue – his obligation to be 'true' to his matter, and urges
those who may be displeased to exercise their freedom to 'turn over the

leaf' and look elsewhere for more edifying material:

> storial thyng that toucheth gentillesse,
> And eek moralitee and hoolynesse.
>
> (I. 3179–80)

In this way, the burden of recognizing 'truth' is left with each individual reader in accordance with his chosen presuppositions, and the blame of those who profess themselves shocked is left where it rests, upon themselves: 'Blameth nat me if that ye chese amys' (I. 3181). The obligation of the author is to the 'truth' of life as it presents itself, not to any partial or selective version of it. 'The Millere is a cherl, ye knowe wel this' (I. 3182); but he was *there*, a member of the company – like the Reeve and others, who also told of 'harlotrie' – and to suppress him in the interests of 'gentility' would be to renounce *truth*. This the author cannot do whilst remaining faithful to what he has seen as the essence of the vocation which makes him an imaginative creator reflecting life, and not the author of a moral treatise imposing abstractions – however venerable, or 'authoritative' – upon it. The last line of this prologue is a recommendation to proportion which is close to Chaucer's central vision. 'Men shal nat maken ernest of game' (I. 3186), because to do this is to be untrue to the nature of art and of life as it is offered to those engaged in the living of it. It is at least possible that the 'gentil' readers who profess themselves scandalized by the Miller's bawdry and exuberance are being excessively susceptible, self-approvingly refined, in their reaction to what their author is giving them; although in accepting this, one may also reflect that 'gentility' can be a humane and civilizing force, that a world which stressed the attributes of the Miller to the exclusion of those of the Knight would be very notably poorer for the choice.

A. The Miller's Tale

The tale told by the Miller stands then in a relationship of contrast to that told by the Knight. In recognizing this, it is important not to see the contrast in terms of mutually exclusive intentions. Chaucer's genius moves habitually, and fruitfully, within the limits indicated by 'high romance' and popular *fabliau*. It is generally unwilling to move beyond these terms, either in the direction of 'tragedy' or of the specifically 'religious' vision which was Dante's concern; and, within these boundaries, it shows a marked preference for avoiding mutually exclusive contrasts between conflicting alternatives. So it is at this point in the pilgrimage. The Knight has just ended his tale, which has been received as a worthy expression of noble and humane aspirations. As such it is allowed to stand, but not to stand alone. If the Miller is allowed to impose his dissenting voice to the extent of disturbing the Host's plan, the effect is not to annul or replace what has gone before, but to provide, through the liberating comedy of a very different, though scarcely less 'artful' story, for the recognition of *other* human needs and for the release of tensions which so much concentration on high-minded abstraction might otherwise foster.

For this compensating intention it is necessary that the new tale should parallel its predecessor.[7] It is most obviously like it in having a 'heroine' who is the object of amorous pursuit by two rival aspirants to her favours: a young wife held in unnatural bondage – 'narwe in cage' – by her gross and jealous husband, the 'riche gnof' (I. 3188) of the opening. The difference that separates this object of desire from the remotely spiritualized Emelye is underlined with exuberant particularity:

> Fair was this yonge wyf, and therwithal
> As any wezele hir body gent and smal.
> A ceynt she werede, barred al of silk,
> A barmclooth eek as whit as morne milk
> Upon hir lendes, ful of many a goore.
> Whit was hir smok, and broyden al bifoore
> And eek bihynde, on hir coler aboute,
> Of col-blak silk, withinne and eek withoute.
> The tapes of hir white voluper
> Were of the same suyte of hir coler;
> Hir filet brood of silk, and set ful hye.
> And sikerly she hadde a likerous ye;
> Ful smale ypulled were hire browes two,
> And tho were bent and blake as any sloo.
> She was ful moore blisful on to see
> Than is the newe pere-jonette tree,
> And softer than the wolle is of a wether.
> And by hir girdel heeng a purs of lether,
> Tasseled with silk, and perled with latoun.
> In al this world, to seken up and doun,
> Ther nys no man so wys that koude thenche
> So gay a popelote or swich a wenche.
> Ful brighter was the shynyng of hir hewe
> Than in the Tour the noble yforged newe.
> But of hir song, it was as loude and yerne
> As any swalwe sittynge on a berne.
> Therto she koude skippe and make game,

As any kyde or calf folwynge his dame.
Hir mouth was sweete as bragot or the meeth,
Or hoord of apples leyd in hey or heeth.
Wynsynge she was, as is a joly colt,
Long as a mast, and upright as a bolt.
A brooch she baar upon hir lowe coler,
As brood as is the boos of a bokeler.
Hir shoes were laced on hir legges hye.
She was a prymerole, a piggesnye,
For any lord to leggen in his bedde,
Or yet for any good yeman to wedde.   (I. 3233–70)

The picture is so rendered in black and white as to stand out with the vivid definition of a realized physical presence against what has gone before. Already we can contrast the firm contours of this elementally sensuous creature with the remote generality of Emelye, who belonged – appropriately in terms of her tale – to the Garden of Love, to a literary convention in which detail of a 'realistic' kind had, at best, a secondary part to play.

Emelye – to put the matter in another way – moves within the framework which her creator has provided, whereas Alison consistently evades hers. Her evasion is related to *nature*, and more particularly to those aspects of it which concern youth, spring, the impulse of the rising sap and the annual rebirth of life. The effect is to bring into play aspects of the pilgrimage to which the tale told by the Knight had hardly allowed expression: the manifestations celebrated, as we saw,[8] in the opening lines of the General Prologue. We are given, as terms of comparison for this vivacious piece of human reality, the swallow's song on its return from the winter migration, the '*newe* pere-jonette tree',[9] the 'kid' or 'calf', 'skipping and making game', discovering at each step the miraculous sense of being *alive* in the company of its mother. These impressions extend naturally to the description of the young wife, who is exuberantly sensual and enticing: she had, we are told, 'a likerous ye' – the implications of the adjective are perhaps more natural and spontaneous, though they refer to the same reality, than the associations of the modern 'lecherous'. She is in fact given an elemental presence, attractively responsive to the touch ('softer than the wole is of a wether') and the other senses:

Hir mouth was sweete as bragot or the meeth,
Or hoord of apples leyd in hey or heeth.

Alison has the primary attraction, the spontaneous vitality, and something of the playful, gambolling quality of a young creature adventuring, with a certain engaging awkwardness, into the spring-time world of light, and conscious of the sheer pleasure of finding herself alive.

These are aspects of life to which Chaucer evidently responded, and to which we respond with appropriate delight. They should not lead us to simplify the complete effect of the description. In giving full value to these aspects of his creation (and reminding us, in the process, of what the Knights left out in presenting *his* heroine), the poet is not requiring us to indulge 'pastoral' sentiment at the expense of reality. We know, because we are told, that the effect which this creature makes upon those around her, and which will enable her in due course notably to evade the rough 'justice' which overtakes those who have been rash enough to covet her body, is compatible with an elemental cruelty which is also an aspect of 'nature'. Not for nothing is she compared to that small bundle of compact predatory energy, the 'weasel', and not for nothing is it made clear that the impression of artlessness which constitutes so large a part of her charm is the result of a deliberate, if unsophisticated exercise of 'art': the 'art' which has led her to pluck those brows, 'bent and blake as any sloo', which has made of her 'so gay a popelote', and which – as we are led to forsee in a final concession to realism – will bring her at the last to the common destiny of her kind: to satisfy the passing appetite of some 'lord' for his 'piggesnye', or, alternatively and more prosaically, to be given in marriage to a 'good yeoman' and to submit to the daily domestic drudgery of the farm.

Looked at more closely the initial 'artless' attraction of this description is seen to bear a variety of implications for the 'pilgrimage' as a whole. It rests upon an awareness that 'nature' and 'art' are inescapable constituents of human life, that for man, even in a state of relative unsophistication, it is natural to be 'artful'; and to this realization it adds a firm sense of the inescapable social realities by which that nature is limited. Some of the implications of the description point beyond the immediate comic intention to raise, as it were in passing, questions which will impose themselves in the course of the pilgrimage. It may not be an accident that the Miller's Alison shares her name with the Wife of Bath:[10] not of course that there can be any direct correspondence between the pilgrim 'character' and the 'heroine' of a tale told within the framework of pilgrimage, but as though by choosing to give her *this* name Chaucer is indicating to those who care to read that he is introducing in her person aspects of human nature which will be seen to raise fundamental questions in relation to the design as a whole.

Like Emelye, the 'heroine' of the new tale is favoured with the attention of a pair of lovers who differ from Palamon and Arcite in being aware, exactly and precisely, of the tangible physical nature of their desires. Nicholas, the self-reliant young man upon whom her favours are conferred, declares, in the act of holding her 'harde by the haunchebones', the pressing nature of his need:

> Ywis, but if ich have my wille,
> For deerne love of thee, lemman, I spille.   (I. 3277–8)

The language he uses indicates his *non*-aristocratic status, and it can hardly be an accident that the word he uses to address his mistress – 'lemman' – is one which the Knight would surely have rejected as inappropriate to his tale. Nicholas' rival in love, Absolon, aspires more pretentiously, and with less success, for what is ultimately the same thing. As the Miller puts it,

> I dar wel seyn, if she hadde been a mous,
> And he a cat, he wolde hire hente anon.   (I. 3346–7)

The Miller's world differs from that proposed by the Knight in being one in which men are aware of the compulsions of the flesh, and in which they are brashly confident of their ability so to contrive matters as to satisfy them. *These*, the tale would seem to propose, are the forces which govern the 'loves' of men in the *real* world, and *these* – we shall add, after reading its conclusion – are the preposterous ends to which their pursuit is apt to lead them: purposes and ends which the Knight largely excluded from his more rarefied and ultimately 'tragic' understanding of the conduct of human affairs, but which impose themselves with the saving force of comic incongruity upon those who, in their consistent high-mindedness, tend to be impatient of intractable human realities.

That saving force operates through Alison's consistently successful evasion of moralizing judgements and limiting categories. Through her treatment of her husband and her pair of 'lovers' a kind of 'destiny', far removed from that of the Knight but not to be understood in abstraction from it, works itself out in the course of a marvellously vivid and controlled exercise in tale-telling. The nature of this 'destiny' is made clear by the 'fate' which has overtaken the carpenter-husband, and which the tale requires us to see as belonging to the natural order of things:

> But sith that he was fallen in the snare,
> He moste endure, as oother folk, his care.   (I. 3231–2)

The effect is to introduce a main theme of the pilgrimage. Marriage, and the conditions upon which men and women embark upon it, is to be a central concern in what follows: a concern especially associated with the Wife of Bath and the effect of her presence upon the company. If anything emerges from the development of this theme, it can be summed up in the need to exercise 'patience': the 'patience' which, in many of the tales, will be enjoined, as a recognition of inescapable and limiting fact, upon *all* men engaged in their journey through life. The recognition, which was required of Emelye's aristocratic lovers in the high seriousness of *The Knight's Tale*, finds its comic counterpart in the situation of the 'sely' carpenter who has imprudently contracted a marriage which has turned into a 'snare', or trap, which he shares after his fashion with the rest of men and with which – like them – he must live as best he may.

The 'snare' into which the carpenter has fallen is the result of his own error. He has assumed that he can hold his young wife – 'unnaturally', as the tale would have it – in bonds of possession: and the result is that he is inevitably, naturally, deceived. A passage near the opening of the tale brings home to us by vivid juxtaposition the element of vital contradiction, the refusal to be bound or limited by restricting social forms, which makes Alison's betrayal of him inevitable. No sooner have Nicholas' exploits with her been given in festive terms –

> Whan Nicholas had doon thus everideel,
> And thakked hire aboute the lendes weel,
> He kiste hire sweete and taketh his sawtrie,
> And pleyeth faste, and maketh melodie –   (I. 3303–6)

than the narrative, in a typically effortless transition, moves on to place her in a directly contrary light:

> Thanne fil it thus, that to the paryssh chirche,
> Cristes owene werkes for to wirche,
> This goode wyf went on an haliday.
> Hir forheed shoon as bright as any day.   (I. 3307–10)

Once again we see Chaucer's genius working through contrast and compensation, holding together different 'realities' whilst allowing none to be overcome or replaced by another. The first pair of couplets has already given us the contrast between the plain, prose reality of Nicholas' 'thakking', or 'stroking', of Alison 'aboute the lendes', and the 'sawtrie', or 'melodie', which constitutes a kind of *bourgeois* equivalent of the aristocratic accomplishments so dear to the teller of the previous tale. Now, as though in response to the 'black and white' quality of this story, its preference for clear contours and sharply defined contrasts, the difference between 'Cristes owene werkes', on which this 'good wife' is presently engaged, and the 'sweetness' which she has just enjoyed with her uninhibited lover, answers to a sense of 'real', *given* human nature which Chaucer was particularly concerned to convey in this tale.

The body of the tale, as it proceeds with a consummate skill far beyond anything we might expect from the Miller to balance successive 'blocks' of narrative matter against one another in a beautifully contrived crescendo of mounting comic suspense, follows Alison's two 'lovers', through their alternatives of energetic and self-confident contriving, to the incongruous ends to which their aspirations lead them. From the first, Absolon's efforts are doomed to failure. His pretensions to gentility, his attitudes, alternately supercilious ('of speche daungerous') and ridiculously squeamish ('somdel squaymous / Of fartyng') in relation to his less dignified bodily functions, make him less attractive to Alison than his more uninhibited rival. Try as he may, it is useless for him to exhibit himself in church, 'jolif' and 'gay',

> with a sencer on the haliday,
> Sensynge the wyves of the parisshe faste;
> (I. 3340-1)

useless to eye the object of his desire – 'so propre and sweete and likerous' – with his pressing but consistently vain attentions. 'Trippe and daunce' though he may, energetically casting 'his legges to and fro' in feverish imitation of 'the scole of Oxenforde' (I. 3329-30), Absolon is subject to a 'fate' hardly less arbitrary, though notably less solemn, than that which moved Palamon and Arcite to their respective ends.

The story of his rejection, given with a full measure of exuberant and liberating comedy, occupies the early stages of the tale. Moved by the pressure of his urgent need, he embarks on a midnight serenade:

> He syngeth in his voys gentil and smal,
> 'Now, deere lady, if thy wille be,
> I praye yow that ye wole rewe on me,'
> Ful wel acordaunt to his gyternynge.
> This carpenter awook, and herde him synge,
> And spak unto his wyf, and seyde anon,
> 'What! Alison! herestow nat Absolon,
> That chaunteth thus under oure boures wal?'
> And she answerde hir housbonde therwithal,
> 'Yis, God woot, John, I heere it every deel.'   (I. 3360-9)

The 'joly' wooing, the 'gyternynge' and 'descantynge' under the 'bower's wall', are evidently conceived as a parody of the courtly lover's traditional endeavours, which are sufficiently placed both by the strenuous implications of the words which describe them and by being addressed to this most uncourtly of mistresses in the presence of the grossly unimaginative husband who shares her bed. Alison's exquisitely non-committal recognition of this voice of unrequited passion is marked by the detachment, the freedom from judgement and moralizing categories which the tale, for its duration, requires of us. Thus, it would seem, in essential indifference to the idealizing constructions which men seek to impose upon it, do the ends of life variously assert themselves. If

Alison exercises her privilege of choice in rejecting Absolon, it is certainly not out of any obligation which a morality essentially foreign to the tale might suggest to her, but for the simple reason that the satisfaction of her physical need requires her to look elsewhere.

Under these circumstances Absolon suffers the indignity of a rejection which amounts to his 'destiny'. In the words of the narrator, which fall at this point with a sense of detachment that we must surely associate less with the Miller than with the poet: 'This passeth forth; what wol ye bet than weel?' (I. 3370). Here, we may think, is something like an answer, given in the fashion appropriate to the story, to the question so eloquently raised by the Knight at the culminating point of his invention: 'What is this world? what asketh men to have?'[11]The answer, it would seem, though advanced in a very different key, is not finally unlike that put forward in the avowedly 'philosophical' tale. When men have exhausted their best endeavours to obtain whatever end, of the many possible, they have proposed to themselves, they are required to accept the reality which limits their desires. Failure to recognize this, which led Palamon and Arcite to tragedy, and finally to a Stoic acceptance of their respective fates, finds its comic reflection in Absolon's determination to press his ridiculous suit. His frenzied activity transposes into the comic key the aristocratic lovers whom he so absurdly aspires to emulate:

> Fro day to day this joly Absolon
> So woweth hire that hym is wo bigon.
> He waketh al the nyght and al the day;
> He kembeth his lokkes brode, and made hym gay;
> He woweth hire by meenes and brocage,
> And swoor he wolde been hir owene page;
> He syngeth, brokkynge as a nyghtyngale;
> He sente hire pyment, meeth, and spiced ale,
> And wafres, pipyng hoot out of the gleede;
> And, for she was of town, he profred meede.
> For som folk ben wonnen for richesse,
> And somme for strokes, and somme for gentillesse.
> Somtyme to shewe his lightnesse and maistrye,
> He pleyeth Herodes upon a scaffold hye.   (I. 3371–84)

The effect of all this activity is to make Absolon ridiculous and, in the process, to cast a measure of absurdity upon the antics of his more 'poetical' betters. His 'woes' and his sleeplessness are a comment upon theirs. His recourse in his wooing to 'meenes' and 'brocage' – legal mediation and contract – reflects upon their more 'spiritual' aspirations, and the gifts he proffers answer to the social level appropriate to him and to the tale in which he plays his part.

The 'philosophy', if such we can risk calling it, which makes of this story a brilliant corrective to its predecessor, is stated with disarming directness in the form of the proverbial reflections appropriate to its kind:

> But what availleth hym as in this cas?
> She loveth so this hende Nicholas
> That Absolon may blowe the bukkes horn;
> He ne hadde for his labour but a scorn.
> And thus she maketh Absolon hire ape,
> And al his ernest turneth til a jape.
> Ful sooth is this proverbe, it is no lye,
> Men seyn right thus, 'Alwey the nye slye
> Maketh the ferre leeve to be looth.'
> For though that Absolon be wood or wrooth,
> By cause that he fer was from hire sight,
> This nye Nicholas stood in his light.   (I. 3385–96)

The lovers of *The Knight's Tale*, we may recall, were left in Theseus' view to 'go pypen in an ivy leef'.[12] The Miller's luckless aspirant is left, rather more roughly, to 'blowe the bukkes horne'. The feeling contained in the phrase differs, but the sense is ultimately much the same. Such, according to the anti-romantic, but not implausible view of this narrator, is the nature of things as Chaucer – less no doubt in correction of the Knight's point of view than by way of compensation – allows him to advance it as a foot-note to the elaborate doctrinal patterns so tenaciously pursued through the development of the previous tale. Men do well to remember that they have bodies as well as 'souls' and that their desires are apt to move them in directions hardly less arbitrary, irrational, or even absurd, than any which mysterious 'gods' may be thought to control. The results are apt to impose themselves in ways that must strike them as obscure, disconcerting, and refractory to their desires to think consistently well of themselves. The favours of Fortune, offered in this instance through Alison's highly physical presence, are conferred with no special regard for the aspirations – or the deserts, as they may like to believe – of her devotees. 'Patience' – by which is meant no demeaning self-abasement, but the exercise of a saving realism in the face of a reality which consistently and inevitably exceeds the compass of man's will to reduce it to his own image – is enjoined upon him as a necessary and chastening condition. It is a condition which may affect him in tragic, 'Boethian' terms – as in the case of the rival lovers of the Knight's conception – or with a sense of comic incongruity to save them from the excesses of solemnity and self-pity to which the 'serious' lovers of high romance are notoriously prone. It is the function of comedy both to recall men and women from an excess of devotion to their ideal constructions and to make the process of recall humanly tolerable by endowing it with the saving quality of humour.

If Absolon represents one aspect of man's efforts to follow his desires to a satisfying conclusion, Nicholas stands for another. Unlike his rival, and in marked contrast to the protagonists of *The Knight's Tale*, he exhibits the practical virtues to a high degree. He is, above everything, 'hende' – handy and self-reliant – to the point of effrontery; the adjective sticks to him with an iteration that reminds us, in their very different world, of those applied as inseparable personal attributes to the heroes of ancient epic. Broadly confident of his ability to manipulate circumstance, Nicholas sets up an elaborate contrivance to bring him to the end he has in view. He revels in the power he exercises over his dupes and – by a final twist which answers to the tale's special quality of saving irony – is brought, in the process of overreaching himself, to the reward appropriate to his particular brand of presumption.

For the execution of his plan Nicholas relies on the self-satisfied obtuseness of his victims. The outcome amply confirms his estimate. Confronted with the report of Nicholas' 'disappearance' the carpenter expresses his astonishment ('greet merveyle') at the news and delivers himself of an important 'truth' concerning life as he has observed it:

> I am adrad, by Seint Thomas,
> It stondeth nat aright with Nicholas.
> God shilde that he deyde sodeynly!
> This world is now ful tikel, sikerly.
> I saugh to-day a cors yborn to chirche
> That now, on Monday last, I saugh hym wirche.
>
> (I. 3425–30)

The tone is absurdly sententious, naive to the point of farce; but it takes us, in a way that is very characteristic of this tale, beyond farce, relating it to that sense of death in life, of the sheer precariousness of the human situation, which played so prominent a part in the medieval imagination.[13] It is a sense which Chaucer, with his habitual sanity, consistently refuses either to ignore or to exploit to ends of moral exhortation. Here, of course, it is defused of solemnity by the evident obtuseness with which the speaker delivers himself of it: but the motif will be developed to a variety of ends in the tales to follow – notably by the Pardoner and the Nun's Priest[14] – and constitutes an integral thread in the complete design.

What follows is given, of course, in rejection of seriousness of any kind. The carpenter, in no mood to put up with 'mystery' and nonsense, sends his 'knave', or servant – clearly a man after his own heart – to discover the plain truth of Nicholas' condition. Presenting himself before the closed door 'ful sturdily', as befits a man sure of his ground, the 'Knave' knocks and calls as if he were 'wood' – mad – but gets no response. Then, with one of those vivid touches which contribute so effectively to the life of the tale, he bends to peep 'ful depe' through a hole low in the door, through which the cat 'was wont in for to crepe', and is rewarded by the sight of a 'transformed', an apparently alienated Nicholas, gaping upright, 'As he had *kiked*' – peeped – 'on the newe moone' (I. 3445). The news prompts the carpenter to a further self-congratulatory delivery in his best moralizing vein:

> This carpenter to blessen hym bigan,
> And seyde, 'Help us, seinte Frydeswyde!
> A man woot litel what hym shal bityde.
> This man is falle, with his astromye,
> In some woodnesse or in som agonye.
> I thoghte ay wel how it sholde be!
> Men sholde nat knowe of Goddes pryvetee.
> Ye, blessed be alwey a lewed man
> That noght but oonly his bileve kan!'   (I. 3448–56)

The comment stands in close relation to attitudes which will be in evidence among the pilgrims. After his fashion, the carpenter is advancing the injunction to 'patience', acceptance by men of their necessarily limited knowledge; but his expression of this recurring theme is marked by the very accent of 'right-minded' complacency upon which – we can hardly fail to remember – the Miller reflected in his recent observations on the danger of probing too closely into 'goddes pryvetee' in the matter of marriage.[15] Once again the comedy bears implications for our sense of the enterprise as a whole. To ask probing questions, in the matter of marriage as in others related to the conduct of human life, is to indulge an uneasy human compulsion which runs the risk of turning up disconcerting answers, or – it may be – no satisfying answer at all; but *not* to ask the questions, simply to fall back on a 'patient' acceptance of things as they are, may be to live, like the carpenter, in a comfortable state of invincible self-congratulation.

Read in this way, the carpenter's attitude has implications for the 'religious' assertions which, from time to time, are advanced in the tales and which are inseparable from the very concept of 'pilgrimage'. It is not Chaucer's intention to ridicule, or even to play down these assertions, which are central to his design; but it *is* his purpose – or part of it – to induce us to exercise a certain probing detachment in their regard, and the presence in this tale of a persistent 'religious' echo answers to this intention. Having marked out clearly his own sense of 'certainty', and rejected whatever may be outside it, the carpenter is no man to be daunted by the irritating presence of 'mystery'. He causes Nicholas' door to be 'heaved up' with the help of his servant: whose name – 'Robyn' – is, by a coincidence which is at least suggestive, that of the Miller himself, who has been presented in the General Prologue as adept in breaking down doors.[16] Like the Miller who conceived him, the carpenter is ready to remove inconvenient obstacles, irritating 'mysteries', by the simple, but often self-damaging process of running at them, metaphorically if not physically, with his head. The limits of this obstinate assertion of the tangible and the concrete, this repudiation of everything that lies, like the matter of *The Knight's Tale*, beyond the Miller's habitual terms of reference, are made clear when the carpenter, in his determination to arouse Nicholas from his 'trance', falls back on an absurdly disconnected patter of half-remembered spells and exorcising conjurations:

> What! Nicholay! what, how! what, looke adoun!
> Awak, and thenk on Cristes passioun!
> I crouche thee from elves and fro wightes.
> Therwith the nyght-spel seyde he anon-rightes
> On foure halves of the hous aboute,
> And on the threshhold of the dore withoute;
> 'Jhesu Crist and seinte Benedight,
> Blesse this hous from every wikked wight,
> For nyghtes verye, the white *pater-noster*!
> Where wentestow, seinte Petres soster?'   (I. 3477–86)

This hotch-potch of disconnected nonsense reflects sharply on the nature of the carpenter's understanding of the common-sense 'certainties' which he assumes that he shares with all right-thinking men. There is considerable irony in the fact that, priding himself on his hard-headed view of life, he is unable to see what his wife is doing under his nose and falls back on a mixture of base superstition and unintelligible gibberish. It is not that Chaucer, here or elsewhere, is asking us to reject the 'certainties' themselves, which – on balance – he would no doubt find civilizing and beneficent in their effect upon human lives. Rather, he requires us to understand how precarious these affirmations of daylight 'reason' are, how much of what has been ostensibly subdued is still there, and how it answers to elements in human experience which do not readily respond to tidying-up or to suppression. 'We have the answers', such as the carpenter – and, we might add, the Host – affirm when confronted by 'facts' that seem to challenge their assumptions. The 'answers' are those which support their aspiration to live, comfortably and unimaginatively, in the world they have fashioned for themselves; but, at the back of the 'certainties' which they so confidently assert, we recognize, in their unguarded reactions, the existence of a 'mystery' which, expressed in the form of incoherent gibberish, nevertheless undercuts the solidly un-breakable assumptions on which they rest the conduct of their lives.

Throughout this part of the story Nicholas remains the confident contriver in arrogant control of the intrigue he has set in motion. The ingenuous docility of his victim is given by contrast to admirable comic effect. When Nicholas has 'prophesied' the coming of the Last Day – the day which is to bring the end of *all* life on earth: 'Thus shal mankynde drenche, and lese hir lyf' (I. 3521) – the carpenter's reaction clings to that part of the loss which directly concerns himself:

> Allas, my wyf!
> And shal she drenche? allas, myn Alisoun!   (I. 3522–3)

The couplet rhyme ('lyf': 'wyf') points to a contrast which is, once again, central to the tale. It establishes, almost pathetically, the attachment of this 'sely' husband (but are not all men in some measure 'sely'? and is not the carpenter as much pathetic as stupid?) to the wife who, as *we* know, is engaged in betraying him.

The advice offered by the manipulator to his victim has a full measure of the tale's exuberant dedication to absurdity. John is to save himself and his wife from the deluge to come by following the example set by none other than the patriarch Noah. Let them, he proposes, prepare on the roof three separate 'troughs', of the kind used in the kneading of bread; and let each be fastened by a rope, ready to be severed when the flood water has risen. In this way all three – husband, wife, and betrayer will float safely, like Noah, upon the face of the waters. Above all, Nicholas insists, with a flourish of imaginative comedy, husband and wife are to remain separate, so that no sin may pass between them at a time crucial for their salvation:

> Thy wyf and thou moote hange fer atwynne;
> For that bitwixe yow shal be no synne,
> Namoore in lookyng than ther shal in deede.
> (I. 3589–91)

The 'advice', rounded off with what reads like the parody of a confessor's dismissal of his penitent ('This ordinance is seyd. Go, God thee speede!'), answers to Nicholas' absolute and all too human confidence in his own ingenuity. Beyond that, it may not be altogether fanciful to relate what he says to counsel which the Parson – who, for all his virtue, is something less than a realist – will give in respect of similar matters in his concluding sermon.[17]

These contrivings lead to a culminating triumph of comic invention, as Nicholas paints an ecstatic picture of the fulfilment to which his advice will bring all concerned:

Thanne shaltou swymme as myrie, I undertake,
As dooth the white doke after hire drake.
Thanne wol I clepe, 'How, Alison! how, John!
Be myrie, for the flood wol passe anon.'
And thou wolt seyn, 'Hayl, maister Nicholay!
Good morwe, I se thee wel, for it is day.'
And thanne shul we be lordes al oure lyf
Of al the world, as Noe and his wyf.   (I. 3575–82)

The comic contrasts in which this tale abounds are never shown to better effect. By setting the reality of age and youth, naively jealous possessiveness and brisk amoral contriving, in relation to 'Noe' and his 'wyf' looking out on the receding waters and seeing themselves as lords of the creation, the tale elevates itself to the status of a comic reflection of universal human incongruity. The contrast between the pretensions which Nicholas' mocking words encourage in his dupes, and the reality of the 'white doke' following the 'drake', is such as to tie the tale in spirit to some of the deeper human purposes mirrored in the pilgrimage. It is to see Chaucer, in his comedy, simultaneously affirming and limiting the part which the transforming imagination plays in human life, at once constituting man's specifically humanizing gift and leading him to overreach himself and to be left exposed in the absurd situations which he has contrived.

This kind of incongruity, indeed, constitutes the heart of Chaucer's comedy in this tale. It expresses itself, very particularly, in the skill shown in using the couplet form both to advance the narrative and to point the contrasts within it which answer so compellingly to the sense of its comedy. Now, when Absolon is about to be brought back into the story, one more example of this skill answers to the present state of the intrigue. 'And thus', as the narrator puts it, rounding off one 'block' of matter to introduce the next,

lith Alison and Nicholas,
In bisynesse of myrthe and of solas,
Til that the belle of laudes gan to rynge,
And freres in the chauncel gonne synge.   (I. 3653–6)

In four lines at once sharply distinguished in their defining contours and tied together by the onward movement which the rhyming couplets impose, we are given the different levels on which the comedy operates. Alison and Nicholas take their pleasure – the 'myrthe' and 'solas' which, in another of the tale's most frequently stressed adjectives, they find so 'sweet' – in mutual 'bisynesse' at the expense of the husband who is so blissfully unaware of what is going on under his nose: at the expense, too, of 'this amorous Absolon',

> That is for love alwey so wo bigon   (I. 3658)

and who has removed himself temporarily to Osney. The lovers' contrive to savour the 'sweet' fruits of Nicholas' ingenuity until the break of dawn: that moment in which the more serious lovers imagined by poets traditionally voice their 'complaints' against the prospect of day and separation. This, by a further juxtaposition, is also the time at which the celibate clerics in the nearby monastery rise to salute another kind of 'love' in fulfilment of their daily obligation to perform the morning Office. The monks affirm the resumption of one kind of life just as another, and very different one, is ending. At the same time, and side by side with these contrasted realities we are required by the onward movement of the couplets to remember that yet another actor in the story, the love-lorn Absolon, has been left waiting in the wings, nursing his unrequited desire and is now ready to re-enter to receive his reward and to provoke the final act of *hubris* by which Nicholas will overreach himself and be subjected to the tale's comic 'destiny'.

For, of course, the ultimate point of the tale, as it proceeds to the wonderfully contrived pulling together of its various threads, is something more than the successful outcome of Nicholas' manipulations. Like the other characters in the story (with the notable exception of Alison, who remains untouched by the compensating action of the tale's comic 'justice') he overreaches himself in his efforts to shape ends to coincide with his desire. Even on their comic stage, men are not meant to ape God or to substitute their own 'purveiaunce' (I. 3566) for the Providence recently celebrated by the Knight in his tale. If they attempt to do this, following an irresistible human urge which in itself serves to qualify the Knight's noble abstractions, they will end by paying in comic terms the price of their presumption. Nicholas in the moment of his success commits the error of allowing his appreciation of his own 'handiness' to lead him one step beyond the point at which he would have done better to stop. To this end, as well as to complete his own undoing, Absolon is brought back into the plot. 'Wo-bigon' for his unrequited love, he thinks he sees his chance in the husband's absence; but he too is rewarded in terms as roughly unpoetical as they are appropriate. There is rich comedy, a combination of natural sensuality and 'literary' self-consciousness, in the parody of the Song of Songs which conveys his plea to the contemptuously indifferent object of his yearnings:

> 'What do ye, hony-comb, sweete Alisoun,
> My faire bryd, my sweete cynamome?

> Awaketh, lemman myn, and speketh to me!
> Wel litel thynken ye upon my wo,
> That for youre love I swete ther I go.
> No wonder is thogh that I swelte and swete;
> I moorne as dooth a lamb after the tete.
> Ywis, lemman, I have swich love-longynge,
> That like a turtel trewe is my moornynge.
> I may nat ete na moore than a mayde.'
> 'Go fro the wyndow, Jakke fool,' she sayde.
>   (I. 3698–3708)

This carries on, in its own way, the imagery of nature, of life and love reborn which we found in the opening picture of Alison; but, of course, it is necessary to the tale's intention that it should not be allowed to stand at its own absurd estimate. Alison's retort, again given for emphasis as the second line of a couplet, is followed by the brutally 'unromantic' jape which cures him of his 'malady'. Absolon's frenzied reaction to the realization of what he has kissed –

> Who rubbeth now, who froteth now his lippes
> With dust, with sond, with straw, with clooth, with chippes,
> But Absolon, that seith ful ofte, 'Allas!' –   (I. 3747–9)

is the counterpart to the preparations for his lover's tryst, as they were given a little earlier in the story:

> Whan that the firste cok hath crowe, anon
> Up rist this joly lovere Absolon,
> And hym arraieth gay, at poynt-devys.
> But first he cheweth greyn and lycorys,
> To smellen sweete, er he hadde kembd his heer.
> Under his tonge a trewe-love he beer,
> For thereby wende he to ben gracious.   (I. 3687–93)

His revenge on Nicholas rounds off the pattern of compensating 'fates' which the tale has so effectively traced. It leaves his arrogant rival in a position no better than his own; for if there is to be a 'moral' to this story it can only be that each of its male principles gets in the end precisely what he deserves: which is as near to a 'lesson' as it needs, or cares, to make. When Nicholas 'anon leet fle a fart / As greet as it had been a thonder-dent' (I. 3806–7), he not only supplies the appropriate comment, in *fabliau* terms, on Absolon's absurd pretensions, but invites the counter-stroke by which he is reduced to the level of his victim. We could say, if we wished to go so far, that a kind of 'destiny' has worked itself out by the end of the tale: a 'destiny' conceived in comic terms as distinct as may be from those proposed by the Knight, but one not less germane to the complete pattern of human life at which the concept of 'pilgrimage' aims:

> Thus swyved was this carpenteris wyf,
> For al his kepyng and his jalousye;
> And Absolon hath kist hir nether ye;
> And Nicholas is scalded in the towte.   (I. 3850–3)

The Knight himself, working with very different material, could hardly have achieved a more harmonious or complete resolution: could hardly have been more justified in rounding off his tale with the Miller's final words, which have in effect something of the finality of his own conclusion: 'This tale is doon, and God save al the rowte!' (I. 3854).

B. The Reeve's Tale

The point of *The Miller's Tale* lies, of course, in its unobtrusive artfulness: the skill which has kept the action moving and brought its separate strands together at the moment when Nicholas utters his cry for 'water' and precipitates the carpenter's cutting of the rope which restores him from his dream of 'Noe and his flode' to the reality of every day. The tale offers a kind of comment on that told by the Knight: though, in saying this, we are to understand that it is not so much that there is a 'dramatic' type of development in question, or that different 'points of view' are seen coming together to form a new vision. There is – the tales between them seem to 'say' – this point of view, this reality, *and* this other. They are seen to exist side by side when we consider the truth of life, and neither can safely be neglected to advance the other. It could be argued that there is an advantage which the medieval method of construction in self-contained blocks or units has over the more 'organic' system preferred by most modern writers, who see a unity growing out of, and finally transcending, its separate parts. Life is apt to present itself in a non-organic way, in the sense that our perceptions are disconnected in relation to one another, and that any 'whole' which we may postulate to unite the separate parts must lie beyond the limits of an experience which is by definition incomplete, constantly shifting and changing in time. Most medieval thought assumed that the 'unity' existed, but also held that it could only be grasped in relation to an end outside and beyond the process itself. This in turn implied, for a writer like Chaucer, the removal of the temptation to make premature connections, or to force 'solutions' which, of their very nature, could not be found in the material of experience as given. It is the ability to use the pilgrimage scheme to point human contrasts, to develop contrasting facets of the real without forcing them into an abstractly imposed unity, that makes the *Tales* so much more than a collection of skilfully told stories: that makes the design in its entirety nothing less than a rich and varied commentary on human life.

The points of contact between the tales told by the Knight and the Miller do not exhaust the implications of Chaucer's design at this stage. *The Reeve's Tale* marks a further stage in the descent into disorder which is so palpably subverting the original seemliness of the Host's declared plan. In the process of developing the rivalry between the two respective tellers, and thus pointing to the pressures which undermine the 'pilgrimage' ideal of ordered 'fellowship', it contrives both to reflect further upon the idealism of *The Knight's Tale* and to subject to a qualifying 'realism' the exuberant display of comic invention just displayed by the Miller.

The Reeve, like the Miller, is no doubt a sensualist, but of a very different kind. Unlike his rival he recognizes himself to be an old man – 'Ik am oold, me list not pley for age' (I. 3867) – who expressly excludes himself from the 'merry', playful aspect of the pilgrim venture. Beneath his attitudes, and the very specific tone which conveys them, we are aware of a bitterly resentful note that expresses itself in a sour concentration that is all his own. 'Gras tyme is doon, my fodder is now forage' (I. 3868). In the General Prologue we have already been given a portrait of the Reeve[18] – dry, withered, disenchanted – which his tale confirms. A characteristic note of unrelenting realism marks his perception of the decline which overtakes human existence in time:

> Foure gleedes han we, which I shal devyse, –
> Avauntyng, liyng, anger, coveitise;
> Thise foure sparkles longen unto eelde.
> Oure olde lemes mowe wel been unweelde,
> But wyl ne shal nat faillen, that is sooth.
> And yet ik have alwey a coltes tooth,
> As many a yeer as it is passed henne
> Syn that my tappe of lif bigan to renne.
> For sikerly, whan I was bore, anon
> Deeth drough the tappe of lyf and leet it gon;
> And ever sithe hath so the tappe yronne
> Til that almoost al empty is the tonne.
> The streem of lyf now droppeth on the chymbe.
> The sely tonge may wel rynge and chymbe
> Of wrecchednesse that passed is ful yoore;
> With olde folk, save dotage, is namoore!   (I. 3883–98)

The theme is one which will occupy an important place in the pilgrimage. Some of Chaucer's outstanding characters – notably the Wife of Bath and the Merchant, each in their very different way – will be concerned with the withering of illusion that accompanies increasing years. An unrelenting moral realism expresses itself here through the recognition of the ungenerous, self-centred sins which belong to old age as the 'stream of life dries up', the 'tap' gives out its final parsimonious drips. As a more modern poet has put it, 'Let me disclose the gifts reserved for age':[19] the Reeve, drawing on a long tradition of moral and literary realism to evoke the 'gleedes', the dying 'sparks' which 'longen unto eelde', is engaged in doing just that.

From a man of these attitudes we must expect a tale very different from that of his rival. If the Reeve is to succeed in exacting revenge on the rival who has exposed him to ridicule, and who is evidently in physical terms more than a match for him, it will have to be by giving vent to the sharp edge of his tongue and free play to his resentful imagination. The tale told by the Miller has imposed itself, no doubt, by its effortless 'art' and by its reflection of real and vital human drives; but, having done so, it calls in turn for a measure of qualification. It has amounted to the imaginative transformation of what was, in realistic terms, a sordid story of animal appetites and gross deceptions; but these unpleasing realities remain, though they can be forgotten in response to the sheer inventiveness and comic verve of the telling, and the Reeve, bitterly resentful both of his rival and of life itself, is well calculated to bring them out.

It is in this light that we need to see the portrait the Reeve draws of *his* miller in the tale he tells. This is a picture of his rival as he might easily be, or become: brutish in character and aspect –

> Round was his face, and camus was his nose;
> As piled as an ape was his skulle: (I. 3934–5)

a 'thief' – '*And* that a sly, and usaunt for to stele' (I. 3940):[20] the Reeve lets no occasion pass, achieves his effects through a concentrated emphasis that corresponds to his bitter, old man's animus – above all a man whose social pretensions, and the dubious foundations on which they rest, are made plain in the masterly sketch of the wife who is intended to support them:

> A wyf he hadde, ycomen of noble kyn;
> The person of the toun hir fader was.   (I. 3942–3)

As so often in Chaucer, the apparently artless second phrase, underlined by being given to a new rhyming couplet, carries a devastating comment on the claim to 'noble kin' which has gone before. The brief sketch in which the Reeve's portrait of the miller's wife terminates is a small masterpiece of social comedy:

> And eek, for she was somdel smoterlich,
> She was as digne as water in a dich,
> And ful of hoker and of bisemare.
> Hir thoughte that a lady sholde hire spare,
> What for hire kynrede and hir nortelrie
> That she hadde lerned in the nonnerie.   (I. 3963–8)

The social realism which leaves so powerful a mark in this tale makes an effect as different as may be from the *joie de vivre*, the sheer comic energy which has characterized the previous tale and in relation to which this kind of pretension is irrelevant; but it remains a reality, and calls as such for representation in the balanced and self-compensating image of life which the 'pilgrimage' is concerned to advance.

The miller's daughter, as the tale presents her, is the best comment on these social ambitions. She can also be seen as exercising a 'placing' function in relation to the Alison whose amoral activities went so conspicuously unpunished in the previous tale; and – we need hardly say – she is as solidly real as the Knight's Emelye was remote and ethereal. Perhaps, indeed, this is an Alison seen, not with the transforming eye of the comic imagination, but as she might have been in real life:

> This wenche thikke and wel ygrowen was,
> With kamus nose, and eyen greye as glas,
> With buttokes brode, and brestes rounde and hye:
> (I. 3973–5)

a vision, such as men have seen since the most primitive times, of the fertility principle in life, whose eyes 'grey as glass' belong to the sensually imagined heroines of romance but whose other attributes answer to a reality at once more direct and more physical than any the poetic imagination can substitute for it. Another aspect of the 'flesh', we might say, prevails here: a reminder of other worlds and other realities, which also play their part in the 'pilgrimage' and which need to be recognized for what they are if it is to be something more than a precarious imaginative illusion imposed upon the reality of things.

Generally speaking, the tale is its own best comment. The two impoverished scholars who come to the mill to buy corn are sharply drawn from the standpoint of the Reeve's own advancing years. 'Testif they were, and lusty for to pleye' (I. 4004): possessed of the vital energies which the speaker knows are his no longer and which inspire his resentment when he considers their continuing existence in others. The miller, well aware of their intention to deprive him of his gains, is confident in the capacity of 'experience' to defeat youthful ingenuity: as he puts it, 'The gretteste clerkes been noght wisest men' (I. 4054). This, once again is a

theme which the tales will be concerned to develop, centring it largely on
the participation in the pilgrimage of a real 'clerk' – he of Oxenford – and,
finally, on his contribution of the tale of the patient Griselda to the
common undertaking.[21]

In the confidence of his superior understanding of the ways of the
world, the miller proceeds to outwit the students without much difficulty.
'Wery and weet, as beest is in the reyn' (I. 4107), the victims return,
painfully disabused of their brash over-confidence, and the miller gives
himself the satisfaction of a parting gibe to celebrate the triumph of realism
over the trumpery deceptions of the imagination and the intolerable
effrontery of youth:

> Ye konne by argumentes make a place
> A myle brood of twenty foot of space.
> Lat se now if this place may suffise,
> Or make it rowm with speche, as is youre gise.
>   (I. 4123–6)

So far, so good. The Reeve has contrived, through his tale, to indulge his
resentment against the careless self-confidence of the young. It is his
intention, however, that *no-one*, young or old, should emerge well from
his story. There is still his grudge against the Miller of the pilgrimage to be
worked off, and beyond that the Reeve, for reasons which perhaps have to
do with his own resentful awareness of age, needs to show that the old are
not less vulnerable than the young to deception and exposure. At this
point, accordingly, his miller overreaches himself. Like Nicholas, he is
moved to take his contrivings just beyond the point at which he would
have done better to desist. By introducing the chastened students into his
narrow quarters he opens the way to his own downfall. As they listen to
the 'melody' of snores rising round them, they prepare their revenge
among the reversed sleeping-places. Aleyn gets into bed with the miller's
daughter, and John, by shifting the cradle from its usual place, induces the
miller's wife to join him. His motive is, quite simply, not to be outdone by
his companion:

> 'He has the milleris doghter in his arm.
> He auntred hym, and has his nedes sped,
> And I lye as a draf-sak in my bed;
> And when this jape is tald another day,
> I sal been halde a daf, a cokenay!
> I will arise and auntre it, by my fayth!'   (I. 4204–9)

The contrast between John and Aleyn, the one immediately successful
and the other uneasily aware of inferiority, reminds us yet again of the
difference which separated practical, 'hende' Nicholas from the eagerly

contriving, but always unsuccessful Absolon. Everything about the tale –
the unsentimentally hard-headed attitudes, the careful reproduction of
North country speech, the embittered old man seeking compensation for
the indignities and forced impotence of age – reads as a counterpoint to the
expansive spirit of the preceding story. There is little 'merriment' – no
'jolly' wooing, no 'gyternynge' and 'descantynge', no exuberant
'melody'[22] – in the prevailing sexuality here, only a hard concentration on
the satisfying of elementary physical needs – 'He priketh harde and depe
as he were mad' (I. 4231) – and a certain sardonic quality in the reference to
the wife's 'myrie fit' with her young bed-fellow. Alison and Nicholas had
been 'merry' too at the expense of her duped husband; but their
'merriment' was such as to strike us, whilst the comic illusion lasted as a
liberation from stuffiness, from the limits imposed by the social
imperatives of conscience. It is the nature of this illusion to be both
salutary, while it lasts, and finally impermanent: and so here, even as John
enjoys the fruits of his appetite, the morning after – the romantic *aubade*
beloved of so many poets – overtakes Aleyn in the arms of his buxom,
amply physical Malyne.

The farewell between them reads, indeed, like a parody of all the
familiar situations dear to 'romantically' minded poets:

> Fare weel, Malyne, sweete wight!
> The day is come, I may no lenger byde;
> But evermo, wher so I go or ryde,
> I is thyn awen clerk, swa have I seel! (I. 4236–9)

The North country tone and phrasing, and the contrast with convention-
ally poetic turns of phrase – 'everemo', 'sweete wight' – tell us how we are
to take this farewell; tell us in addition, how much – or how little – is
implied in the girl's reply: 'Now, deere lemman,' quod she, 'go, far
weel.' (I. 4240). Her final word is to tell her clerk how he can recover in the
form of 'a cake of half a busshel' what he and his fellow student have lost to
the miller. The latter is left to deplore the loss of his dignity at the hands of
the young men whom he deceived and who have turned out to be

> so boold to disparage
> My doghter, that is come of swich lynage. (I. 4271–2)

It is not what has been done to his daughter that rouses the miller's
indignation, but rather the affront to his social pretensions, the fact that he
has been outwitted by two young men whose dialect reflects a mean social
status from which he would like to dissociate himself. Upon them he can
only seek to visit his revenge, as the Reeve would no doubt have wished to
visit it upon *his* rival, in a violent physical explosion true to the spirit of the
story:

> And by the throte-bolle he caughte Alayn,
> And he hente hym despitously agayn,
> And on the nose he smoot hym with his fest;
> Doun ran the blody streem upon his brest;
> And in the floor, with nose and mouth tobroke,
> They walwe as doon two pigges in a poke.   (I. 4273–8)

Much of the art of these tales lies in the convergence of groping action on a detail – in this case a glimmering of light in darkness – which seems to offer an assurance of security, but which turns out to be deceptive. The cry for 'water' in *The Miller's Tale*,[23] the 'white thing' dimly perceived here: these are wonderfully effective devices for focussing the misplaced energies of the human agents of each story upon a deceptive point of certainty. The device carries in each case and without imposing it in any obtrusive way, notably more than it seems to offer. Another kind of 'destiny', very different from that nobly envisaged by the Knight and subjected by the Miller to the action of the released comic imagination, works itself out in misunderstanding and misdirected brutality. Throughout the tale, the Reeve's vision of life imposes itself, bitter, realistic, and convinced of final and necessary futility. Chaucer, having given value to the qualities of the preceding tales – so widely different between themselves, but each asserting in its own way the primacy of the imagination – is now concerned to show that the imaginative view of things also calls for a corrective, a balancing point of view based on a more disenchanted reading of what passes for 'reality'. This *The Reeve's Tale* supplies, not with the effect of destroying the tales which have gone before (the Reeve, after all, is not more detached or less self-motivated in his tale-telling than the Knight and the Miller had been), but with that of joining them in the developing design, and of introducing themes that will weave themselves into the expanding pattern of 'pilgrimage'.

II
MARRIAGE
AND
'MAISTRIE'

V

THE
WIFE OF BATH:
PROLOGUE AND TALE

Most modern editions of *The Canterbury Tales* have followed the conclusion of the extended opening fragment by *The Man of Law's Tale*. This is not one of Chaucer's most immediately appealing performances. The emotions expressed in it may reasonably strike us as remote, lacking in the human concreteness which we expect from him at his best. The tale does, however, occupy a place of some importance in the complete plan, bringing together the themes of *marriage* and *patience* which are variously explored in a series of tales which Chaucer may have intended to follow it[1] and which take us decisively from the realm of myth on the one hand and of rather abstract moralizing on the other into a knot of increasing human complexity. It is as though Chaucer, before embarking on a second long series of interconnected tales, wished to propose a possible *norm* or standard in relation to which the episodes which follow and which move, by development and contrast, increasingly deeply into certain central realities of human life, are to be seen and, in a sense, judged.[2]

It is reasonable to suppose that the end of the Man of Law's story – which ends in a marriage conceived in holiness and leading to spiritual fulfilment – was followed by the series of tales to which many scholars have agreed to give the general description of the 'marriage group': that loosely interrelated series of stories which deal with the question of the dominating party, male or female, in marriage. The term may be accepted, provided that we resist the temptation to impose upon Chaucer's 'plan' a *thesis* which, considered in isolation, is simply not there. The idea that the tales in question constitute a 'dramatically' developed debate rounded off by a conclusion which offers a 'solution' has been argued frequently and at times persuasively;[3] but, carried beyond a certain point, it does not bear examination.[4] In the first place, the alleged propriety of each tale to its teller can hardly be considered to apply consistently to the tales as we have them. It is not easy to see *The Merchant's Tale* as primarily the product of one man's disillusionment with his own marriage; we are simply not given enough 'psychological' or 'character' data to persuade us that this 'autobiographical' content constitutes the principal interest of the tale. *The Franklin's Tale*, again, which has been proposed to provide a 'solution' to the 'problems' of marriage considered in the course of the previous stories, raises at least as many questions as it resolves:[5] nor is it connected in any uniformly consistent way with the portrait of the teller as given in the General Prologue. In *The Wife of Bath's Tale*, equally, there are elements – such as the long discussion on 'gentillesse[6] – which are not, at first sight, what we might expect from a character conceived in the narrow terms which the 'debate' theory implies.

At most, the tales can be said to be generally appropriate to the tellers. Just enough correspondence is given us, in many cases, for the story to get under way; but neither the teller nor the tales can be said to interlock in any way which a modern reader would call 'dramatic'. Each tale rather represents a position, a point of view, which is allowed to stand like a self-sufficient 'block', or unit, in the design. It is followed in each case by another 'block', representing a different and often opposed standpoint; but such resolution as emerges is not primarily obtained through any 'organic' interaction between the 'blocks', but rather by the referring of *all* of them to a point of view outside and beyond the 'action': a point of view which is given, *known* to be true, and from which we can look back to each of the human manifestations seen in the separate tales and see them for the partial and incomplete realities they are. There is a distinction to be made here (one which essentially separates medieval from modern art) between two viewpoints. The first sees human experiences, and the artistic 'symbols' which reflect them, as reacting dynamically upon one another to produce the sense of a 'whole' never completely attained, constantly in a process of development. The second tends to regard each such experience as existing on a 'horizontal' level in its own right, and as differentiated 'vertically' in its approach to, or distance from, the unique and all-embracing end in relation to which all that appears to be partial and incoherent achieves its final meaning.[7]

It must be further stressed that the 'marriage' theme which, we may agree (with these reservations), plays a prominent part in the pilgrimage, does not stand alone. 'Marriage' is only a part of life, an important one admittedly, even a central human relationship, but not one which can be understood in abstraction from the rest of human existence. Part of the difficulty in which we become involved, when we try to apply the 'marriage debate' theory to the tales, arises from a failure to grasp the full scope of the conception of marriage as a medieval mind understood it. On these terms marriage, considered as a union of two persons of different sex, is not a self-sufficient reality. Its ends include, in the first place, the pre-eminent purpose of 'generation', the continuation of the species, and this makes the relationship an incomplete one, in the sense that it is called upon to look beyond itself, to find its fulfilment both in the future and in relation to society as a whole. Beyond this, there is another and perhaps even more important aspect of the matter. The concept of 'marriage' is evoked, for the medieval mind, in connection with practically any relationship of a hierarchical kind in human life. To be baptized is to become part of the 'marriage' between Christ and his Church. It is also to put oneself into a position by which the spirit and the flesh enter into a right relationship – that is, a 'marriage' – of higher to lower. Marriage is the recognition and establishment of a relationship between things which are conceived as forming part of an essentially hierarchical order; and where such order exists, it may be assumed that there is a condition of 'marriage' between the faculties or the realities concerned.

Marriage, then, is part of a larger order of reality and can only be understood in relation to that order. *One* result of recognizing this is to reveal the futility of all the arguments which see human beings as fulfilling their natures by 'domination'; but the lesson is evidently one that goes far beyond the particular problem represented by the relationship between man and woman in marriage, important, even central, as that may be. It is rather one which has to be seen – as Constance, in *The Man of Law's Tale*, saw it after her fashion – in relation to the totality of human life, to the end of *pilgrimage* itself, and its final relationship is to the 'non-literary' tales in prose, told first by the poet himself in *The Tale of Melibeus* and finally taken up by the Parson who, in his sermon on penance, raises the whole project to another, essentially 'eternal' level. Meanwhile, in the course of her prologue and tale the Wife of Bath will simultaneously point to the validity of this wider conception of marriage and, by the power of her stressed and obstinate particularity, call it into question.

A. The Wife of Bath's Prologue

If the *end* to which Chaucer's plan tends lies beyond the creation of character, it is none the less in terms of character that it is rendered actual and specific. The occasion for embarking on this expanding stage in the 'pilgrimage' project is the intervention of the Wife of Bath. The importance given to this is indicated by a reversal of the normal procedure of the *Tales*.

Most of the pilgrims reveal themselves, as far as is required, in the course of telling their tales; the Wife of Bath is remarkable, in her prologue, for overwhelming hers, making of it – for she will have a tale too, and this is an introduction to it, an explanation of its *raison d'être* – the story of the life she led with her *five* husbands. There are only two other cases – those of the Pardoner and, in a rather different way, of the Canon's Yeoman – in which Chaucer departs so conspicuously from his normal pattern by giving unusual length or dramatic prominence to the circumstances that precede the telling of a story. The Pardoner has an introduction and a prologue, the latter of unusual length and complexity, and when he comes to tell his tale it will be divided into a sermon and a uniquely powerful 'example'; moreover his tale will be followed by a tense episode in which the problem of his relationship to the other pilgrims will be placed most uneasily before us.[8] The Canon's Yeoman erupts quite unexpectedly into the pilgrimage like a visitor from some strange and sinister outside world, and raises in the process fundamental questions which reverberate in relation to the entire undertaking.[9] In each of these cases we are left with the sensation that these characters serve as focal points for forces, perverse or at least ambivalent in kind, which make us aware of the presence of precarious, potentially anti-social and obstructive elements which could affect the balance, the sane human normality, which the design as a whole is concerned to ratify.

In the case of the Wife of Bath a good deal of care is needed to distinguish the various strands which make up the monologue. This divides itself naturally enough, at l. 193, into two parts, which may even have been written at different times in the process of enlarging the original conception.[10] The first part, up to l. 192, contains the Wife's comment upon, and her 'refutation' of, the anti-feminine commonplaces contained in many moralizing medieval texts; the greater part of the material is drawn from Walter Map's *Epistola Valerii ad Rufinum de non Ducenda Uxore*, from Theophrastus' *Liber de Nuptiis*, and, less prominently, from St. Jerome's *Epistola adversus Jovinianum*. All these authors advise for various reasons against marriage, and against them the Wife argues by appealing to what she calls her 'experience' supported, where appropriate, by recourse to her own very special reading of 'authority'. Her arguments are those advanced by the heretic Jovinian, who held that marriage was as worthy as virginity in the sight of God and who even expressed himself in favour of a married clergy. To recognize that Chaucer, as an orthodox Christian of his own day, would have held these views to be perverse (they run counter to those of St. Paul and by implication belittle the monastic vocation), whilst at the same time giving them the force which the Wife's presentation ensures, is to respond to the full subtlety of his intention. The Wife prefers the arguments of Jovinian to those of Jerome.[11]

We shall not conclude that Chaucer meant us to follow her in this; but neither shall we deny the force which her statement of these arguments conveys.

In the second part of the prologue, which begins at l. 193 – 'Now, sire, now wol I telle forth my tale' – we have the Wife's version of her life with her successive husbands. This, once more, can be divided into two parts at l. 450: the first deals with her first *three* husbands – those whom she describes as 'good', because they were old, rich, and finally subservient to her will – and the second with the last *two*, who were 'young' and, by her account, to be reckoned as 'bad'. The Wife starts by referring to this part of her prologue as her 'tale', and there are reasons – persuasive if not conclusive – for believing that this is what Chaucer originally intended it to be. If so, he evidently changed his mind and decided to give the Wife a tale outside what now stands as her prologue; but once again there is evidence which tends to indicate a further variation in the plan. The tale at present given to the Shipman must have been written originally to be told by a woman, and in all probability by Alice, from whom it would have come quite appropriately. The two references to 'my joly body' – one in the epilogue to what now stands as *The Man of Law's Tale* (II. 1185) and the other at the end of *The Shipman's Tale* (VII. 423) – seem to be decisive in this respect; and the protest, now given to the Shipman, against the possibility of a tale by the Parson (II. 1178–90) would be a suitable introduction to her version of her own life and married experience.

The Wife opens her monologue with an appeal to 'experience', the result of her long and varied exposure to the married condition:

> Experience, though noon auctoritee
> Were in this world, is right ynogh for me
> To speke of wo that is in mariage.   (III. 1–3)

The words stand in an oddly ambivalent relationship to much of what is to follow. The Wife begins by appealing to 'experience', as she will continue to do throughout her monologue, and by stating her intention of speaking of tribulation – 'woe' – as an inseparable aspect of the married condition; but we shall find, when we come to read her version of her life, that what she is concerned to stress is not 'woe', sorrow or frustration, but the pleasure she has gained, in part from the satisfaction of her physical needs, and still more from the 'maistrie', the domination she has exercised, or sees herself as having exercised, over her husbands. The apparent contradiction is curious and, as we may think, significant in relation to what we are actually told of these relationships. Perhaps, as we follow the speaker through the successive stages of her story, we come to feel that there was more 'woe', more dissatisfaction and tribulation in her 'experience', than she can now afford to recognize; and perhaps, indeed, her whole intervention – prologue and tale – is finally devoted, whether she realizes it or not, to compensating for the increasing bleak reality of her condition.

The Wife, then, in the act of laying stress upon her 'experience', recognizes the existence 'in this world' – and unlike Constance in the previous tale, she wishes to be concerned with no other – of an 'authority', a received body of doctrine, with which she will need to come to terms. She also recognizes that her 'experience' can give support to what this same 'authority' sees as the element of 'woe' in the married state: though this recognition, perhaps, she *needs* to ignore, replacing it by an increasingly shrill affirmation of its opposite. The Wife needs to believe that her successive marriages were what, as we shall see from her own account of them, it is far from certain that they were: an affirmation of life, a gift from God 'that is eterne on lyve' (III. 5), rather than the source of 'woe', of useless frustration, which so many respectable 'authorities' would have them be and which, in her heart, she knows that, to a very considerable degree, they actually were.

The Wife's need to come to terms with the inconvenient realities stressed by 'authority' is at once suggested by her recourse to Christ's words, representing an 'authority' which not even she is ready to question. Christ's presence at a wedding 'in the Cane of Galilee' can reasonably be taken, as it has been traditionally taken, to imply approval of the institution of marriage: not, however, of the Wife's successive attempts at living it. Indeed, the words recorded in another text as spoken by 'Jhesus, God and man' beside a well 'in repreeve of the Samaritan': –

> 'Thou hast yhad fyve housbondes,' quod he,
> 'And that ilke man that now hath thee
> Is noght thyn housbonde' –   (III. 17–19)[12]

carry a damning implication for her way of life. Aware as she is of these uncomfortable texts, and of the unique 'authority' from which they proceed, the Wife is unable either to deal with them or to ignore their existence. 'Thus seyde he certeyn', she says, almost ruefully, for the words have the authority of Scripture behind them, and as such are not to be set aside even by this speaker. All she can do is to confess, uncomfortably, her inability to deal with them – 'What that he mente therby, I kan nat seyn' (III. 20) – and then, since the recognition remains intolerable to her, seek to evade their plain sense in a spirit of almost scholastic disputatiousness. 'But that I axe', she says,

> why that the fifthe man
> Was noon housbonde to the Samaritan?
> How manye myghte she have in mariage?:   (III. 21–3)

questions which seek to evade the condemnation of her way of life by shifting attention to *other* texts which may present themselves as more favourable to the case she needs to advance.

Such texts do, indeed, exist: for it is in the nature of texts, as Chaucer well knew, to offer support for whatever we need to believe. The Wife, once she has placed the most inconvenient ones as safely behind her as she can, proceeds to invoke others more to her liking. She quotes with approval the Biblical injunction in favour of procreation – 'God bad us for to wexe and multiplye' (III. 28); but even here we can hardly think that this 'gentil text' justifies the indifference she expresses to the *number* of marriages a woman may undertake –

> of no nombre mencion made he,
> Of bigamye, or of octogamye –   (III. 32–3)

and there is no sign, here or elsewhere in the course of the Wife's story, that she has been attracted to the married state by the desire for children, or that her successive relationships have led to the births of any.

Evidently the Wife's use of the most august texts is prompted by her need to manipulate an 'authority' which she cannot simply set aside as irrelevant. She is ready to quote the Apostle – Paul – as stating that 'to be wedded is no synne' (III. 51), and argues that this implies that she is

> free
> To wedde, a Goddes half, where it liketh me;
> (III. 49–50)

but she passes over, though she quotes them, the less expansive implications of the words which follow in the same passage: 'Bet is to be wedded than to brynne' (III. 52); and her carefree use of words like 'bigamye' – once absurdly enlarged, as we have seen, to 'octogamye' – to apply to the 'holy' figures of the Old Testament is a pointer to the way in which we are to receive her words. The truth is that the argument rests, not upon any serious concern for the texts, however venerable, or for the truth which most of Chaucer's readers would have been disposed to attach to them, but upon something very different: upon the speaker's compelling urge to justify her obsessive *need* for a 'husband', her inability to live without one. It is this need, the expression of a genuine, if disordered instinct for life, that expresses itself in words which cut across her almost 'scholastic' disposition of the texts and points to the deeper compulsion of her nature:

> Yblessed be God that I have wedded fyve!
> Welcome the sixte, whan that evere he shal.
> For sothe, I wol nat kepe me chaast in al.

> Whan myn housbonde is fro the world ygon,
> Som Cristen man shal wedde me anon.   (III. 44-8)

The rest of the prologue – the refutation of the misogynous authors, and
the following account of her experiences with her husbands – as well as
the tale she eventually tells will be directed to bringing out the force that
resides in the arguments and to revealing their final limitation.

A similar line of thought enables the Wife to turn the tables effectively
on the traditional arguments in favour of the state of virginity. Although
she argues in support of her own special needs, it is hard not to feel that
she is also speaking, even beyond her immediate purposes, in favour of
nature and of life itself. Too great an insistence on theological authority, of
the type advocated by some modern Chaucerians who tend, in reaction
against the contrary views held by preceding scholars, to read the poet's
text in an 'Augustinian' key, is apt to lead to conclusions that savour of the
preposterous. It may be true, in terms of the strictest orthodoxy, and as a
distinguished scholar has put it, that 'the highest use of the sexual organs
is to refrain from their use',[13] and it may even be, as the same scholar
suggests, that the Wife is 'uncomfortably aware' of the texts which
support this view; but she, and her creator, were also undoubtedly
mindful of Jean de Meun's defence of the process of 'generation' as resting
on Nature's creative purpose, and it is hard to believe that Chaucer did not
give, and mean his readers to give, the French writer's arguments the
force that they must certainly have. After all, as he allows Alice to argue,

> certes, if ther were no seed ysowe,
> Virginitee, thanne wherof sholde it growe?;   (III. 71-2)

and in any case, as she also affirms, it seems reasonable to suppose that
the kind of spiritual perfection envisaged by the argument in favour of
perpetual chastity cannot be for everyone:

> For wel ye knowe, a lord in his houshold,
> He nath nat every vessel al of gold;
> Somme been of tree, and doon hir lord servyse.
> (III. 99-101)

The contrast between the preciousness of 'gold' and the solid, down to
earth reality of 'tree' – wood – is calculated to bring out the human
normality of the Wife's position and so to obtain a measure of sympathy
for her.

To go thus far with the Wife, however, is not to relinquish our privilege
of looking rather more closely at her line of argument. This affects the
entire range of human life in society; for, as she goes on to point out, in the
belief that she is strengthening her case,

> Crist, that of perfeccion is welle,
> Bad nat every wight he sholde go selle
> Al that he hadde, and gyve it to the poore
> And in swich wise folwe hym and his foore.
> He spak to hem that wolde lyve parfitly;
> And lordynges, by youre leve, that am nat I.
> I wol bistowe the flour of al myn age
> In the actes and in fruyt of mariage.   (III. 107–14)

The argument is a double-edged one indeed. The Wife is disclaiming for herself any ambition to attain the 'perfection' which the Gospels put before her as before all Christian believers. This, no doubt, is to be considered perverse in her, since it seems clear that we are called upon to recognize the existence of 'perfection' even if we are unable to reflect it adequately in our lives. Evidently the Wife is manipulating her texts to suit her own convenience; and yet – surely – we cannot, in recognizing this, avoid the thought that her 'perversity' is in certain respects very close to the realities of human nature. For how many, she insinuates, of those who are ready to condemn her for worldliness would *really*, when it becomes a question of passing from verbal acquiescence to actual conduct, be ready to make the renunciation – whether of sexual pleasure or, we might add, of the conveniences which possessions bring – which it would seem that Christ's teaching, carried to its logical conclusion, implied? And if it is right, as most men seem implicitly to recognize by the conduct of their lives, to be content with something less than 'perfection' – a perfection, moreover, which might be considered to run contrary to the elementary needs of life – might it not then be logical to conclude, as the Wife at once proceeds to do, that in *nature* the sexual faculties were given to man to be *used*, to serve the natural end of 'generation' by which the continuity of the species is assured and central human needs satisfied?

In advancing this point we must not mistake where we are finally intended to stand in this matter. The Christian, and Pauline, call to chastity is one thing, its interpretation by academic and generally unmarried moralists attempting to relate it to the daily conduct of life, quite another. The Wife's statement concerning 'generation' points to the latter. It derives, no doubt, from Jean de Meun, who developed it in his part of the *Roman de la Rose* at length and with considerable anti-clerical animus. His argument rests on a 'philosophy of plenitude' which, when joined to the equally traditional idea of the Chain of Being, required not only that *all* the possibilities open to the Divine creative purpose be realized but that, once they had been brought into existence, they should be maintained by the unfailing exercise of the reproductive power. By this exercise, controlled by Nature as God's deputy,[14] the creation is maintained in its perfection; and by it, further, the creature fulfils its potential, participates in the creative activity which is the supreme manifestation of the 'goodness' and 'virtue' of the Creator. Generation, as opposed to abstinence or the rejection of life, becomes – according to this 'philosophy' – the means by which a created being approaches the full realization of its nature.[15]

Chaucer, then, by incorporating into the Wife's discourse features drawn from the character of *La Vieille* in the *Roman*, approximates her, up to a point, to these metaphysical considerations. The novelty of his achievement lies in their incorporation into a vivid speaking voice, a character possessed by urgent and conflicting compulsions which bring these theories splendidly to life; but it can scarcely be accidental that there is no suggestion throughout the Wife's long apology that she has herself borne children, no indication of any fruit of 'generation' as having blessed her successive marriages. In this respect, her repeated emphasis on the word 'fruyt' – another key word, used to varying ends throughout the pilgrimage – seems to carry a bitter, if unconscious irony. Her matrimonial adventures, it would seem, have been from this standpoint essentially *sterile*; and this may account in some measure for the dissatisfaction she increasingly shows, willingly or otherwise, with herself and her way of life.

This impression is confirmed by the fact that she wins the keen attention of none other than the Pardoner, whose figure is equally, as we shall see, associated with sterility. He is moved by the Wife's words to 'start up' and to declare his admiration.

> 'Now, dame,' quod he, 'by God and by seint John!
> Ye been a noble prechour in this cas;'   (III. 164–5)

Such a preacher, we may think, as he will himself prove to be when the time comes, and in an even more equivocal cause; for the fact is that the Pardoner, besides being excluded from grace by the way of life he has adopted, is also physically incapable of achieving the 'fruits' of marriage.[16] It is interesting to note that the Pardoner's interruption prompts the Wife, in reply, to accentuate the note of strident aggressiveness which is to be so powerfully asserted in the story of her marriages:

> 'Abyde!' quod she, 'my tale is nat bigonne.
> Nay, thou shalt drynken of another tonne,
> Er that I go, shal savoure wors than ale.
> And whan that I have toold thee forth my tale
> Of tribulacioun in mariage,
> Of which I am expert in al myn age,
> This is to seyn, myself have been the whippe, –

> Than maystow chese wheither thou wolt sippe
> Of thilke tonne that I shal abroche.'   (III. 169–77)

There is something about the Pardoner that brings out the elements of perversity and excess, of unconfessed and uncontrolled motivation, in those who come into contact with him. This will be apparent in the Host's savage reaction to the conclusion of his tale.[17] Here it is the Wife who seems to be moved by the urge to flaunt her assertiveness, to stress her *need* to exercise domination in relation to a being whose way of life excludes him from any human or positive relation with his fellow-pilgrims. Seasoned traveller that she is, the Wife is, of course, expressing *bonhomie*, projecting herself in rough and loud-voiced humour; but there is more than this to her reaction. Her tone is, beneath the banter, hard and aggressive, the reflection of her desire to see herself as inflicting, rather than as suffering, the 'tribulation' that seems to be inescapable in the married state which she has so variously, and so vainly experienced; and there is something not far from blasphemy in her reference to the 'tonne', the wine cask, from which she will force the Pardoner to drink in bitterness – it shall 'savour' to him, she says, 'worse than ale' – and which recalls the miracle at Cana, which she has already mentioned as conferring divine approval upon the married state,[18] and the words recorded as spoken by Christ to his disciples in anticipation of his Passion.[19]

The brief, tense exchange between these two is a revealing prelude to the story of misdirected, and finally self-consuming efforts at self-assertion to which it leads. If the Pardoner, of all people, is going to talk about marriage, the Wife will let him know in no uncertain terms what he is letting himself in for. Let him, she says, hear out what she has to say and *then*, if he so wishes, proceed with his absurd intention. The motive which prompts her to go over the story of her married life is from the first frankly stated, even aggressively flaunted before her fellow-pilgrims: almost as though she felt the need to cover by the emphasis of her self-assertion what she recognizes, albeit unwillingly, as the perversity, the sterility, of the position in which, at the end of her long and varied exposure to 'experience', she finds herself. That the first intimation of the reality which underlies her bold aggressiveness should be insinuated through her jesting, but not *only* jesting, confrontation with the Pardoner – himself the manifestation of sterility, of exclusion from the creative human reality of love – is a master-stroke of Chaucerian subtlety and penetration.

In the second part of her prologue the Wife seeks to back up her self-justifying argument in what, as we have already suggested, Chaucer may originally have intended to be her contribution to the pilgrimage. This is the story, according to her version, of her five successive marriages. This, again, can be divided into two parts at l. 450: parts which answer to

two distinct but logically connected stages in her story. The first part
concerns the *young* woman who married three *old* husbands and, as she
remembers it, held the whiphand over them; the second focusses
attention on the *aging* woman who married two *young* (or younger) men
and who became engaged in a battle – which she needs to believe ended in
her victory – to maintain her control over them. Chaucer may have become
aware of the full possibilities of his theme in the process of developing it
over an extended period of time. He may have begun by using the Wife's
marital story to illustrate the attitudes (those which stress feminine
domination) put forward in the first part of the monologue and to
insinuate in the process his own double-edged comment on the attitude to
women contained in the writings of so many respected (and respectable)
moral 'authorities'. He may, however, have come in so doing to be
increasingly concerned with the point at which the attitudes so defiantly
defended by the Wife come up against the inconvenient realities of
increasing years and declining physical attractiveness. Perhaps – he may
have come to reflect as he considered the splendidly vivid character he had
brought into being – *domination* is ultimately a fantasy, and a pathetic one
at that: a fantasy that existed principally in Alice's mind and which she is
unwillingly forced, in the course of her story, to see for what it is: a
projection of human need and an implicit confession of equally human
inability, on these terms, to meet it.

There are a number of indications that the Wife's version of her married
life is not to be taken at her own estimate. It is no accident that her
husbands have been precisely *five*; we shall not overlook the parallel,
which she has herself mentioned and somewhat evasively dismissed,[20]
with the Gospel incident of the Samaritan woman at the well who had also
'married' five times and who was told that the partner with whom she was
then living was not her husband.[21] The Wife found this text hard to
understand and we may, if we will, feel some measure of human
sympathy with her, whilst reflecting at the same time that the woman in
the Gospel was unable to draw 'living water' from her well and conclude
that Alice is similarly excluded from any true understanding of the nature
and implications of 'love'.

This is confirmed by the way in which she introduces her story. Of the
five husbands to whom she has admitted, 'withouten oother compaignye in
youthe',[22] 'three', she says, were 'good' and two 'bad'. The criterion she
uses to differentiate between them is in itself an indication of her inability
to understand what the married relationship, on any serious view,
involves. The three 'good' husbands were those whom, as we have seen,
she succeeded in dominating, the 'bad' those who resisted her
determination to impose her will upon them. That in the course of the
story she consistently treats the 'good' husbands with contempt, and that

her respect finally turns out to be reserved for the one who, by her own standards, treated her *worst* is some measure of her confusion and of the complexity with which we are required to come to terms in reading the tale.

For, of course, it is no simple or merely 'moralistic' judgement that we are asked to make in response to the Wife's vivid narrative. Her first three husbands – the 'good' ones, in her declared estimation – were *old*, whereas she was *young*. The fact is in itself a comment on the kind of 'goodness' she saw in them and on her own attitude to the married relationship. She projects herself as a women confident in her youth and physical attractiveness who accused her elderly husband of avarice, jealousy, and mistrust: 'sins' which are the accompaniment of old age[23] and which are apt to go with the kind of virtue that the moralists so insistently praise. The Merchant, as he will eventually reveal himself through the 'hero' of the tale he tells, is an outstanding example of the type.[24] The Wife's words addressed to this old man capture, in her report, the very inflections of domineering, self-assertive and calculating protest:

> Sire olde kaynard, is this thyn array?
> Why is my neighboures wyf so gay?
> She is honoured over al ther she gooth;
> I sitte at hoom, I have no thrifty clooth.
> What dostow at my neighebores hous?
> Is she so fair? artow so amorous?
> What rowne ye with oure mayde? *Benedicite*!
> Sire olde lecchour, lat thy japes be!
> And if I have a gossib or a freend,
> Withouten gilt, thou chidest as a feend,
> If that I walke or pleye unto his hous!
> Thou comest hoom as dronken as a mous,
> And prechest on thy bench, with yvel preef!
> (III. 235–247)

This, no doubt, is the kind of thing that the Merchant found himself confronted with in his own new, and bitterly disappointing experience of marriage;[25] and, if the fact does not excuse his own brand of self-centred resentment, it does account for the disturbing tone of his intervention. In much the same way the Wife is at this point recognizing, in effect if not in intention, the element of exploitation, of calculated aggression, in her indignant diatribe against the old man whom, for reasons which no doubt include a large measure of self-interest, she took for her husband.

The husband's reply, as reported by the Wife, is hardly attractive. It amounts to saying that *all* desirable women, and *all* the men who desire them, go deservedly to the devil: a conclusion which leaves her sceptical –

'Thus goth al to the devel, *by thy tale*' (III. 262) – and which surely enlists Chaucer's sympathy (and ours) in her concluding retort:

> What eyleth swich an old man for to chide?   (III.281)
> Thus seistow, olde barel-ful of lyes!   (III. 302)

To some extent, however, and no more: for this is not a feminist tract, or even simply the vivid piece of character drawing by which it achieves its effect. What is being conveyed, behind all the traditional aspects of the Wife's presentation, is something that amounts to a comment upon marriage, upon what happens to the relationship between men and women when it is considered in terms of one-sided 'maistrie'. What is shown is the replacement of the essential quality of 'trust', which requires mutual forbearance in the exercise of 'patience',[26], by the *jealousy* which follows when marriage, or indeed any important human relationship, is considered arbitrarily and one-sidedly in terms of *possession*. This is what the Wife, by her insistence on exercising domination, has in fact ensured that she has got out of the married condition. Whether it is what she really wanted, or whether the pleasure of the battle was sufficient compensation for what on these terms she missed, the rest of her story, and the tale to which it leads, will call into question; but meanwhile, perverse and even unnatural as her reactions must appear, they have not prevented her from seeing the real defects of those who have responded to her egoism by asserting their own.

Jealousy, in fact, is the other face of possession, and it is thoroughly explored in the course of the Wife's discourse as the belittling, self-annihilating reality it is. Yet even this does not exhaust the sense of this great portrait. If the Wife accuses her old husband of avarice, a mean attachment to property, and of spying upon her in an essential (if no doubt deserved) lack of trust, this is of course part of her game of self-assertion; but there are other aspects of her determined onslaught on masculine deficiencies which read like the truth, and the final impression may be that life – even monstrously assertive and domineering in the following of its own compulsions – will have its way, and that all attempts to hold it in check, or to reduce it to a merely theoretical order (one, moreover, which covers elements of selfishness and impotent resentment under the guise of moralizing) will ultimately fail. The Wife and her husbands were, in effect, made for one another. She chose them as they chose her, each in the illusion of obtaining what was not really there, until each party in the relationship turned into an appropriate scourge for the other.

As we pass in the course of the monologue from the first three husbands to the last two there is a notable change of emphasis. The Wife succeeded, by her own account, in asserting 'maistrie' over the former, but it cannot be said that the result has been to make her, in any acceptable sense of the term, fulfilled or 'happy'. The last two husbands – the 'bad' ones, as she declares that she sees them – are so described by her because they were those whom she found it most difficult to bring under her rule. There is in this respect an important change in her situation. Her relations with her first three partners have been presented, again by herself, as those of a relatively *young* woman to men *older* than herself, whose various egoisms and cupidities she was able, by exploiting her physical assets, to dominate and *use* for ends of her own. We may reasonably think that they deserved her, and she deserved what was missing, as sharers in a human relationship, in them. The point about the last two husbands is that they, with whom by her own account she fought most bitterly, were also those whom, after her own very special fashion, she came to respect. The perception is one which, like many of Chaucer's, reflects a common-sense understanding of the way men and women react to their situations; and it is none the worse for that. What he has done is to take up the perception, incorporating it into his own distinctive, and far from common, sense of reality. As she recalls the details of her unending battles with these later husbands, we come to see (even if she does not) that the Wife is grasping at the shadow of her vanished youth. She needs to believe that these struggles were a continuing affirmation of the same fundamental instinct for life – as she sees it – that led her to insist on her dominant role in marriage. The reality, unwilling though she is to recognize it, is turning into something very different. She is – we might say – finally speaking out of her *need*, pleading through her self-projection to be taken at her own estimate; and at the same time, we sense that she is aware in spite of herself that her words contain a large element of fiction, that they no longer correspond – if, indeed they ever did – to any real truth about herself as a woman and as a human being.

These complex, and largely contradictory intuitions provoke the Wife, in the later stages of her self-revelation, to a mood which answers to her increased sense of her real situation. It is a mood in which the memory, and the nostalgia of past pleasure – real or imaginary? we cannot be certain, and are perhaps not meant to be – blend with the present reality of age and a sense of irretrievable loss:

> And I was yong and ful of ragerye,
> Stibourn and strong, and joly as a pye.
> How koude I daunce to an harpe smale,
> And synge, ywis, as any nyghtyngale,
> Whan I had dronke a draughte of sweete wyn! . . .
>   But, Lord Crist! whan that it remembreth me
> Upon my yowthe, and on my jolitee,
> It tikleth me aboute myn herte roote.

Unto this day it dooth myn herte boote
That I have had my world as in my tyme.
But age, allas! that al wole envenyme,
Hath me biraft my beautee and my pith.
Lat go, farewel! the devel go therwith!
The flour is goon, ther is namoore to telle;
The bren, as I best kan, now moste I selle.
(III. 455–9: 469–78)

Once again we are in the presence of commonplaces everywhere present in medieval and indeed in classical thought: commonplaces brought to life by being placed in the mouth of the superbly particularized figure who utters them, conferring upon them the immediate and unmistakable authority of her own speaking voice.

The passage, indeed calls for that appreciation of tone and inflection which turns moral commonplace into the subtly varied expression of an individual utterance. It is the sense of such a voice, perceptible to any reader who is ready to respond to the marriage of rhythm and sense, that is the measure of Chaucer's achievement in relation to the conventional material which he uses and transforms. It conveys, as nothing else could, the reality of the Wife's condition, as it has been brought home to her in terms of hard, unwilling submission to experience. When she looks back on the past in which – as she would like to think – she was able to impose her own sense of life on the elderly men she married, there is significance in the terms of her recalling. In her youth, she says, she was 'ful of *ragerye*', 'stubborn' and 'strong': this gave her the capacity to enjoy her life – to be as 'jolly' as the lively, inconstant, and thieving magpie to which she compares herself – but at the same time indicates the limits of her kind of self-assertion. 'Ragerye' answers to the kind of sensual restlessness that ends in dissatisfaction, and to be 'stubborn' and 'strong' may be – in a certain sense, is – to affirm a powerful attachment to life, but to do so with a kind of obstinate insensitivity that defeats its own ends.[27] Her dancing and singing she remembers – justifiably – as manifestations of her joy in life, of her share in the 'pith', the sap, of her spring season; but she is, after all, *remembering*, and her memories are made, at best, ambivalent by their association with the draught of 'sweet wine' which seems to have been required to stimulate them.

Here again, of course, we are called upon to avoid easy simplifications. It is not that we are meant to see the drinking of wine – or the other pleasures which the Wife associates with it – as 'sinful'. The wine is 'sweet', for it too is a gift of life, and so are the sensual pleasures she remembers; but the effects are in each case passing, impossible to hold beyond the experienced moment, and to make our happiness depend upon them is to invite the disillusionment, the emptiness, which everywhere follows on the acceptance as final and self-sufficient of what is by its very nature impermanent and transitory. By the time the Wife has reached her present state her pleasures have become a thing of the past, recreated nostalgically in her memory: 'whan that it remembreth me'; and there is a deep if unconscious pathos in her reference to the 'lord Crist' who was, for Chaucer and his age, the very foundation of permanence. Her 'youth' and 'jollity' return from the past to her thought, and 'tickle' the heart with intense evocations of what is, and of its nature can be, no longer there. These thoughts are still capable of reviving dying embers of remembered pleasure ('*Unto this day* it dooth myn herte boote'), but there is a sense that they have become a refuge to which the speaker clings in the face of a present which is increasingly desolate and dispiriting. By the end of the passage the real has asserted itself at the expense of the imaginary. '*I have had* my world as in my tyme', the Wife says, recognizing that what she had – or perhaps likes to *think* she had – in the past is no longer available to her. The present reality is faced, at last, in the bitter reference to 'age' that *poisons* all things: age against which there is, within the terms of reference by which she has chosen to live her life, no remedy, and which has left her, once the 'jollity' and the 'stubbornness' of the past have failed her, with nothing but the 'bran', the empty husk of a life which presents itself as devoid of meaning, empty of true fulfilment.

It is in the light of this crucial turning-point that we are to read the wife's account of her life with her last two husbands. Her fourth partner died on her return from a pilgrimage to Jerusalem; we know from the General Prologue that she was by way of being a professional pilgrim, and we may think that there is an implied comment here on her relationship to the general conception of 'pilgrimage' as an image of human life. The Wife, we have already been told, 'koude muchel of wandrynge by the weye' (I. 467): perhaps, we may reflect, because the urge to exercise domination has left her with no centre of stability, no abiding place upon which to fix her uneasy and urgent desires. To give this latest husband a respectable funeral would, in her view, have been a waste of what is better bestowed upon the living:

> It nys but wast to burye hym preciously.
> Lat hym fare wel, God yeve his soul reste!
> He is now in his grave and in his cheste.   (III. 500–2)

The implications are, once again, more varied than they may immediately appear to be. On one level, the most superficial, the Wife sees herself in her favourite role: asserting the claims of life against a useless concentration on the ceremonies which seek to make tolerable the reality of death. Let the dead bury their dead, she might be urging (and there would be high authority for this in the Gospels,[28] if she cared to use it), and let the processes of life follow their course; which is to leave what is *dead* behind, and to carry on the present business of living. Yet, on the other hand, if death is a part of life, indissolubly connected with it, this cannot be *all* the truth; for there is a human obligation laid on the living to give the dead what is due to them, and in the process to contribute, through their prayers, to the welfare of their souls. It is a fundamental reality of human life, as the Christian sees it, that the living and the dead are bound together in a common *society* and that the obligations of the former towards the latter do not cease when they reach the end of their temporal journey. From this point of view the Wife is denying her duty towards the dead, rejecting an essential human obligation and in effect renouncing her humanity and the bond that joins the living to the generations that preceded them.[29]

To make these points is not, naturally, to deny the essential comedy of the situation, but rather to add to it an extra dimension, a more broadly human meaning. The Wife, in any case, had more immediately compelling reasons for not dwelling on the past. It was at this funeral that her eyes fell upon Jankin, who became the fifth – and, thus far, the last – of her husbands: Jankin, whose presence at the grave-side she recalls in a revealing moment of nostalgic memory:

> To chirche was myn housbonde born a-morwe
> With neighebores, that for hym maden sorwe;
> And Jankyn, oure clerk, was oon of tho.
> As help me God! Whan that I saugh hym go
> After the beere, me thoughte he hadde a paire
> Of legges and of feet so clene and faire
> That al myn herte I yaf unto his hoold.   (III. 593–9)

The processes of life and death are at this point interwoven in a way which takes the Wife decisively out of the role of moral exemplar – which, perhaps, is where she began – and confers upon her the full immediacy of a realized human individual. The effect is certainly, and richly, comic, but – like all great comedy – at the same time something more. The occasion is the funeral of the man whom she likes to call her 'husband'. Having reached the end of his journey he is borne 'to church' to the accompaniment of appropriate manifestations of grief: for he was, after all, a man, and as such the member of a society for whom the public offering of sorrow on the part of his fellows is appropriate. Even in the presence of death, however, the continuing reality of life asserts itself. The Wife remembers how her eye, turning aside from grief, lighted on the 'pair of legs', so 'clean' and 'fair', of the living man who was their 'clerk'; and the thought rouses in her memories of a rare tenacity, affirmations of life in the presence of mortality, conveyed with a human poignancy that exists side by side with comedy and corresponds very closely to her intimate situation in the present. The memory of the past, returning with stressed immediacy after her intimations of decline, makes the Wife declare herself once more a follower of Venus, leads her to sum up the content of her memories in a single brief phrase that bears within itself the vital contradiction on which the whole monologue rests: 'Allas! allas! that evere love was synne!' (III. 614). 'Alas, alas', indeed, but 'sin', as the Wife in spite of herself conceives it, it was: a 'sin', however, bound up with the onward processes of life, and one which only a more adequate conception of 'love' could finally resolve.

It should be noted that this new, and last 'husband' – as he soon came to be – was a 'clerk': worth noting, among other reasons, because we have already been introduced to a *real* clerk in the General Prologue, and because it will be the Wife's treatment of 'clerks', and her contempt for what they represent, that will in due course prompt him to make his own reply to her prologue and tale. As a 'clerk', Jankin was – after his own fashion – a man of books, who was able to find in his favourite texts 'authority' for the low opinion of women which he was determined to inflict, day by day and hour by hour, upon his formidable partner. Her reply to this attempt to subjugate her by weight of learning is a characteristic, if one-sided assertion of 'nature', of 'experience', against erudite 'authority':

> For trusteth wel, it is an impossible
> That any clerk wol speke good of wyves,
> But if it be of hooly seintes lyves: (III. 688–90)

a comment which has some bearing on *The Man of Law's Tale* and will be found to reflect on the Clerk's story of the 'patient' Griselda. The threads of the 'pilgrimage' are beginning to draw closer in ways that advance our sense of a growing design. When his turn comes, the Clerk will 'speke good' of at least one wife; but he will do so by postulating a wife whose virtue is out of this world, the contrary – impossible, as the Wife would think, and as the Clerk himself eventually recognizes[30] – of everything for which she herself stands. As she says again, even more succinctly: 'Therfore no womman of no clerk is preysed' (III. 706), for the simple reason that Mercury, who 'loveth wysdam and science', is the natural enemy of Venus, who 'loveth ryot and dispence' (III. 700).

The Wife is not content to leave the contrast in these simple terms: for it is not abstract doctrine, but *experience*, the realities of life engrossingly accepted and followed, that she believes to be her strength. Women too, she says, were they in the habit of writing books, could tell of men

> moore wikkednesse
> Than al the mark of Adam may redresse,   (III. 695–6)

and Mercury is not less partial than Venus, in so much as the alleged 'wisdom' of scholars in respect of womanly behaviour springs in no small part from age and the impotence which it brings with it.

The culmination of this last stage in the story is a splendid exercise in farce, which is also something more: an unconscious admission, on the part of the Wife, of exactly where the urge to exercise 'maistrie' has brought her. Exasperated by the endless repetition of proverbial 'wisdom' and clerkly admonition, she tells how the 'Martian', aggressive side of her nature drove her to rise up against this treatment to the extent of tearing a leaf from the offending book. Moved to anger, he struck her; the incident shows them to be a pair expressly fitted to act one upon the other. It is significant that, in her version, as she now recalls it, the Wife sees herself as having turned the tables on her tormentor:

> 'O! hastow slayn me, false theef?' I seyde,
> 'And for my land thus hastow mordred me?
> Er I be deed, yet wol I kisse thee.'
> And neer he cam, and kneled faire adoun,
> And seyde, 'Deere suster Alisoun,
> As help me God! I shal thee nevere smyte.
> That I have doon, it is thyself to wyte.
> Foryeve it me, and that I thee biseke!'
> And yet eftsoones I hitte hym on the cheke,
> And seyde, 'Theef, thus muchel am I wreke;
> Now wol I dye, I may no lenger speke.'   (III. 800–10)

The presence in this episode of a large and very successful element of common farce should not blind us to the presence of other, and deeper, elements in the comedy. It is worth noting that the Wife, in her mock charge of 'murder', accuses her partner of the intention to gain possession of her 'land'. Where the urge to dominate is paramount it is likely that there will be 'property', a material motive, not too far behind. Further, and more importantly, the Wife's attitudes combine 'Mars' and 'Venus' in a particularly complex way. She *wants* the revenge which she savours when she has struck her tormentor, but it is not without meaning that what she asked of him in order to get him into her power was – a kiss. We find ourselves asking whether this incident really occurred, at least in the form in which the Wife describes it; or rather, to what degree does it represent a fantasy, the product of her need to assert a power that she knows has long been beyond her reach, a power which she can – by now – only savour in her imagination? At all events, and however this may be (and we are left rather with the question than with any clear-cut answer to it), as a result of this parody of a marital relationship the Wife ended – or so she claims to believe – by getting her way. The husband, she tells us, gave her what she always desired, 'the bridel' in her hand (III. 813), and recognized her 'sovereyntee': after which – as she again tells it – all went perfectly between them:

> After that day we hadden never debaat.
> God helpe me so, I was to hym as kynde
> As any wyf from Denmark unto Ynde,
> And also trewe, and so was he to me.   (III. 822–5)

Whether this conclusion can be taken at its face value, or whether the Wife knows at heart that it is a nominal 'solution', the terms of which in effect contradict the whole trend of her argument, or at least evade the *real* underlying questions, is something that will become clearer in relation to the tale she has chosen to tell.

B. The Wife of Bath's Tale

Ultimately, it may be true to say that when Chaucer created the Wife of Bath he was recognizing the existence, side by side with the Christian view of marriage, of older and pre-Christian elements: what the Wife herself more than once is said to appreciate as 'the olde daunce'.[31] She represents from this point of view an attitude towards sexual relationships which, for all her use of Christian commonplaces in support of her positions, was old before Christianity came into being and which survived in the 'Christian' world in which the poet lived and for which he wrote: partly driven underground, partly taken up into the sacramental view which he certainly accepted, but still powerfully present as a factor in human lives. The conflict, which runs through the art and thought of the Christian Middle Ages, could be summed up as being between the 'two Venuses', the 'legitimate goddess' and the 'goddess of lechery'.[32]

After she has finished her prologue, and as she is about to start on her tale, the Wife indicates her sense of this opposition in striking terms:

> In th'olde dayes of the Kyng Arthour,
> Of which that Britons speken greet honour,
> Al was this land fulfild of fayerye.
> The elf-queene, with hir joly compaignye,

Daunced ful ofte in many a grene mede.
This was the olde opinion, as I rede;
I speke of manye hundred yeres ago.
But now kan no man se none elves mo,
For now the grete charitee and prayeres
Of lymytours and othere hooly freres,
That serchen every lond and every streem,
As thikke as motes in the sonne-beem,
Blessynge halles, chambres, kichenes, boures,
Citees, burghes, castels, hye toures,
Thropes, bernes, shipnes, dayeryes –
This maketh that ther ben no fayeryes.
For ther as wont to walken was an elf,
Ther walketh now the lymytour hymself
In undermeles and in morwenynges,
And seyth his matyns and his hooly thynges
As he gooth in his lymytacioun.
Wommen may go now saufly up and doun.
In every bussh or under every tree
Ther is noon oother incubus but he,
And he ne wol doon hem but dishonour.   (III. 857–81)

It is relevant to this, of course, that the words are spoken in the presence of
a 'lymytour', a preaching friar: one who, indeed, has shown an interest in
the Wife and her story, and who will be involved in a dispute with the
Summoner in the course of which a tale will be told which confirms what is
said here about the insidious ubiquity of his kind.[33] The Wife's attitude to
the Friar is ambivalent, and she is well able to grasp the reality beneath the
plausible, sociable surface; but it is perhaps an attitude which reflects a
deeper opposition, something like an alternative view of life from which
she derives her own definite, if largely misconceived power to fascinate
us.

It has even been suggested[34] that there is a sense in which we may
believe the Wife herself to be the queen of the fairies; but we need hardly
go as far as this. What she says is that the 'elf-queen' has departed with her
'joly compaignye' – the adjective is one that we have already heard,
applied to herself and her 'body', from her own mouth – and has taken
with her the last memories of what she calls 'fayerye'. The place of the
'elf-queen' has been taken by the preaching friar, who journeys round the
country blessing everything there is to be blessed: sanctifying in the name
of the new faith and profiting for himself and his Order in the process. The
friar – the Wife rather ruefully recognizes – has won the battle against the
'old dance' and all that it implied. The result, Chaucer is likely to have

wanted us to feel, has been that the chances for secure and civilized living have been extended under the protection of the new faith. This has been, in itself, a beneficent change, in so far as the world has been saved from the *incubus*, the threat, that once lay behind every bush or under every tree: saved, we may agree, but at the expense of producing in the person of the friar a new *incubus*, who replaces the old order of things with a new one – more plausible and ingratiating, but almost equally dangerous – of its own.

Important as it may be, however, there is more than this to the Wife's tale. The story is set, as we have just seen, in remote times, in 'th'olde dayes of the Kyng Arthour'. The effect is to take it out of the realm of common experience and into that conveyed by one of Chaucer's most significant words: 'fayerye' or, as he sometimes also refers to it, 'fantasye'. In telling her tale the Wife, who has exhibited herself so stridently and hard-headedly in her prologue, is reliving her own experience, adapting it in the telling to make it conform more closely to what she would like to be the reality of things. In this mood of 'fantasy', which contrasts so oddly with the stressed, even over-emphatic realism of her prologue, the masculine affirmation of physical force, and the masculine readiness to assert it, are stressed from the first. This, or something like it, is the reality with which the teller's dream of feminine 'maistrie' would have to come to terms in a society where 'maistrie', based on brute force, is the ultimate reality.

The 'hero' of the tale is a 'lusty bachiller', a brash and even brutal young man who begins by imposing his sensual will upon a 'mayde' whom he has chanced to meet and whom he uses in terms of open brutality:

> Of which mayde anon, maugree hir heed,
> By verray force, he rafte hire maydenhed.   (III. 887–8)

'By verray force': this is the reality with which the world of 'fantasy' – whether envisaged in terms of old romance or in theories of female domination – has perforce to accommodate itself. It is an important part of the *incubus* from which the arrival of the 'lymytour', or at least of what he is supposed to stand for, has, with whatever ambivalence, saved the world. It is certainly not the only world there is, and no doubt to be human in any full sense is to pass beyond it; but it is there, and no theory of life which rests on 'maistrie' – especially when asserted by the physically weaker party in the relationship between men and women – is likely to escape its inconvenient consequences.

In the world of romance, however, which is in this notably unlike that of reality, women are given the opportunity to pass judgement on the men who have wronged them. The erring knight, condemned by law to die, is handed over by Arthur to the queen and her court, who impose upon him the task of finding out 'What thyng is it that wommen moost desiren' (III. 905). In the record of the conflicting things he is told we can scarcely hear clearly enough the voice we have already heard in the preceding prologue:

> He seketh every hous and every place
> Where as he hopeth for to fynde grace,
> To lerne what thyng wommen loven moost;
> But he ne koude arryven in no coost
> Wher as he myghte finde in this mateere
> Two creatures accordynge in-feere.
> Somme seyden wommen loven best richesse,
> Somme seyde honour, somme seyde jolynesse,
> Somme riche array, somme seyden lust abedde,
> And oftetyme to be wydwe and wedde.
> Somme seyde that oure hertes been moost esed
> Whan that we been yflatered and yplesed.
> He gooth ful ny the sothe, I wol nat lye.
> A man shal wynne us best with flaterye;
> And with attendance, and with bisynesse,
> Been we ylymed, bothe moore and lesse.   (III. 919–34)

This is the voice of 'experienced' common-sense, commenting shrewdly on what the Wife has observed – and not least by the practice of self-observation – to be the reality of things. Her findings, though they apply immediately to the situation she knows best as a woman, go considerably beyond this and can readily be related to main underlying themes of the *Tales*. These, roughly, are the things that, in one form or another, *all* human beings – and not only women – tend to look for in the course of their 'pilgrimage': forms of self-justification, distractions variously and often speciously attractive, from the obligation to make serious choices with a clear sense of the ends in view. The element of deception, or self-delusion, which accompanies the search for these objectives is implied by the Wife when she qualifies her findings with the wry implications of her concluding word: 'Ylymed'. What the Wife has perhaps discovered in the course of her long and varied 'pilgrimage' is something that she is only ready to recognize at certain moments of unusual candour: moments when her habitual defences are down and when she recognizes that the normal destiny of her sex is – after all her assertions of 'maistrie', and perhaps indeed on account of them – to be caught, like the bird on a limed twig, in the trap which inescapable circumstances, life itself, seem to have disposed.

The teller of this tale, indeed, is shrewdly realistic concerning the weakness of her sex. Women, she affirms, live for appearance; perhaps, on further thought, their behaviour in this respect is not unlike that of the majority of human beings on their 'pilgrimage'. However 'vicious' within they may be, they wish to be considered 'stable' and 'in o purpos stedefastly to dwelle' (III. 947). On this kind of aspiration the Wife makes her disenchanted comment – 'that tale is nat worth a rake-stele' (III. 949) – and follows it with a retelling of the famous story, from Ovid, of Midas,[35] whose wife knew that her husband had asses' ears, but who was unable to repress her need to reveal the secret, if only to her own image in a well:

> She swoor him, 'Nay,' for al this world to wynne,
> She nolde do that vileynye or synne,
> To make hir housbonde han so foul a name.
> She nolde nat telle it for hir owene shame.
> But nathelees, hir thoughte that she dyde,
> That she so longe sholde a conseil hyde;
> Hir thoughte it swal so soore aboute hir herte
> That nedely som word hire moste asterte;
> And sith she dorste telle it to no man,
> Doun to a mareys faste by she ran –
> Til she cam there, hir herte was a-fyre –
> And as a bitore bombleth in the myre,
> She leyde hir mouth unto the water doun:
> 'Biwreye me nat, thou water, with thy soun,'
> Quod she; 'to thee I telle it and namo;
> Myn housbonde hat longe asses erys two!
> Now is myn herte al hool, now is it oute.
> I myghte no lenger kepe it, out of doute.'   (III. 961–78)

Throughout this part of the tale the writing is sharp and pointed, the adaptation of the couplets to the rhythms of speech unobtrusively effective. The tones are those we have learnt to associate with the Wife in her prologue, an unmistakably personal voice – not altogether divorced, at this point, we may think, from the poet's own – intimately involved in the telling of the story.

After this vivid excursion we return to the adventures of the erring knight who comes, in the course of his search, upon the solution to his problem. The setting is once again the world of 'fayerye' which moves the fancy but is apt to vanish when looked upon with a dispassionate eye:

> And in his wey it happed hym to ryde,
> In al this care, under a forest syde,
> Wher as he saugh upon a daunce go
> Of ladyes foure and twenty, and yet mo;
> Toward the whiche daunce he drow ful yerne,
> In hope that som wysdom sholde he lerne.

But certeinly, er he cam fully there,
Vanysshed was this daunce, he nyste where.
(III. 989–96)

What he saw, instead of the fascinating but evanescent beauty of the
'dance' – is it, we wonder, the 'old dance' by which the teller's mind is so
preoccupied? – was an old, an unbelievably ugly woman: 'A fouler wight
ther may no man devyse' (III. 999). From this witch, the knight learns the
secret which he needs to save his life.

Returning to the court and subjected to judgement, the knight produces
the 'solution' to the problem which has been set him: the solution, we are
not surprised to learn, which has already been put forward by the Wife in
her prologue:

Wommen desiren to have sovereynetee
As wel over hir housbond as hir love,
And for to been *in maistrie* hym above.   (III. 1038–40)

This 'solution' is clearly the Wife's own; but it is significant that she, who is
no longer young, puts it in the mouth of a woman who has reached the
stage of life she can only look forward to in regret and horror. The answer,
however, strikes the assembled 'court' of women as true, and the knight is
duly forgiven.

All this belongs, as we have said, to the world of 'fantasy': a world in
which the teller of the tale is by now deeply involved. In a certain sense,
the 'hag' of the story represents the Wife's own perception of the prospect
of old age which lies before her: and it is not too fanciful to think of the
youthful and brutally assertive knight of the tale as a kind of
representation of her latest husband: younger than herself, upon whom
her only hold is that provided by the desire she inspires in him, and which
is destined to vanish with her advancing years. As we have already
learned from the prologue to the tale:

The flour is goon, ther is namoore to telle;
The bren, as I best kan, now moste I selle.   (III. 477–8)

The process of 'selling', we may feel, is one increasingly attended with
bitterness; and to make tolerable this reality the Wife is here caught in the
process of retreating into her world of 'romantic' fantasy, where the
disenchanting prospects of a life dedicated to impossible, because unreal,
ends of 'maistrie' can be held at bay, for a time and while the imagination
imposes itself upon the real.

The whole of the latter part of the story is set increasingly in the realm of
'fantasy'. The old woman reminds the knight that he promised, in his time
of need, to place himself in her power. She now says, quite simply, that

she wants to become his wife. The terms of her request are significant in relation to the deeper sense of the story. 'For thogh that I be foul, and oold, and poore', she says,

> I nolde for al the metal, ne for oore,
> That under erthe is grave, or lith above,
> But if thy wyf I were, *and eek thy love*.   (III. 1064-6)

What the old woman asks for is not simply marriage and the domination which, according to the Wife, that state should bring with it for the woman, but something more, something which no exercise of 'maistrie' can bring with it: that is, quite simply, the *love* which the old woman feels is passing beyond her power to obtain and which she *desperately* needs and can only hope to achieve by a suspension of the normal rules which govern real life: in other words, by a *miracle*.

The knight replies to this plea with churlish contempt: ' "My love?" quod he, "nay, my dampnacioun!" ' (III. 1067). He also sees the old woman's claim upon him as a slur upon his social standing:

> Allas! that any of my nacion
> Sholde evere so foule disparaged be!   (III. 1068-9)

This, or something not altogether unlike it, is the reality which underlies the Wife's highly fictional account of her success in moulding her later husbands to her will. It has been perhaps the Wife's tragedy to look for the wrong thing at the wrong time. When she was young she used her sexual advantages to exploit the concupiscence of older men with money and to bind them to her short-sightedly selfish purposes. In her old age, or in the prospect of it, she is involved in a sterile sexual war with men increasingly younger than herself: men whom she now *needs*, if only to persuade herself that she can still exercise domination over them.

The situation has an important meaning for the exploration of the nature of 'love' with which, in one form or another, the whole pilgrimage is concerned. Love, confined to sexual attraction and exploited in the interests of an unnatural and impossible 'sovereignty', has become reduced to a state of warfare, an unending struggle in which the Wife – because she is finally, on the terms she has chosen, the *weaker* party, inexorably subjected to the passage of time – has everything to lose. Precisely because she knows that she has lost, or is in the process of losing, the attractions on which she has placed her trust, she needs to assert – in the world of the imagination, where alone she can assert it without contradiction from the 'facts' – her continuing capacity to *win*; but the game is in the process of becoming empty and unreal, and at heart she – 'realist' as she has always claimed to be – knows it.

The rest of the tale develops the final pathos of this situation. The knight turns in disgust on his bed as he lies beside his unwanted and despised bride. 'He walweth, and he turneth to and fro' (III. 1085), perhaps not altogether unlike what the Wife has come to fear will be the attitude of her own husband when faced by her unwelcome importunities in bed. The 'fantasy' wife, however, is notably gentle, even humorously forbearing, in her protests against her treatment:

> Fareth every knyght thus with his wyf as ye?
> Is this the lawe of kyng Arthures hous?   (III. 1088–9)

In the world of 'fantasy', unlike that of harsh reality, the wife can afford to be reasonable and to reprove her unwilling partner for his uncouth attitudes.

The knight responds unattractively, stressing the old woman's 'loathliness' and the insult that he feels has been offered to the superior lineage which means so much to him:

> Thou art so loothly, and so oold also,
> And therto comen of so lough a kynde,
> That litel wonder is thogh I walwe and wynde.
>   (III. 1100–2)

The Wife's reply is a long discourse on the difference between *true* and merely inherited 'nobility': a favourite medieval theme for which Chaucer has drawn, as he expressly states,[36] on Dante's treatment of the same subject. The passage has been seen as both out of character and irrelevant, but it is in fact neither. The Wife, in her advancing years, and aware of what faces her with the passage of time, is finding yet another compensation for the reality of the situation in which she finds herself. She is aware, perhaps, that 'gentillesse', aristocratic courtesy, is not altogether an appropriate yardstick to apply to the stridently assertive personality put before us in the General Prologue and confirmed in her own version of her life-story. Beyond that, if it is true that in terms of 'maistrie' she is only receiving what her own choices have implied (for, in a world where domination is the only reality 'gentility' and mutual respect have no place), she is now aware – realistically speaking – of all that 'maistrie' cannot give her. She is also asserting, however pathetically, the existence of other values: values which she is only now – too late – being brought to appreciate for what they are, on which a humane and reasonable view of relationship might rest.

'Gentillesse' of the kind which the 'husband' of the 'loathly' hag favours based on established property – 'olde richesse' – is, she asserts, nothing more than a cover for inhumanity and presumption: 'Swich arrogance is nat worth an hen' (III. 1112). The truly 'gentle' man is he who shows his virtue in his own deeds: for 'vertuous livyng' cannot be inherited, but is an expression of personal moral worth:

> Thy gentillesse cometh fro God allone.
> Thanne comth oure verray gentillesse of grace;
> It was no thyng biquethe us with oure place.
>
> (III. 1162–4)

To think otherwise is to imply that the principle of *choice*, of moral responsibility, is meaningless. Once again, we are touching upon the main theme of 'pilgrimage', by which all human virtue is ascribed, beyond the necessary best efforts of men, to 'grace'. The truth is, though the lives of men are largely spent in seeking to forget it, that 'He is gentil that dooth gentil deedes';[37] and, as to poverty, for which her 'husband' has scorned her, it should never be forgotten that 'Jhesus, hevene kyng', chose to lead a poor life on earth and to show that 'glad' – that is willingly and positively accepted – 'poverte' is 'an honest thyng, certeyn' (III. 1183). What is needed – and here again we return to a recurrent theme running through the *Tales* – is to accept this condition in a spirit of 'patience'.

At the last, in the 'solution' she offers, the Wife takes the tale fully, and significantly, into the realm of 'fantasy'. Once she has obtained the recognition of the 'maistrie' over her 'husband', the 'hag' will be restored to her original youthful beauty. The teller of the tale will obtain, in her imagination, what it is impossible for her, or for any human being, to obtain in reality: a condition which will harmonize the irreconcilable, unite domination and 'gentillesse', age and youth, in what amounts to a suspension of the laws that govern *real* life: the laws of which the Wife has been made aware by the process described in her own prologue and which she has been brought, however unwillingly, to contemplate for what they are. In the fictional world – so different from, so opposed to that of every day – the knight is converted to a recognition of true 'gentility'. He salutes the old woman as 'My lady and my love, and wyf so deere' (III. 1230) and grants her the wish by which her life – and that of the teller of the tale – has been dominated: 'I put me in youre wise governance' (III. 1231).

Having obtained 'maistrie' in a way as different as it can be from that achieved by the Wife in her 'real' relationship with Jankyn, the fictional 'wife' is able to do what the 'real' one has never done: that is, to bring together irreconcilable opposites, to be both 'fair', like the young, and 'good' like those whom age has left only 'goodness' to live by. When we use the word 'irreconcilable' we mean it, of course, in terms of the standards by which the teller of this tale has chosen to govern her life: standards which now present themselves as the prison she has achieved for herself. It is clearly not impossible to be both 'fair' and 'good': Constance, after all, in *The Man of Law's Tale* had been both, though –

admittedly – only in the world of legend. The possibility, at all events, is at least envisaged within the 'pilgrimage' design. What *is* impossible is to use 'fairness' to achieve the end of 'sovereynetee', or domination, which is incompatible with any valid or even 'realistic' understanding of the very nature of human relationship; and doubly so for a woman who can only pursue that end by denying the *real* facts of her nature. Those who pursue 'maistrie' to the exclusion of the remaining factors in life will find, when 'fairness' has been taken from them by the irreversible processes of time, that the other term in the equation – 'maistrie' itself – has turned into a delusion.

The Wife of Bath, in short, has used her story, consciously or otherwise, to resolve a dichotomy which her attitudes in 'real' life have placed beyond her power to harmonize. The tale she has told, far from being imperfectly suited to her character as presented in the General Prologue and extensively revealed in her own, proceeds from what is there most deeply and seriously implied. In the 'real' world she and Jankyn reached a kind of uneasy balance – the only one open to them, given their respective attitudes – through the violence they inflicted upon one another. In the 'imaginary' world things are more encouraging: old women are magically restored to their lost youth and brutal husbands arrive at a more 'gentle', civilized conception of the married relationship:

> And whan the knyght saugh verraily al this,
> That she so fair was, and so yong therto,
> For joye he hente hire in his armes two,
> His herte bathed in a bath of blisse.
> A thousand tyme a-newe he gan hire kisse,
> And she obeyed hym in every thyng
> That myghte doon hym plesance or likyng.   (III. 1250–6)

Having obtained her will, the fictional wife renounces – but only in the world of the imagination – her ends of domination for the 'obedience' based on mutual trust which the *natural* relationship between man and wife entails; and the situation against which the teller has struggled through the whole course of her life becomes, in her 'fantasy', a reality.

This, however, is not what happens in the 'real' world, where the Wife of Bath, having indulged her compensating dream of what *might* be – the dream in which her *real* wish is perhaps reflected – returns with a typically Chaucerian stroke of irony to her original position:

> And thus they lyve unto hir lyves ende
> In parfit joye.   (III. 1257–8)

In the world of the imagination, perhaps: but in the 'real' world the Wife's final wish is expressed in quite a different way:

Jhesu Crist us sende
Housbondes meeke, yonge, and fressh abedde,
And grace t'overbyde hem that we wedde;
And eek I praye Jhesu shorte hir lyves
That wol nat be governed by hir wyves;
And olde and angry nygardes of dispence,
God sende hem soone verray pestilence! (III. 1258–64)

The tale ends, as all tales undertaken in a pilgrimage should do, with a prayer: a prayer, however, that in this case shows the unwillingness of the teller to accept the full implications, for herself and her own attitudes, of the tale she has told. It is ironical, but surely true to the spirit of the whole episode, that the Wife, stepping out of the fiction by way of commentary, should pray to Jesus Christ, the source of 'patience', and with it of everything that 'maistrie', as a possible way of life, is *not*, to request, from this of all sources, the kind of success to which she has dedicated her life and which both her prologue and her tale have shown, by implication, to run against the very nature of things. This is a stroke of irony as fine, and as varied in its implications, as any that even Chaucer – a master of this kind of effect – achieved.

VI

THE
CLERK'S TALE

The tale told by the Clerk is not bound by any direct link to the immediately preceding matter. It is connected, however, more especially by the so-called 'Envoy' at its close, to the intervention of the Wife of Bath. It has accordingly been taken to form a part of the 'marriage group' and to constitute a reply to the Wife's defence of feminine 'maistrie'.[1] The connection certainly exists, and it is also true that the tale leads into *The Merchant's Tale*, in which the subject of marriage is taken up under a very different light.

To confine our reading of *The Clerk's Tale* to this aspect would seem, however, to lead to difficulties. In the first place, it is doubtful whether the heroine of the tale – the 'patient' Griselda – is of a kind to constitute an adequate response to the Wife's stressed particularity and wealth of human detail. If her story does contain an answer of a kind to the claims of the Wife, that answer is not put forward in terms of marital clashes between husband and wife. Rather does it seem to look back to some aspects of the story of Constance in *The Man of Law's Tale*, with a view of incorporating them into a discussion that includes, but notably surpasses, the consideration of the behaviour of married men and women to point to more general, more universal themes.

The tale is notably more spare, less involved in sentiment, than that of the Man of Law. As befits the teller, it is more firmly held to its intellectual plan, more concerned to subdue thought and feeling to the strictly defined limits of its purpose; and to that purpose everything which might seem subsidiary or irrelevent is either excluded or set in strict subjection.[2] The Wife of Bath has put forward her views on marriage in terms of 'maistrie', asserting her desire to see the woman as the dominating party in the relationship. The clerk is concerned not so much to argue against this position in favour of an opposite extreme, as to stress that the Wife has essentially mis-stated the problem, that the logical conclusion of her position is such as to make *any* valid relationship impossible. To see not only marriage, but any other relationship in her terms is to misunderstand the nature of relationship itself, placing a humane and reasonable reading of life beyond the reach of men. Griselda, like Constance, is strong in her exercise of 'patience'; and 'patience', in the form of mutual understanding and forbearance, is a necessary aspect of any human bond. In both stories, it is a 'patience' based not on an unnatural submissiveness but rather on a recognition of things as they necessarily are, that the teller is finally concerned to advocate.

The story, originally told by Boccaccio[3] and incorporating older elements from folk-lore, was taken by Chaucer from Petrarch's Latin version,[4] probably mediated through a French translation, and this stresses the essentially 'allegorical' nature of the tale. The assumptions which govern it are largely those of the Book of Job, to which reference is more than once made in the course of it. Griselda can be seen as a representation of the human soul, mysteriously exposed to trials and meeting them with faith in the workings of a Providence which no one-sided exercise of reason can compass. The conception is not without its difficulties in relation to the story told. It is one thing to be tested, however mysteriously, by God, and quite another for a virtuous wife to be treated with unnatural cruelty by her human husband. God's ways are by definition beyond comprehension, but it is hard to see Walter's arbitrary decisions in any other than a perverse human light. The story is told by an academic, and shows the readiness of an academic to pursue his theoretical purposes at the expense of mitigating human sympathy. There are signs that Chaucer intended us to be aware of the difficulties presented by his material, and that in fact he hesitated between the strict pursuit of his 'allegorical' aim and his natural instinct as a teller of tales to humanize the story by stressing the pathos of Griselda's sufferings. By so doing he allows the Clerk to run the real risk of making Walter's conduct not so much beyond comprehension as simply and unnaturally cruel, thereby creating an insoluble dichotomy at the heart of his story.

It is significant in this connection that, in the introduction to the tale, Chaucer makes reference to a theme which runs recurrently through the *Tales*: the theme of clerkly, scholarly concern and its relationship to the common understanding and desires of ordinary men. As usual the spokesman for common-sense is, by his own appointment, the Host. Calling upon the Clerk to tell his tale, he expresses himself with some superiority concerning this man of book-learning, whom he sees as a bloodless scholar, occupying his thoughts with 'som sophyme', some lifeless and finally untrustworthy abstraction, and as riding with the pilgrims,

> as coy and stille as dooth a mayde
> Were newe spoused, sittynge at the bord,   (IV. 2–3)

virgin of the kind of experience which, in his bluff and aggressive view, constitutes normal humanity and the absence of which is a matter of ridicule and slightly uneasy repulsion. Claiming to represent the consensus of opinion among the pilgrims, he exhorts the Clerk to be of 'bettre cheere' and to tell 'som myrie tale' (IV. 9), calling upon him to set aside his learning and sense of sophisticated literary art by addressing himself to ordinary men and speaking plainly 'That we may understonde what ye seye' (IV. 20). Here as on other occasions, the Host shows some pretension to literary criticism. He advances his ideas with the plain-speaking confidence that belongs to his nature, which is at once a link binding him to his fellow-men and his chief limitation as self-appointed guide of the company.

Responding to this challenge, the Clerk expresses his readiness to accept the charge laid upon him. He answers 'benignly' and confesses that he is 'under youre yerde' (IV. 22). He will tell a tale appropriate to the occasion: one which – as, almost in spite of himself, he cannot resist saying – he has learned from Petrarch,

> whos rethorike sweete
> Enlumyned al Ytaille of poetrie,
> As Lynyan dide of philosophie,   (IV. 32–4)

but who – as equally he cannot refrain from recalling – has fallen to the common destiny of all men:

> deeth, that wol nat suffre us dwellen heer,
> But as it were a twynklyng of an ye,
> Hem bothe hath slayn, and alle shul we dye.   (IV. 36–8)

Once again Chaucer is maintaining a balance essential to his purpose. Like the rest of humanity, the pilgrims follow their journey in a spirit which largely ignores their common temporal destiny; and, like other men, they live generally, and naturally, by putting inconvenient truths out of their minds. The poem is concerned to give full value to *this* human reality and, at the same time, to remind us, as readers, of another, which the Clerk from his scholarly perspective is disposed to keep in mind: the 'reality' that lies beyond the 'shadow' and to which the human 'pilgrimage' of its very nature tends.

The Clerk's Tale is, in its own way, a contribution to that *other* dimension which is, whether men choose to recognize it or not, inseparable from the concept of 'pilgrimage' as the poem conceives it. The Clerk declares that his telling of it will follow the Host's requirements to the extent of being stripped of the elements of 'high style' which were appropriate to

Petrarch's intention but which would be out of place on the road to
Canterbury:

> And trewely, as to my juggement,
> Me thynketh it a thyng impertinent,
> Save that he wole conveyen his mateere.   (IV. 53–5)

The Clerk declares that he will 'convey his matter' in a more suitable way,
adapting to his audience by devoting himself to plain narration. What he
will *not* do (and here there is, implicitly contained, a reply to the Host's
demand for unvarnished entertainment) is surrender to the request for a
'myrie tale' which would be foreign to his nature and to his conception of
the seriousness of the issues which confront human life and which he
senses as being subject to challenge in his person. In the brief exchange we
can sense that Chaucer is both introducing a typically oblique comment on
the following tale and, in the process, raising in this new context questions
concerning the 'seriousness' of his art, its relation to 'truth' and to
morality, which he had already advanced in the General Prologue[5] and
which are being progressively woven into the texture of his design to
issue, finally, in the enigmatic retraction.[6]

As the tale opens Walter, a worthy and just ruler 'thurgh favour of
Fortune' is being urged by his subjects to fulfil the duty which his position
imposes by contracting marriage. As their spokesman puts it in words
which underline the conception of the married relationship which the
'moral' tales are concerned to advance:

> Boweth youre nekke under that blisful yok
> Of soveraynetee, noght of servyse.   (IV. 113–14)

To contract marriage is to accept a yoke which is not however one of
servitude but of natural and 'sovereign' fulfilment. The yoke is to be
accepted in a spirit of patience which answers to a recognition of the
nature of things and which, once accepted, is destined to further the ends
of life by leading – most obviously – to the creation of new life and thus to
the safeguarding of a ruler's divinely delegated heritage, his responsibility
towards those over whom he exercises just authority.

Here we have an answer, as the Clerk sees it, to the challenge thrown
down by the Wife of Bath. The answer implies a removing of the entire
issue from the partial terms in which it has, in his view, been stated.
Above all, marriage is in some sense an answer to the reality of human
subjection to time: the subjection which, once recognized for the reality it
is, renders the Wife's dilemma unreal. As the spokesman for Walter's
subjects goes on to say:

> For thogh we slepe, or wake, or rome, or ryde,
> Ay fleeth the tyme; it nyl no man abyde,   (IV. 118–19)

and – as we might add – it destroys every human pretension to exercise domination making of it an illusion. The only valid response to this situation lies, in terms of the tale, in the recognition that men live by relationship, and in the creation of the new life to which the most central of human bonds of its nature tends. Walter, in his reply, recognizes this obligation. Indeed, as a ruler he can hardly do otherwise. He also asserts, however, that it is his will to exercise the privilege of choice in taking a wife, rather than to have a bride chosen for him. Once again with reference to the underlying theme he stresses that 'Bountee comth al of God', and states, even more emphatically, 'I truste in Goddes bountee' (IV. 159). How he shows this 'trust', and how the 'bounty' of God's design works itself out in spite of and beyond his human perversity, the rest of the tale will show.

The wife Walter chooses comes in fairy-tale fashion from a 'throp', a village 'of site delitable' in the environs of his palace; for it is a part of the intention of the tale to show that

> hye God somtyme senden kan
> His grace into a litel oxes stalle.   (IV. 206–7)

The implied reference to the Nativity is the first of several in the tale and gives some indication of what we are intended to read into it. On Griselda, living in a way appropriate to these surroundings – 'A fewe sheep, spynnynge, on feeld she kepte' (IV. 223)[7] – Walter has often 'sette his ye', and now he decides to call her to become his wife. The call is of its nature gratuitous, divorced – as are the divine elections – from any corresponding deserving in the person chosen. The suggestion is that of the calling of the soul by God to its vocation: a parallel which it would be wrong to press too far, but which already existed in Chaucer's Petrarchan source and which lends an additional dimension to the story.

Griselda receives Walter's decision, as she will receive all that befalls her, 'with reverence, in humble cheere' (IV. 298). Even so – we may reflect – the Virgin Mary received the salutation of the angel announcing the birth to her of the Christ child. Walter then puts forward his proposal, which the father receives in a spirit of proper submission:

> my willynge
> Is as ye wole, ne ayeynes youre likynge
> I wol no thyng: (IV. 319–21)

the parallel with an act of religious acceptance is evident. Griselda, again like Mary, is astonished 'To seen so greet a gest come in that place' (IV. 338), and to hear the marquis address her as 'this benigne, verray, feithful mayde' (IV. 343).

The terms of Walter's proposal follow logically from these implied parallels. He requires of his wife absolute submission, much as God can properly receive it of his creature. His demand amounts to a solemn challenge:

> I seye this, be ye redy with good herte
> To al my lust, and that I frely may,
> As me best thynketh, do yow laughe or smerte,
> And nevere ye to grucche it, nyght ne day?
> And eek whan I sey 'ye', me say nat 'nay'.   (IV. 351–5)

No human husband, we may think, can properly demand so much, and in such terms, of the most faithful wife. The words clearly constitute something more than the Clerk's answer to the Wife of Bath's assertion of 'maistrie', though the terms on which he believes that such an answer may rest are implicit in them. Walter speaks less as a human husband than as the Creator addressing the creature he has brought into being; and the reply he receives is worded to meet this situation. Griselda says,

> Lord, undigne and unworthy
> Am I to thilke honour that ye me beede,
> But as ye wole youreself, right so wol I.   (IV. 359–61)

Just so did Mary accept the message of the angel, and the reply goes far towards establishing the spirit and meaning of the tale. Submission, 'patience', is referred here to something more than a relationship between human beings. It is, beyond this and inclusive of it, a recognition of human dependence, of the infinite distance that – on any providential reading of life – separates the divine purposes from all possible human understanding,[8] and it is in this light that the very human questions raised by the 'marriage tales', as well as others of even wider application, have to be considered in the spirit of 'pilgrimage'.

With his 'challenge' answered by the proper gesture of acceptance, at once 'feudal' and 'religious' in kind, Walter takes Griselda as his bride. Before he does so, she is dressed for her role. Her poor rags are taken from her body by the court ladies who, we are told, with one of the touches of humour by which Chaucer contrives to humanize his tale,

> were nat right glad
> To handle hir clothes.   (IV. 375–6)

She then undergoes a kind of fairy transformation in the process of being 'translated'. Once again a parallel with the Nativity is insinuated into the teller's comment:

> I seye that to this newe markysesse
> God hath swich favour sent hire of his grace,

> That it ne semed nat by liklynesse
> That she was born and fed in rudenesse,
> As in a cote or in an oxe-stalle,
> But norissed in an emperoures halle.   (IV. 394–9)

The emphasis on the 'new' condition into which Griselda has entered carries with it, at least by implication (it would be unwise to take the point too far) a certain parallel with the Christian soul entering, after an act of proper submission, into the 'new' life for which the divine purpose has chosen it.

To Walter's subjects the transformation comes as a kind of miracle: 'Hem thoughte she was another creature' (IV. 406). The tale goes on to affirm that Griselda in her new state was found to be in possession, as a fairy-tale princess should be, of all the aristocratic virtues:

> She was encressed in swich excellence
> Of thewes goode, yset in heigh bountee,
> And so discreet and fair of eloquence,
> So benigne and so digne of reverence,
> And koude so the peples herte embrace,
> That ech hire lovede that looked in hir face.   (IV. 408–13)

The 'increase' is a natural accompaniment of the new, 'redeemed' life, a spontaneous response of the divine generosity to the soul's unreserved commitment. Walter, we are told, has wedded 'lowely' indeed, but also 'roially'. His new spouse shows not only the virtues of 'wifly hoom-linesse', but also those appropriate to a ruler:

> eek, whan that the cas required it,
> The commune profit[9] koude she redresse;   (IV. 430–1)

so that she was able to conjure all 'discord, rancour, ne hevynesse' and bring Walter's subjects to live 'in reste and ese', as far as these desirable states are compatible with the realities of man's temporal condition. With the birth of a girl child to the marriage the first, fortunate side of the tale is complete.

At this point there begins the story of Griselda's 'trials', the result of her husband's determination to 'tempt' – in the sense of 'test' – his wife. He begins by stressing that he found her 'in povre estaat ful lowe' (IV. 473) and raised her, by his unaided decision, to her present dignity. The implication, of course, is the familiar one – 'the Lord hath given, the Lord hath taken away' – and it is the sense of the tale that this is a realistic, indeed a necessary deduction from the facts of human life. Walter then goes on to take Griselda's daughter from her, and to lead her to believe that both this child and the son whom he also subsequently removes have been killed on account of their lowly origin. Griselda's response is an assumption of unlimited 'patience', which can only appear acceptable – if, indeed, it can ever be so – in terms of religious submission. *Nothing* that her husband wishes can be displeasing to her, as she insists – 'This wyl is in myn herte, and ay shal be' (IV. 509) – in the act of 'Conformynge hire to that the markys lyked' (IV. 546). It is some indication of the intention which moves the Clerk's telling of this story that, far from seeking to make Griselda's attitudes 'psychologically' plausible, he goes out of his way to underline the arbitrary quality of Walter's decisions. He acted, we are told, 'As lordes doon, whan they wol han hir wille' (IV. 581): no doubt because, in some measure at least, he represents the most incomprehensible and absolute of *all* 'lords'.

There are signs that Chaucer, if not the Clerk, intends us to feel the strain which acceptance of the story on these terms imposes. He allows the Clerk to go out of his way to humanize his tale by underlining the pathos of Griselda's situation as she bids farewell to her children:

> And thus she seyde in hire benigne voys,
> 'Fareweel my child! I shal thee nevere see.
> But sith I thee have marked with the croys
> Of thilke Fader – blessed moote he be! –
> That for us deyde upon a croys of tree,
> Thy soule, litel child, I hym bitake,
> For this nyght shaltow dyen for my sake.'
>   (IV. 554–60)

There is a sense throughout all this that Chaucer, by stressing the element of pathos in the Clerk's story, is inducing us to consider the difficulties in its nature. To be incomprehensible in his dealings with men, like the God of the Book of Job, is one thing, but to be arbitrary and cruel, as Walter is more than once asserted to be –

> wedded men ne knowe no mesure,
> Whan that they fynde a pacient creature –   (IV. 622–3)

is quite another matter. It is hard to believe that Chaucer can have held this to be a true statement of the attitude of all, or most 'wedded men' to the 'patient' wives they have taken to themselves. Even the presentation of Griselda is not entirely free from this kind of difficulty. The story seems to hesitate between making her a symbol of conformity to the divine purposes –

> I wol no thyng, ne nyl no thyng, certayn,
> But as yow list –   (IV. 646–7)

and developing the human pathos of her position as a victim.

To stress pathos in this way, indeed, is to create an intractable problem which cannot fail to end by affecting our attitude to the tale. If Walter emerges as cruel and arbitrary in his human dealings with his wife, it becomes hard to avoid feeling that Griselda is unnatural, almost perverse, in the degree of her submission. To find her acceptable we need, presumably, to share the allegorical assumptions which seem to govern the Clerk's telling of his story. There are indeed times – when, for example, she accepts Walter's decision to remarry for reasons of state – when she seems to speak with the accents of the soul conforming to the will of its Maker:

> And she agayn answerde in pacience,
> 'My lord,' quod she, 'I woot, and wiste alway,
> How that bitwixen youre magnificence
> And my poverte no wight kan ne may
> Maken comparison'.   (IV. 813–17)

In these terms she recognizes, as every soul reasonably may, when it considers itself in relation to a God who is defined as *other* than his creation and only approachable through the operation of his grace, that she has been placed 'Where as I was noght worthy for to bee' (IV. 829).

At the same time there are indications that Chaucer – and here it would seem that we are dealing with the poet rather than with the teller of the tale – does not wish us to see the story quite consistently in these terms. His natural instinct, as we may feel, is to make Griselda not a symbol but a feeling and suffering person; and to do this he was obviously tempted to stress the pathos of her situation to a degree which induces us, as readers, to protest at the way in which an all too human – or inhuman – husband has 'tested' her. We need not necessarily think of this as a failure, though it is certainly an inconsistency; for it may be that the inconsistency is a sign of the problem involved in any providential reading of life and that Chaucer, in expressing it, was in fact recognizing a reality which a more 'transcendentally' minded poet – or a dedicated and consistent academic like the Clerk – might find it possible to exclude but which is apt to insinuate itself as a specifically human reaction. We begin to see why the Host, claiming to represent the point of view which prevails in many of his fellow-pilgrims, has expressed himself with a certain bluff distrust of the Clerk and what he stands for.[10] We shall not identify ourselves in any simple way with this point of view, which reflects real limitations in the Host's own way of looking at life; but we shall recognize that it possesses, within these limits, a certain validity which also has a part to play in the complete conception.

It is, perhaps, in accord with a reality of this kind that we find Griselda reminding her husband that, when she came to him, she brought him nothing but the virtues and attributes of poverty:

> To yow broghte I noght elles, out of drede,
> But feith, and nakednesse, and maydenhede,
>
> (IV. 865–6)

going on to say, with a combination of allegorical sense and underlying human reproach,

> 'Naked out of my fadres hous,' quod she,
> 'I cam, and naked moot I turne agayn.
> Al youre plesance wol I folwen fayn.'   (IV. 871–3)

The reference to the Book of Job is evident,[11] and answers to the basically religious content of the tale. Mortal man is born 'naked' and, as every medieval writer knew, returns to 'nakedness' when he dies; but to this recognition, with its implication of the need to live by 'patience', Griselda adds a human note when she goes on to say,

> But yet I hope it be nat youre entente
> That I smoklees out of youre paleys wente.   (IV. 874–5)

But: there is perhaps a large part of the ultimate sense of the tale in that reservation. In Griselda's immediately following words there is something very like a forcible protest against the way in which she has been treated:

> Ye koude nat doon so dishonest a thyng,
> That thilke wombe in which youre children leye
> Sholde biforn the peple, in my walkyng,
> Be seyn al bare; wherfore I yow preye,
> Lat me nat lyk a worm go by the weye.
> Remembre yow, myn owene lord so deere,
> I was youre wyf, though I unworthy weere.   (IV. 876–82)

Perhaps we can fairly say that Chaucer is using the Clerk's story to underline the central difficulty raised by any 'providential' solution to the problem involved in the existence of man's unmerited – or so it seems – suffering in life. The soul is called upon to 'conform', perhaps, but also to respect its sense of its own dignity. By her words Griselda has become, at least for a moment, something more than an unnaturally submissive female: has become a soul aware of the real questions which her recognition of her created and therefore dependent condition raises.

To understand her in this way it is necessary to see the 'marriage' aspect of the story as no more than a part, however important, of its significance. Through his tale the Clerk is offering a comment on the values represented by the Wife of Bath, in which he sees a challenge to his own; but he is in effect resolving the problem by raising it to a different level, placing it in a wider context. So much is made clear in the tale's explicit reference at this point to the story of Job:

> Men speke of Job, and moost for his humblesse,
> As clerkes, whan hem list, konne wel endite,
> Namely of men, but as in soothfastnesse,
> Though clerkes preise wommen but a lite,
> Ther kan no man in humblesse hym acquite
> As womman kan, ne kan been half so trewe
> As wommen been, but it be falle of newe.   (IV. 932–8)

The Clerk seems to be dissociating himself, in his own scholarly way, from the kind of 'misogynous' authority so extensively quoted by the Wife. No doubt he is recalling the statement in her prologue that

> it is an impossible
> That any clerk wol speke goode of wyves:[12]

and again: 'Therefore no womman of no clerk is preysed'.[13] He is defending women, as the Wife thought she was, but from his own, distinctly 'clerkly', scholarly point of view. 'Maistrie', as he sees it, is no answer on either side to the problems raised by the relationship of the sexes. Any such answer, to be effective, must rest rather on a realistic acceptance of the nature of things, and beyond this – and here reason can take us no further – on a recognition of that humility which the human condition imposes. This is the aim of Griselda's story, the reason which, from the Clerk's point of view, justifies its telling: and though his way of telling it may be open to the kind of objection which is implied in the Host's suspicion of all academic, theoretical narration, it stands in its own right, not exclusively indeed, or unchecked by the existence of largely incompatible reactions, as an element in the complete 'pilgrimage' plan.

In this spirit Griselda pursues her path consistently to the end, receiving her husband's new wife, abandoned by the fickle populace, whose concern is ever with 'novelty', and finally receiving Walter's admission that she has been 'tried' enough:

> I have thy feith and thy benyngnytee,
> As wel as evere womman was, assayed,
> In greet estaat, and povreliche arrayed.
> Now knowe I, dere wyf, thy stedfastnesse.
>   (IV. 1053–6)

In this recognition, he 'hire in armes took and gan hire kesse' (IV. 1057).

He then explains, somewhat surprisingly in relation to what we have read, that he has acted

> For no malice, ne for no crueltee,
> But for t'assaye in thee thy wommanheede,
>   (IV. 1074–5)

and receives in return an expression of loving gratitude which, if it cannot in realistic terms convince us, is yet true to the Clerk's intention in telling his tale. Griselda refers to her husband, in the presence of the children whom she thought she had lost and who are now restored to her, as 'your *benyngne* fader', who has kept her 'tendrely'; and finally she states her constancy in unequivocal terms:

> Sith I stonde in youre love and in youre grace,
> No fors of deeth, ne whan my spirit pace!   (IV. 1091–2)

The very emphasis of these statements is calculated – no doubt deliberately – to raise doubts in our minds as readers in relation to what has gone before; but, seen from the Clerk's logical if academically abstracted standpoint, they aim at the expression of a necessary truth. To accept death in humility and patience is the final expression of what he sees as a realistic understanding of the human situation. His is the expression of a point of view which has nothing exclusive or final about it – the tale, as we have seen, almost forces us to question it, and many of the other pilgrims will reject it, either directly or by implication – but which belongs, as an element among others, to the complete pattern of the journey. Having declared her acceptance with due solemnity, Griselda is reunited to Walter 'in heigh prosperitee', in 'concorde and in reste', for the term of their natural lives and when Walter dies he is succeded by his son, again in accordance with the nature of things.

Having told his story, and as though aware of the difficult – indeed unanswerable – questions raised in it, the Clerk is careful to point the moral as Petrarch originally gave it. The story, he stresses, as though in reply to the likely objections of those who share the attitudes of the Host, has *not* been told so that Griselda may be an example for other wives to follow. This, indeed, cannot be: 'it were inportable, though they wolde' (IV. 1144). The real moral, as the Clerk presents it, is less immediately applicable to ordinary conduct. It asserts that every man should, in his degree, 'be constant in adversitee', and this for the simple reason that 'adversity' is an inescapable aspect of real life:

> For, sith a womman was so pacient
> Unto a mortal man, wel moore us oghte
> Receyven al in gree that God us sent;

> For greet skile is, he preeve that he wroghte.
> But he ne tempteth no man that he boghte,
> As seith Seint Jame, if ye his pistel rede;
> He preeveth folk al day, it is no drede,
> And suffreth us, as for oure excercise,
> With sharpe scourges of adversitee
> Ful ofte to be bete in sondry wise;
> Nat for to knowe oure wyl, for certes he,
> Er we were born, knew al oure freletee;
> And for oure beste is al his governaunce.
> Lat us thanne lyve in vertuous suffraunce.   (IV. 1149–62)

For its final 'solution' the tale turns, appropriately enough given the teller, to 'authority', and more precisely to the Epistle of St. James.[14] The answer to the questions raised by the Wife of Bath lies, for the Clerk, in raising the whole 'debate' to a level beyond her understanding of it; lies in relating the behaviour of men and women to what his philosophy poses as accordant to the nature of reality. Only once this has been done, and once it has been recognized that what is required of all men is – once the proper resources of reason have been exhausted – an act of *faith* in what lies, necessarily and inevitably (as reason itself can tell us), beyond comprehension, can all lesser problems be seen as falling in some measure into place. In the real world there are no Griseldas – or, at best, only 'thre or two' – to be found; but the point, for the Clerk, does not lie there, or in any mere stating of the need for domination. Only once the question has been removed from this order of consideration, seen for what – again in the Clerk's assumption – we know to be true by express revelation, and so to answer to the final *end* of life, only then will the lesser problems be seen for what they are. Seen, in other words, as incomplete and partial aspects of the *natural*: that is, of the *real*. It is from this point of view that the tale, in what is described as *Lenvoy de Chaucer*, but is in fact an appropriate conclusion, allows the Clerk to throw down his challenge to the Wife of Bath and so to make his own contribution to the so-called 'marriage debate'.

VII

THE
MERCHANT'S TALE

We have argued thus far that a large part of the central portion of *The Canterbury Tales* is organized, definitely if loosely, round the intervention of the Wife of Bath. The Wife gathers round herself a number of themes central to the *Tales*, and her attitudes are at once alive, intractably assertive of permanent aspects of human nature, and destructive of a 'natural' attitude to the business of living. The answer to her attempt to base the whole of her conduct on the securing of 'maistrie' is implicit in the final recognition that a life lived on these terms can give no lasting satisfaction; we have seen that this is what her tale, which confirms the deeper implications of the story of her life as insinuated in her prologue, really amounts to. An answer to the Wife's 'challenge' is given by the Clerk in academic terms which correspond to his own reading of 'authority', but which end by raising questions inseparable from the nature of the tale he has chosen to tell. It is seen to lie in the mutual, and human, exercise of 'patience': not the impossible subjection which the story of Griselda seems to imply, but a realistic understanding of the given facts of the human situation and of the kind of fruitful relationship which they do imply.

It is in these terms that we are to understand the final Envoy put into the mouth of the Clerk. At the end of his story of what, as he recognizes, may strike his audience as incredible and unnatural submission, he addresses himself ironically to the attitudes defended by the Wife and, even as he admits that there are no more Griseldas in the world (but were there ever?) echoes the Wife's advice in what amounts to a ferociously ironic recognition by the man of book-learning of the way of the world:

> O noble wyves, ful of heigh prudence,
> Lat noon humylitee youre tonge naille,
> Ne lat no clerk have cause or diligence
> To write of yow a storie of swich mervaille
> As of Grisildis pacient and kynde,

Lest Chichevache yow swelwe in hire entraille! . . .
Ye archeẅyves, stondeth at defense,
Syn ye be strong as is a greet camaille;
Ne suffreth nat that men yow doon offense.
And sklendre wyves, fieble as in bataille,
Beth egre as is a tygre yond in Ynde;
Ay clappeth as a mille, I yow consaille.

(IV. 1183–8: 1195–1200)

We are asked here to respond to a variety of inflections. The Clerk seems to be venting upon the Wife his resentment at the way in which men of learning (and by implication himself) have been treated in her prologue. He is also recognizing what the Wife's attitude has implied, that patience such as that shown by Griselda is not for this world, that in this world it must seem grotesque and unnatural. At the same time, he is insisting on a greater truth, one which the poet himself would surely be inclined to share: the truth that the end of domination, carried to the extreme which its very nature implies, is mutual destruction, and that some measure of acceptance of the traditional view of the married state – and of the exercise of humanity and common forbearance in this and, indeed, in all relationships between persons – is necessary if marriage itself, and with it, maybe, the society in which it occupies a central position, is not to collapse into a welter of conflicting and self-destroying rivalries. The 'truth' contained in the Clerk's position, and the failure of his tale to convey it in a humanly convincing way, leave the so-called 'debate' unresolved and the way open for further contributions. Accordingly, as soon as the Clerk has had his say, The Merchant's Tale carries on the theme of sexual domination and deepens it into a consideration of the place occupied by self-assertion, the claim to one-sided and obstinate possession, in the relationship between men and women.

It would be wrong to overstress the element of personal experience involved in the Merchant's telling of his tale. The description we have been given in the General Prologue (I. 270–84) contains touches of irony but scarcely reveals much that is relevant to an understanding of his character. It seems that what we have not been told there begins to emerge, and to emerge disconcertingly, as soon as the tale gets under way. In his brief introduction the Merchant tells his audience that he has been deeply disillusioned in his marriage; though we also learn that he has only been wedded 'thise monthes two' (IV. 1234). The first words he speaks echo those with which the Clerk has just ended his tale:

Wepyng and waylyng, care and oother sorwe
I knowe ynogh, on even and a-morwe.   (IV. 1213–14)[1]

They lead to the conclusion that his married experience has been long enough to convince him that

> Were I unbounden, also moot I thee!
> I wolde nevere eft comen in the snare.   (IV. 1226–7)

The comment has just enough propriety to the teller (and just as much relation to what has gone before) to set this particular 'block' of matter into the general scheme.[2] The tale could be seen as bearing some relation to previous matter: to the Reeve's remarks on the disenchantments of age[3] and, more closely, to The Shipman's Tale – which, we recall, may originally have been intended for the Wife of Bath[4] – of an old merchant who was betrayed by his young wife with a monk who is expressly described in the tale as 'yonge' (VII. 28). It also stands in a relation of more fundamental significance to the previous intervention of the Wife, to which indeed it may be seen as offering a bleak and disenchanted masculine counterpart. A further aspect of 'marriage' is going to be presented: not with a view to modifying what has gone before but in order to explore another of the elements that will have to be fitted into their place in the pattern and to be reconciled, not on earth or within the scope of a poet's 'makyng', but where alone all opposites are reconciled: in the heavenly 'Jerusalem' where all that is among men separate, partial, and contradictory can be thought of as united, complete, and consistent.

Harmony and consistency can hardly be called the outstanding qualities of a tale which presents itself as a series of disparate elements, put together in ways that sometimes seem awkward, but which evidently correspond to aspects of human experience which stand in an uneasy relationship to the 'pilgrimage' design as a whole. The Merchant's telling of his story is broken and uneven, contorted like the mind of the man who tells it. Scarcely has it been set in motion than it is interrupted by a long parenthesis (IV. 1267–1392) in which the Merchant gives vent to the ferocious animus which colours his attitude to marriage. The next part of the tale (IV. 1393–1688) shows the 'hero' coming to a decision in respect of his own marriage by bending reason to his senile importunity. It is followed by a segment (IV. 1689–1865) which shows the marriage grotesquely consummated. The rest of the story deals firstly, with the deception of the infatuated husband by his young wife and her lover (IV. 1866–2218) and, finally, with an intervention by the 'gods' of classical and folk-lore memory (IV. 2219–2418) which relates these events to the Merchant's special view of the male-female relationship and to the theme of 'sight' – of the way in which men 'see' what their desires condition them to 'see' – which is a recurrent theme in the general plan.

The tale, then, is the story of an old man who thinks of his marriage in terms of possession, and suffers the disillusionment which his outlook makes inevitable. The two central figures are Januarius, 'a worthy knight' of Pavia, and May, the wife whom he decides to marry in his old age. The names, with their suggestion of winter and spring, death and life, place the story within a frame of reference which has made itself felt in the 'pilgrimage' since the opening lines of the General Prologue.[5] At this point, however, it seems that the spring season can indeed be 'cruel' to those who are no longer in harmony with its compulsions and who seek to impose upon the 'natural' processes of life the impossible and distorting demands which reflect their 'wintry' condition.

That the Merchant is moved, for whatever reason, by a concentrated animus against his 'hero' is evident from the start. It is not enough to present Januarius as an absurd old man in the comic manner established for this kind of tale. He has to be a vicious egoist who, after sixty years of convenient unattachment, during which he 'folwed ay his bodily delyt' (IV. 1249), has come to feel – inappropriately, out of season – 'a greet corage . . . to been a wedded man' (IV. 1254–5). Whether his motive can be called 'hoolynesse', or whether it represents 'dotage', a simple failure to recognize his failing physical powers, is left in ironic suspense. In either event, it leads the old man to believe that

> 'Noon oother lyf,' seyde he, 'is worth a bene;
> For wedlok is so esy and so clene,
> That in this world it is a paradys.'   (IV. 1263–5)

'Thus seyde this olde knyght, that was so wys' (IV. 1266): wise in his blind self-estimate and supremely foolish in the eyes of the Merchant and of those of the audience whom he is inviting to join him in the sour pleasures of demolition. Whether 'paradise' is so easily to be attained, or whether it is available to those who seek in it the 'easy' and 'clean' satisfaction of their desires remains an open question to which the Merchant – in whose mind both these adjectives ring with a note of bitterness which the following development of the tale underlines – will provide *his* answer in the course of the telling.

Having introduced his 'hero' the Merchant proceeds, in the course of an extended parenthesis (IV. 1267–1392), to a comprehensive depreciation of marriage and of the teachings concerning it advanced by the most respected authorities. He has heard the Clerk speak of a 'blissful' yoke of 'sovereignty' and proposes, in reaction, to advance his own view of what that 'yoke' in reality entails. 'And certeinly', he observes, 'as sooth as God is kyng', it is a glorious thing for a man who finds himself 'oold and hoor' to take to himself a wife to become 'the fruyt of his tresor',

> On which he myghte engendren hym an heir,
> And lede his lyf in joye and in solas.   (IV. 1272–3)

Contemplation of this prospect leads the Merchant into an impassioned mock 'celebration' of the 'joy' which this happy condition is said to offer to those who are so fortunate as to have entered upon it:

> Wel may his herte in joy and blisse habounde,
> For who kan be so buxom as a wyf?
> Who is so trewe, and eek so ententyf
> To kepe hym, syk and hool, as is his make?
> For wele or wo she wole hym nat forsake;
> She nys nat wery hym to love and serve,
> Thogh that he lye bedrede, til he sterve.   (IV. 1286–92)

The effect of this outburst is of some complexity. The Merchant seems to be expressing sentiments which might be found appropriate in the mouth of the Clerk, or even the Parson. It is only when we reflect, in relation to the sorry 'hero' of this tale, upon these aspirations to build upon the state of wedlock a life 'blisful and ordinaat',[6] or consider the subtly depreciative effect of the romantic term 'make' as applied to the partner who is said to offer these conveniences, that we begin to sense the peculiar animus that underlies these eminently respectable sentiments. The point has some relevance for our understanding of the 'pilgrimage' *motif* as a whole. To achieve 'bliss', a measure of personal fulfilment, by setting our lives in 'order' is, indeed, the end to which the journey is directed and to which those engaged in it may reasonably aspire: but the men and women who undertake it have in each case their own sense of that 'order' and not a few of their aspirations are flawed by the blindly self-seeking motives which govern their seeking.

The force – and the frustrating nature – of these self-serving drives are powerfully reflected in what follows. After summarizing the opinions of the 'clerks' – including that 'Theofraste' whose prudent but unattractive views were faithfully dealt with by the Wife of Bath,[7] and who is on record as holding that

> A trewe servant dooth moore diligence
> Thy good to kepe, than thyn owene wyf –
> (IV. 1298–9)

the Merchant urges those who hear him to 'Deffie Theofraste, and herke me' (IV. 1310). 'A wyf', he concludes, 'is Goddes yifte verraily' (IV. 1311): what kind of gift he will faithfully reveal in the course of his tale. Marriage, it seems, proposes itself to the incautious as a bargain of more lasting quality than the material gifts of Fortune – land, rents, pasture, 'moebles', and the like – which have been the speaker's concern and which 'pass', as generations of moralists have warned, 'as a shadwe upon a wal' (IV. 1315). A wife will offer an investment more durable than any of these: one which may even turn out to be more lasting than the man who has so incautiously taken her may have anticipated, which may well 'endure . . . lenger than thee list, paraventure' (IV. 1318).

These observations lead the Merchant into a more extended 'celebration' of the institution of wedlock as Christian teaching conceives it. Marriage is – for so we have been told, again on the best authority – 'a ful greet sacrement', offering conveniences and delights which no man would willingly forgo:

> He which that hath no wyf, I holde hym shent;
> He lyveth helpless and al desolat, –
> I speke of folk in secular estaat.
> And herke why, I sey nat this for noght,
> That womman is for mannes helpe ywroght.
> The hye God, whan he hadde Adam maked,
> And saugh him al allone, bely-naked,
> God of his grete goodness seyde than,
> 'Lat us now make an helpe unto this man
> Lyk to hymself'; and thanne he made hym Eve.
> Heere may ye se, and heerby may ye preve,
> That wyf is mannes helpe and his confort,
> His paradys terrestre, and his disport.
> So buxom and so vertuous is she,
> They moste nedes lyve in unitee.
> O flessh they been, and o flessh, as I gesse,
> Hath but oon herte, in wele and in distresse.
>
> (IV. 1320–36)

In the course of advancing the traditional account of the institution, the Merchant contrives to involve it in his rancorous, depreciative view of life. He presents Adam in his solitary state as 'bely-naked', helpless and stripped of dignity, requiring the support which his Creator, by what turned out to be rather a dubious joke at his expense, provided for him in the person of a companion. In mitigation of his original state of defenceless wretchedness God offered Adam a support 'like to himself': a support which turned out, in the event, to be – Eve! She was created, according to the divine intention, to be his 'help', the adornment of his 'paradise' on earth; and because he was incautious enough to receive her as such she became the occasion for his fall. Adam *fell*, lost his 'paradise', and lost it – in the Merchant's view – because he sought it in 'disport', in the 'buxom' attractions which Eve offered in his original state of pathetic solitude and which turned out, when tested by the event ('heerby may ye *preve*'), to cover an illusion. What Adam found at the expense of his lost innocence was a forbidden fruit which became, for all men after him, an aspect of their changed, *un*paradisal condition. It is interesting to recall that Januarius has just been said to think of his marriage as a 'paradise' in this world:[8] interesting also to reflect that he will in due course suffer a 'fall' from his own grotesque kind of 'innocence' under a tree and in a 'paradisal' garden of his own contriving.[9]

Having delivered himself of this doctrinal excursion the Merchant returns to his theme. The 'joke' played upon Adam is the origin of one from which succeeding generations of men have suffered at the hands of the women they married. It remains none the less an illusion to which human nature is obstinately attached and from which the Merchant no doubt bitterly resents his own awakening. His resentment expresses itself in the ecstacies which he visits upon his creature:

> How myghte a man han any adversitee
> That hath a wyf? Certes, I kan nat seye.
> The blisse which that is bitwixe hem tweye
> Ther may no tonge telle, or herte thynke.
> If he be povre, she helpeth hym to swynke;
> She kepeth his good, and wasteth never a deel;
> Al that hire housbonde lust, hire liketh weel;
> She seith nat ones 'nay', whan he seith 'ye'.
> 'Do this,' seith he; 'Al redy, sire,' seith she.
>
> (IV. 1338–46)

The Merchant is evidently engaged in building up a 'fantasy' of things as an old man is determined to see them. He seems also, in the last lines quoted, to be reflecting back in bitterness on the submissiveness of the Clerk's Griselda. The 'fantasy' involves a confusion between two different orders of 'reality' which is presented as common to the generality of mankind. By confounding the desire for material comfort with the happiness that 'Ther may no tonge telle, or herte thynke',[10] men involve both terms in the equation in their own kind of equivocation. The recognition of man's tendency to will his deception, to see things not as they are, but as his desire to think comfortably of himself prompts him, runs as a recurrent theme through the pilgrimage. It is often the occasion for the easy, spontaneous *bonhomie* of Chaucer's tale-telling, but it can also produce the more bleakly sardonic picture of a man who prides himself on the 'realism' of his vision, but who is unaware of the extent to which his attitude reflects a blindness to what human life can offer.[11] It could be said that the end of 'pilgrimage' is to explore the forms of 'blindness' by which men and women in some measure conduct their lives, and beyond this to indicate how their eyes may be opened, how they may be restored to a proper sense of what really is, and to rest the conduct of their lives on this true perception.

It is characteristic, in this connection, of Chaucer's pilgrims that they should speak on occasion more wisely than they know.[12] So is it at this point with the Merchant. He has described, for reasons of his own, a valid ideal which other men, not necessarily foolish or self-seeking, have thought to be of possible attainment:

> O blisful ordre of wedlok precious,
> Thou art so murye, and eek so vertuous,
> And so commended and appreved eek
> That every man that halt hym worth a leek,
> Upon his bare knees oughte al his lyf
> Thanken his God that hym hath sent a wyf,
> Or elles preye to God hym for to sende
> A wyf, to laste unto his lyves ende.   (IV. 1347–54)

According to this view, there is a life-giving aspect to marriage and there exists 'authoritative' support for it. The fact that neither the Merchant nor the Wife have made a success of their attempts to enter into this relationship can be seen as pointing, in typically Chaucerian fashion, in separate directions. Their presence in the pilgrimage has the effect of making us aware of the gap that separates venerable theory from refractory fact, the real behaviour of men and women from the statement of what should be. It does not, however, constitute a valid negation of the truth which it calls into question. Both the Merchant and the Wife, whom he seems to have in mind at this point,[13] have sought to bend the 'truth' to ends which answer to tenaciously negative aspects of their respective natures. Both bear unwilling testimony, through the tales they tell, to the 'truth' which has evaded them. The Wife, by the end of her story, seems to have glimpsed, however unwillingly, this reality concerning herself, whereas the Merchant's 'hero' – and perhaps the Merchant himself – remains invincibly blinded to it.

The point is one which must affect our sense of the 'pilgrimage', and of the place of this tale within it. Behind it there lies the fundamental question of what men *love* and in what they seek their fulfilment. As significant as anything in the Merchant's extended digression is the conclusion in which he equates the 'love' which men hope to find in the wives they have chosen with love of self. Once again, an impressive text is subjected to distortion. 'Love wel thy wyf', he says, echoing the Apostle,[14] as 'Crist loved his chirche' (IV. 1384). So far, so good; this is both orthodox and acceptable. What follows, though still expressed in authoritative terms, is – in the Merchant's mouth, and in relation to the story he is about to tell – an example of the subtle and creative ambivalence that marks Chaucer's handling of texts. 'If thou lovest thyself, thou lovest thy wyf' (IV. 1385). The apostolic injunction amounts, properly

understood, to an assertion of the need for giving, for unreserved
commitment as the foundation on which all relationship rests. The text,
however, is twisted to the convenience of the self-serving motives which
are expressed and ridiculed in the course of the tale. Christ evidently did
not love the society he founded in any spirit of self-affirmation, but rather
in one of creative generosity, even to the point of sacrificing his human life
to lay its foundations. Similarly, and by analogy, for a husband to love his
wife 'as himself' is to take the idea of unreserved and mutual dedication as
far as it can be conceived to go. It is *not* to see the other party to the
relationship as a convenience, the simple extension of a man's egoism.
This the Merchant in his 'blindness' cannot see; and that is why his tale,
which is intended by him to expose the inability of others to 'see' reflects
more truly than he can understand upon the reality which, to his own loss,
he has refused to make his own.

Having established to his own satisfaction the terms of illusion within
which he proposes to operate the Merchant is ready to return to his 'hero',
as he summons his friends to announce his decision to enter upon

> The lusty lyf, the vertuous quyete,
> That is in mariage hony-sweete.   (IV. 1395–6)

Recognizing that he is

> hoor and oold,
> And almoost, God woot, on my pittes brynke,
>   (IV. 1400–1)

he is convinced that the young bride to whom he aspires will be a docile
instrument to minister to his comfort. 'But *certeynly*', he says, with a trust
in his illusion as firm as it is misplaced,

> a yong thyng may men gye,
> Right as men may warm wex with handes plye.
>   (IV. 1429–30)

The image of wax as a medium pliant to the contrivings of human will and
human hands will reappear to play its part in the final resolution.[15]

In all this the emphasis rests on Januarius' confidence that his way of life
can be 'amended' to suit the realities of his 'wintry' condition. Reflecting
on those who 'lyve in chastitee ful holily', he denies any application to his
own case:

> But sires, by youre leve, that am nat I.[16]
> For, God be thanked! I dar make avaunt,
> I feele my lymes stark and suffisaunt
> To do al that a man bilongeth to;

> I woot myselven best what I may do.
> Though I be hoor, I fare as dooth a tree
> That blosmeth er that fruyt ywoxen bee;
> And blosmy tree nys neither drye ne deed.
> I feele me nowhere hoor but on my heed;
> Myn herte and alle my lymes been as grene
> As laurer thurgh the year is for to sene.
> And syn that ye han herd al myn entente,
> I prey yow to my wyl ye wole assente.   (IV. 1456–68)

Januarius' words, with their emphasis on the living manifestations of nature – the blossoming tree that is neither 'dry' nor 'dead', the evergreen that keeps its foliage through the year – point, by contrast, to the *un*natural content for his determination. Even the 'laurel' to which he compares himself in his conviction of youthfulness of heart suggests a specious comparison in as much as its continued greenness is not subject to the annual rhythm of seasonal life, where each phase occupies its natural place in the cycle of the year. 'By their fruits ye shall know them': if the old man compares himself to a tree which continues to bear 'fruit' in defiance of the passage of time, it is appropriate that the fruits which he will gather in due course will come to him from a flowering tree in the spring season and in a garden of his own creation, but which will bear nothing but bitterness and betrayal.[17]

With these purposes in mind, and prevented by the pursuit of them from seeing things as they are, Januarius calls on two 'brothers', Justinus and Placebo,[18] to confirm him in his resolve. Placebo, true to the compliant implications of his name, tells him that 'youre owene conseil is the beste' (IV. 1490). Justinus counters with the warning that it is

> no childes play
> To take a wyf withouten avysement,   (IV. 1530–1)

and by referring to his own bitter experience of marriage. The old man, of course, rejects this voice of prudence. 'Straw' he says, 'for thy Senek, and for thy proverbes!' (IV. 1567): words which, in a very Chaucerian manner, convey a repudiation of academic 'authority' in the act of indicating that the speaker, in this as in so many cases where infatuated self-will is in question, might have done well to heed the advice he is so rashly determined to reject.[19]

'Heigh fantasye and curious bisynesse' (IV. 1577), indeed, inspire Januarius' absurd resolve. They bear fruit in a series of elusive images which haunt his dreams, and which point to the nature of his infatuation:

> Many fair shap and many a fair visage
> Ther passeth thurgh his herte nyght by nyght,

> As whoso tooke a mirour, polisshed bryght,
> And sette it in a commune market-place.   (IV. 1580–3)

The 'mirror', naturally enough, reflects what its author requires it to show:

> Thanne sholde he se ful many a figure pace
> By his mirour; and in the same wyse
> Gan Januarie inwith his thoght devyse
> Of maydens whiche that dwelten hym bisyde.
> (IV. 1584–7)

Januarius' night-time imaginings represent his particular variation on a more ample theme with which the tales are largely concerned: the tendency, common to men, to indulge their fantasies to the point of finding them reflected in the 'mirrors' which they set up for themselves to give back the shadows of their intimate desires.[20] Januarius is determined to live in the world of illusions which he is 'busily' constructing for his own gratification: and so – though, no doubt, he failed to recognize it – was the Merchant when he set up for himself a 'shadow' of marriage, only to awaken bitterly to a reality which failed to sustain it.

The absurdity of these aspirations is brought out in an admirable display of ironic comedy. Once he has chosen his bride 'of his owene auctoritee' – for, as generations of poets have known, 'love is blynd alday, and may nat see' (IV. 1598)[21] – Januarius indulges himself in the obsessively physical imagination of delights to come:

> He purtreyed in his herte and in his thoght
> Hir fresshe beautee and hir age tendre,
> Hir myddel smal, hire armes longe and sklendre,
> Hir wise governaunce, hir gentillesse,
> Hir wommanly berynge, and hire sadnesse.
> (IV. 1600–4)[22]

Such is the imaged content of the 'mirror' he has set up for his own gratification, and upon it he is determined, in invincible self-esteem, to confer the illusion of reality:

> And whan that he on hire was condescended,
> Hym thoughte his choys myghte nat ben amended.
> For whan that he hymself concluded hadde,
> Hym thoughte ech oother mannes wit so badde
> That inpossible it were to repplye
> Agayn his choys, this was his fantasye.   (IV. 1605–10)

In presenting the old man's vision of himself as 'condescending' to the passive and grateful object of his pleasure, the Merchant requires his audience to see him as indulging a 'fantasy' which reflects his determination to think well of himself and to see the world as responding comfortably to his needs: a determination from which, to his creator's satisfaction, he is to be rudely awakened to a less gratifying reality.

To emphasize the inevitability of this awakening the Merchant returns to the 'paradisal' theme which has from the first provided an underlying thread in his narrative. Januarius reflects that, once he has married, the only problem will be that of dealing with a happiness too perfect to endure. As he sees it he is going to enjoy in this world a bliss which the most venerable 'authority' reserves for the life to come. 'I shal have myn hevene in erthe heere', he reflects, in the process of leading

> now so myrie a lyf,
> So delicat, withouten wo and stryf. . . .
> How sholde I thanne, that lyve in swich plesaunce
> As alle wedded men doon with hire wyvys,
> Come to the blisse ther Crist eterne on lyve ys?
>
> (IV. 1645–6: 1650–2)

The question is posed by Januarius in terms which answer to the content of his 'fantasies' and which he rashly assumes to be readily available to all married men. Beyond the patent absurdity, there lies a serious question which must affect our understanding of the human 'pilgrimage' and the fulfilment to be expected from it. The 'bliss' that Christ offers is available, as even Januarius has heard, to those who know that the end of the journey cannot, of its nature, lie *here*: that *here*, in the order of time, it is liable to be involved in impermanence and tribulation.

To make this point is not to involve the tale in any overtly moralizing or theological reading. The Merchant is as unlikely as any of the pilgrims to be concerned with any religious conception of 'heaven'. 'Heaven', for him, is the mirror of his immediate pleasure, and other human beings the means to procure its satisfaction. His attitude is prompted, it seems, by disappointment at finding that his partner has, as he thinks, let him down, that 'heaven', in this sense of it, is simply not available. His wakening from illusion inspires a comment in which Justinus steps somewhat illogically out of the limits of the tale to reflect on aspects of the 'marriage' theme already treated by the Wife of Bath. 'I hope to God', he tells his brother,

> hereafter shul ye knowe
> That ther nys no so greet felicitee
> In mariage, ne nevere mo shal bee,
> That yow shal lette of youre savacion,
> So that ye use, as skile is and reson,

The lustes of youre wyf attemprely,
And that ye plese hire nat to amorously,
And that ye kepe yow eek from oother synne.
My tale is doon, for my wit is thynne.
Beth nat agast herof, my brother deere,
But lat us waden out of this mateere.
The Wyf of Bathe, if ye han understonde,
Of mariage, which we have on honde,
Declared hath ful wel in litel space.
Fareth now wel, God have yow in his grace.
(IV. 1674–88)

This counsel of prudence might come appropriately from the Parson; but
the disclaimer which follows – 'for my wit is thynne' – reads like an
intervention by the poet in his pilgrim-narrator guise. The comment is
offered on a down-beat that amounts to a disclaimer of finality. What is
certain is that the warning against expecting too much, and expecting it in
the wrong way, involves a truth which has already been implied in the
Wife's story – delivered briefly, 'in litel space' (!) – of her unending battle
with her husbands, and of her final failure to impose, in the 'real' world,
her own 'fantasy' upon reality. Januarius similarly fails on the terms he
has chosen; and so, we may suppose, did the Merchant when he
discovered through his own bitter experience that the 'paradise' of his
imagination was not to be had for the asking.

In this spirit of 'proprietory' self-assertion Januarius marries his young
wife. When his brothers see that the incongruous outcome is not to be
avoided – 'that it moste nedes be' – they make the best of it, arranging 'by
sly and wys tretee' for May to marry her grotesque man 'As hastily as evere
that she myghte' (IV. 1694). What follows wraps the event in the sarcastic
depreciation which colours the Merchant's telling of his story:

But finally ycomen is the day
That to the chirche bothe be they went
For to receyve the hooly sacrement.
Forth comth the preest, with stole aboute his nekke,
And bad hire be lyk Sarra and Rebekke
In wysdom and in trouthe of mariage;
And seyde his orisons, as is usage,
And croucheth hem, and bad God sholde hem blesse,
And made al siker ynogh with hoolynesse.   (IV. 1700–8)

The effect is to involve the 'truth' of the 'holy sacrament'[23] in something
like a bitter sarcasm on marriage itself. May is enjoined to follow the
example of Sara and Rebecca in 'wisdom' and in the 'truth' of her new

state: how she will follow this injunction, and what kind of 'truth' her conduct will reveal, the Merchant takes it upon himself to reveal at the outcome. When the priest has spoken the customary prayers, 'as is usage', he ends by 'crouching' the incongruous pair: that is, he makes the sign of the Cross over them in blessing and exorcism of evil. The word, which suggests the carrying out of a vulgar superstition,[24] has the effect of reducing the minister of the Church, 'with stole aboute his nekke', to something like the level which the Pardoner will in due course make his own.

Januarius, meanwhile, as he presides over the wedding banquet at the side of his notably withdrawn May, feels himself 'ravysshed in a traunce', transported into an imagination of fulfilled bliss: 'Hire to biholde it semed fayerye' (IV. 1743). After he has struggled to contain himself in patience – 'I wolde that al this peple were ago' (IV. 1764) – the moment of truth is given in a passage which is a masterpiece of savage demolition:

> The bryde was broght abedde as stille as stoon;
> And whan the bed was with the preest yblessed,
> Out of the chambre hath every wight hym dressed;
> And Januarie hath faste in armes take
> His fresshe May, his paradys, his make.
> He lulleth hire, he kisseth hire ful ofte;
> With thikke brustles of his berd unsofte,
> Lyk to the skyn of houndfyssh, sharp as brere –
> For he was shave al newe in his manere –
> He rubbeth hire aboute hir tendre face,
> And seyde thus, 'Allas! I moot trespace
> To yow, my spouse, and yow greetly offende,
> Er tyme come that I wil doun descende.   (IV. 1818–30)

A large part of the effect of these lines rests on the controlled build-up which leads to the unlovely climax. Januarius, preparing to take his silent bride into his arms, dwells on the romantic commonplaces which are supposed to govern this kind of situation. She is, in his mind, the 'fresshe' May who will bring him to the enjoyment of bliss: the adjective, which will be stressed almost to obsession in what follows,[25] falls sourly, stalely, upon our ears, to colour Januarius' further references, in what amounts to a mockery of ecstasy, romantic and religious, to his 'paradise', the 'make'[26] of his senile ardours. For, by a parallel which runs through the tale and which conveys a large part of its deepest sense, May's 'freshness' recalls that of Eve and the 'paradise' she offers to her incongruous 'Adam' will become the setting for a 'fall'.

Entering into the 'paradise' of his heated 'fantasy' Januarius conducts himself as a man engaged in the parody of a religious rite. He is, after all, preparing to enter into the 'heaven' his imagination has prepared for him. He sees himself 'descending' from the bed which is to be the altar of his impotent endeavours; but meanwhile, under the forms of solicitous apology, he savours the pain which he expects to inflict by his 'offending' of the 'spouse' whose imagined virginity he sees as obediently and passively disposed for his taking. The passage, like much else in the tale, is cruel, and has been found distasteful. The cruelty, however, is no indulgence, but the recognition of an unlovely reality. Januarius is an extreme case; but his sorry obsession adds a necessary note to the 'marriage theme', reflects one more aspect of the tendency of men to distort the central realities of life to accommodate their possessively self-serving ends. Later on, in the tale to be told by the Nun's Priest,[27] this eminently 'masculine' compulsion will be presented in a more generous comic perspective, seen as absurd rather than as vicious. In this way it will be assimilated into the prevailing comic vein of the pilgrimage; but Chaucer did not create his masterpiece by passing over the darker places of man's nature, and the tone of this story makes it a bleak counterpart to the more vivacious exposure of feminine self-assertion presented in the Wife of Bath.

To be at ease in his grotesque situation, Januarius needs to be convinced that the 'deed' he is about to perform is both natural and appropriate. He sees himself as a good 'workman' (IV. 1832): one who, in satisfying his appetite, will follow the example of the craftsman who proposes to work 'well' in refusing to be 'hasty'. What is to be done will be done 'perfectly', extracting the last imagination of pleasure lingeringly, 'at leyser' (IV. 1834); for, after all, he can satisfy himself with the thought that the saving concept of 'wedlock' exists to cover every excess that his selfish sensual 'will' can propose to him:

> A man may do no synne with his wyf,
> Ne hurte hymselven with his owene knyf.[28]
>
> (IV. 1839–40)

All this prepares the way for a return to May, the passive victim – thus far – of these advances:

> But God woot what that May thoughte in hir herte,
> Whan she hym saugh up sittynge in his sherte,
> In his nyght-cappe, and with his nekke lene.   (IV. 1851–3)

This is a recall from 'fantasye' to reality, indeed: a recall stressed by the urbane understatement which follows: 'She preyseth nat his pleyyng worth a bene' (IV. 1854).

Already, in one of those inset narrative 'blocks' upon which Chaucer so often relies to establish contrasts germane to his purpose, we have heard of a 'squire' named Damian, who – in a line which echoes the description of the Knight's son in the General Prologue[29] – 'carf biforn the knyght ful many a day'. As befits a creation of the Merchant's Damian turns out to be very different in reality from what he is in appearance. Externally, he is not unlike the pilgrim Squire, or unlike the poetical lovers whose reverential attitudes that young man so ardently cultivates. He too is 'ravisshed' at the sight of his 'lady': so much so

> That for the verray peyne he was ny wood.
> Almoost he swelte and swowned ther he stood,
> So soore hath Venus hurt hym with hire brond.
>   (IV. 1775–7)

The emotions are not unlike those which the Knight's son may be expected to have felt. They are, indeed, given expression at some length in his unfinished tale, in which the attractions and deceptions of 'romantic' love constitute a central theme.[30] The difference reflects the Merchant's malevolence, the consistently negative reading of life which will make *his* squire a fitting companion for the 'fresh' May whose image is to be so effectively tarnished – like that of 'love' itself – in the course of this story.

The Merchant, indeed, contrives with considerable skill to destroy practically everything to which he directs our attention. Between them, *this* squire and *this* 'lady' plan the deception of the old man who is, respectively, *his* lord and *her* husband. 'Sike' in 'Venus' fyr' and burning 'for desyr' (IV. 1875–6), Damian is ready to 'putte his lyf in aventure' (IV. 1877) by penning a letter, 'In manere of a compleynt or a lay' (IV. 1881), to declare his devotion to 'his fayre, *fresshe* lady May' (IV. 1882). The constant repetition of this last epithet in relation to the notably evasive object of these urgent attentions has the effect of casting doubt on the reality which it ostensibly represents. The Merchant, clearly, is no advocate of 'romantic' sentiment. It is his purpose to reduce it – and, in the process, 'love' itself – to a shabby and unlovely delusion. Januarius is to be the unpitied author of his own deception; and so, 'good man' that he is said to be (and we are left wondering precisely what sense, other than that of infinite gullibility, the adjective can have in this context), the thought enters his mind to enquire after his squire's health, and to send his wife to look into his condition.

'Fresh' as she may be, May proceeds dutifully to Damian's bed-side, leaving her husband in impatient expectation of her return. He will not, he says, be able to rest 'Til that ye slepe faste by my syde' (IV. 1928). Damian uses the occasion to convey his letter into May's hands, enjoining her to the secrecy which is, as every reader of poetry knows, an inseparable aspect of romantic love; and May returns to Januarius with the letter hidden on her person. Here the reality which the Merchant intends his

audience to see beneath his heroine's beauty emerges in a deliberate
expression of his anti-romanticism. No sooner is her husband asleep than

> She feyned hire as that she moste gon
> Ther as ye woot that every wight moot neede;
> And whan she of this bille hath taken heede,
> She rente it al to cloutes atte laste,
> And in the pryvee softely it caste.   (IV. 1950–4)

We must surely feel that the Merchant's reticence concerning the place in
which May seeks refuge to read her *billet-doux* and to which she consigns it
'softly' once read, answers in a very special way to his vision of life. *That*,
he seems to be moved to insist, is the need which men have in common
and which makes their 'romantic' pretensions grotesquely unseemly. The
attitude is one which seems to catch Chaucer in an unwonted 'Swiftean'
mood. It spills over onto May herself, tarnishing her iterated 'freshness'
and involving the relationship which men like to dignify by the name of
'love' in stealth and deception.

Throughout this part of his story the balance of the Merchant's animus
is held evenly between his characters. If May's treatment of Damian's
letter has revealed her in ways which contrast strikingly with her
'freshness' – it is no accident that this glimpse into her intimacy is followed
by a repetition of the epithet[31] – it is still true that she is under the
obligation to return to her husband and to submit to his unwelcome
attentions. Wakened by the persistent coughing that answers to his
physical condition Januarius requires her to offer her nakedness to his
pleasures: for, as he puts it, 'hir clothes dide hym encombraunce' (IV.
1960), and she is required to acquiesce in their removal, 'be hire lief or
looth' (IV. 1961).[32] That, under these circumstances, she should look for
relief in her 'squire' is hardly surprising: though it is typical of the spirit
which the Merchant imposes on his matter that he should take the
opportunity to ironize on the doctrine of the 'clerks' who tell us that 'alle
thyng hath tyme' (IV. 1972) and on the relation of May's conduct to the
ends of

> grete God above,
> That knoweth that noon act is causelees.   (IV. 1974–5)

It is not the first time – as it will not be the last[33] – that Chaucer allows a
character to comment sceptically on the doctrines of the Schools; but that
he should do so in relation to *this* story, making of the Merchant his
'philosopher', is unique and disquieting.

May, meanwhile, has taken an 'impression' of pity from the visit to
Damian (IV. 1978): we remember, in connection with the choice of word,
that Januarius has already thought of her as pliant wax to be moulded by

his hands,[34] and we shall shortly see her fashioning, also in wax, the image of a key to bring about his betrayal.[35] The 'pity' she feels for her 'squire' leads her to indulge her desire in a way that the poets of 'love' have made familiar:

> 'Certeyn,' thoghte she, 'whom that this thyng displese,
> I rekke noght, for here I hym assure
> To love hym best of any creature,
> Though he namoore hadde than his sherte.'   (IV. 1982–5)[36]

Evidently no romantic heroine could speak more feelingly in dedicating herself to the object of her desire: and none, we might add, could express herself more carelessly with regard to the restraining force of established and prudent opinion. Such, in terms of naked and self-fulfilling desire, is the true nature, as the Merchant is concerned to show it, of the impulse that conceals itself under the forms of devotion and 'pity'. As he puts it, with an irony that falls the more devastatingly for remaining unstressed, 'Lo, pitee renneth soone in gentil herte!' (IV. 1986).[37] Far be it from the teller of the tale to approve the possible attitude of 'som tyrant' who – with the consensus, no doubt, of the more uncompromising moralists – would allow this 'gentle' squire to 'sterven in the place' (IV. 1991) without the benefit of so 'fresh' a creature's grace.

Moved by these sentiments, and by the terms of his letter, May prepares an answer for Damian in which 'she graunteth hym hire verray grace' (IV. 1997): the 'verray', which habitually carries so much more weight in Chaucer than its modern equivalent, reads with a special irony in this application. 'Sotilly', 'secretely', she conveys her answer to him under his pillow, and 'twists' his hand in hidden collusion; and, after assuring him that

> Ther lakketh noght, oonly but day and place,
> Wher that she myghte unto his lust suffise;
> For it shal be right as he wole devyse,   (IV. 1998–2000)

she returns to her husband in a demure show of wifely obedience. Similarly Damian, in the process of going through the motions of the lover who approaches the fulfilment of his desire, shows himself as 'lowe', servicably obedient to his old master, 'As evere dide a dogge for the bowe' (IV. 2014).

Januarius, meanwhile, continuing on the path he has chosen, 'Shoop hym to lyve ful deliciously' (IV. 2025). 'Busily', moved by officious self-indulgence, he contrives a setting for his unseasonable lust in the form of an old man's version of the Garden of Love:

> He made a gardyn, walled al with stoon;
> So fair a garden woot I nowher noon.

For, out of doute, I verraily suppose
That he that wroot the Romance of the Rose
Ne koude of it the beautee well devyse;
Ne Priapus ne myghte nat suffise,
Though he be god of gardyns, for to telle
The beautee of the gardyn and the welle,
That stood under a laurer alwey grene.
Ful ofte tyme he Pluto and his queene,
Proserpina, and al hire fayerye,
Disporten hem and maken melodye
Aboute that welle, and daunced, as men tolde.

                                        (IV. 2029–41)

It is important to respond to the various elements that go to the making of this garden. It is, as we have said, a special version of the Garden of Love, at the heart of which is to be found the 'rose' which the suitably disposed 'gentle' lover may aspire to pluck. It is a spring-time garden, the reflection of the May season, and a human 'May' will represent for the old man the 'canker'[38] which awaits him at its centre. It is said to excel the garden inhabited by Priapus, the double deity who is at once the patron of civilized cultivation and the embodiment of the sexual drives which lurk, hidden and potentially menacing, in its darker corners. It is the setting of immemorial folk-lore, where the ancient 'gods', 'Pluto amd his queene', winter and spring, death and rebirth, may fugitively present themselves, leaving their destined underworld to join in the pre-Christian ecstasy of the 'dance'. Like most medieval gardens, it carries memories of the Fall, of the worm of corruption at the heart of the fruit offered to Eve which turned to ashes in her mouth and, through her, in Adam's. Beyond all these echoes, and for the immediate ends of the tale, it is a garden which a selfish and impotent old man has conceived and for which he proposes to hold the key, shutting his young wife from the world and seeking impossibly to maintain over her his unnatural 'rights' of property.

The security which Januarius builds on these foundations of illusion – and on the walls within which he seeks to enclose his most prized possession – cannot last. As the Merchant puts it,

                worldly joye may nat alwey dure
        To Januarie, ne to no creature:

                                        (IV. 2055–6)

a moral beyond exception, but adapted in the context of this story to the peculiarly destructive ends proposed by the teller. Januarius, after living 'in this wyse, many a murye day' (IV. 2053), is struck blind 'al sodeynly'. The effect of his blindness is to feed 'the fyr of jalousie' in his heart, exasperating his determination to cling, even beyond his own life-time, to his rights of possession:

> For neither *after his deeth*, nor in his lyf,
> Ne wolde he that she were love ne wyf.   (IV. 2077–8)

Jealousy – the survival of possessiveness in human relations after the death of the 'truth' which expresses itself in trust – is presented in this tale as the ultimate manifestation of man's impossibly self-centred vision of things. It is a 'sin' which combines the mean, the pathetic, and the ridiculous, and as such has a special appeal for the Merchant. We are told that Januarius was 'jalous everemoore',

> Which jalousye it was so outrageous,
> That neither in halle, n'yn noon oother hous,
> Ne in noon oother place, neverthemo,
> He nolde suffre hire for to ryde or go,
> But if that he had hond on hire alway.   (IV. 2087–91)

Where nothing is given, where there is no mutual commitment of self or faith in life, there can be no true 'marriage'. Januarius, with his obsessive anxiety to keep his hand always on the wife he can no longer see, is in effect denying the nature of all relationship and inviting betrayal upon himself.

Seen through these eyes of disenchantment, it is no surprise that May is no better than she turns out to be. To achieve her freedom she takes advantage of her husband's blindness to steal the key to the garden, to have a copy made in impressionable wax,[39] and to convey it to her lover. What follows is a masterpiece of destructive tale-telling. We may, are indeed required to find it distasteful; but we shall do well to reflect that Chaucer is a great poet because his sense of the human 'pilgrimage' recognizes the existence of darker realities without which it would not be the penetrating, inclusive image that it is. Possessiveness, in the form of 'jealousy', has been a central feature of the Wife of Bath's contribution, as it is of the Merchant's; and, if the masculine form of this deformation of life is more unlovely, less redeemed by comic energy, than its feminine counterpart, that may be because Chaucer found that man's more presumptuous claim to 'authority' gave him the greater distance to travel in his fall from 'grace'.

Moved by May's contriving – by 'eggyng of his wyf' (IV. 2135) – Januarius calls her to join him in the garden, where they may 'pleye' alone, with 'no wight but they tweye'. His invitation parodies the sensual ecstasy of the Song of Songs:

> Rys up, my wyf, my love, my lady free!
> The turtles voys is herd, my dowve sweete;

> The wynter is goon with alle his reynes weete.
> Com forth now, with thyne eyen columbyn!
> How fairer been thy brestes than is wyn!
> The gardyn is enclosed al aboute;
> Com forth, my white spouse! out of doute
> Thou hast me wounded in myn herte, O wyf!
> Ne spot of thee ne knew I al my lyf.
> Com forth, and lat us taken oure disport;
> I chees thee for my wyf and my confort.   (IV. 2138–48)

The intimations of spring call us back powerfully to central themes of the pilgrimage; but, of course, their sense lies at this point in their relation to an old man who is clinging to the embers of a life he can no longer enjoy, who is determined to make of the wife whom he cannot hope to satisfy an exclusive, self-gratifying possession. The emphasis lies throughout on self, on '*my* wife', 'whom *I* chose', 'for *my* comfort'; and where these attitudes prevail life refuses to be subjected, seek its way to escape from the 'prison' into which the 'garden' has been turned.

The exchange in the garden is conducted with a full share of the Merchant's concentrated malevolence. Januarius addresses May in terms which in another situation would be those of 'love'. 'Thou art the creature that I best love' (IV. 2161), he tells her, and says that he would die rather than offend his 'trewe deere wyf' (IV. 2164). It is necessary to the Merchant's intention that his absurd creature should be rendered for a moment pathetic, in order to emphasize to better effect the cruelty of his deception. The old man pleads with his wife to remain faithful to him: pleads with reasons that combine an appeal to the highest motives – 'love of God' and respect for his 'honour' – with a promise, which amounts to a bribe, to make over to her 'al myn heritage, toun and tour' (IV. 2172).

'Fresh' May answers this speech 'benignly', as is her wont. Her ostentatious weeping is backed by the appeal of a respectable woman to her reputation. She too has 'a soule for to kepe' (IV. 2188), 'honour' to maintain. 'I am', she insists, 'a gentil womman and no wenche' (IV. 2202), adding a complaint against the way in which all men treat the women who are faithful to them:

> Why speke ye thus? but men been evere untrewe,
> And wommen have repreve of yow ay newe.   (IV. 2203–4)

Her words are immediately followed, in typical underplayed but devastating juxtaposition, by a couplet which underlines the contrast between them and the reality they conceal:

> And with that word she saugh wher Damyan
> Sat in the bussh, and coughen she bigan.   (IV. 2207–8)

She signs to Damian to climb into the tree at the centre of the garden. The tree, we are told, was 'charged with fruyt' – what kind of 'fruit' we are about to see – and the time is the morning – 'Bright was the day, and blew the firmament' (IV. 2219) – as though to provide an appropriate background to May's 'freshness' and to recall the traditional season of the Fall: and she and January are 'romynge ful myrie', like Adam and Eve, or indeed any pair of romantic lovers, along the paths of the garden which the old man's 'fantasy' has created as a refuge from reality.

The garden, beneath all its other associations, harbours other than human dwellers:

> And so bifel, that brighte morwe-tyde,
> That in that gardyn, in the ferther syde,
> Pluto, that is kyng of Fayerye,
> And many a lady in his compaignye,
> Folwynge his wyf, the queene Proserpyna,
> Which that he ravysshed out of Ethna
> Whil that she gadered floures in the mede.
>
> (IV. 2225–31)

The exchange between these 'deities' takes up the debate between the sexes introduced by the Wife of Bath. Pluto argues that daily 'experience' proves the 'tresoun' which women inflict on men. Their proverbial 'untrouthe' and 'brotelnesse' – to which testimony is borne by the best 'authorities' – are about to be confirmed under their eyes when Januarius' wife will allow Damian, his 'owene man', bound to him by solemn ties of feudal obligation, to make a cuckold of him. As the 'god' puts it with a blunt brutality close to the Merchant's heart: 'Lo, where he sit, the lechour, in the tree!' (IV. 2257).

Like the Wife, Pluto's queen has a ready reply to these accusations. She will put 'sufficient answer' into May's mouth: for all women,

> though they be in any gilt ytake,
> With face boold they shulle hemself excuse,
> And bere hem doun that wolden hem accuse.
>
> (IV. 2268–70)

'For lak of answere noon of hem shal dyen' (IV. 2271): for they will so bear themselves in untruth as to make their men 'lewed as gees' (IV. 2275). She goes on to argue that there are many 'Wommen ful trewe, ful goode, and vertuous' (IV. 2281), and offers in testimony those who dwell as nuns 'in Cristes hous' and those who in former times suffered martyrdom for their faith. Something of the same argument will be advanced in Chaucer's own prose tale of Melibeus,[40] and we shall not deny it force on its own terms; but here it is put forward in defence of deception and Proserpina is almost as waywardly feminine in her attitudes as the Wife of Bath has been in defending her sex:

> I am a womman, nedes moot I speke,
> Or elles swelle til myn herte breke;   (IV. 2305–6)[41]

and her attitude to Solomon, whom she dismisses as 'a lecchour and an ydolastre' (IV. 2298), interestingly recalls the use of the same name by her pilgrim counterpart.[42]

The end of a 'marriage' watched over by 'deities' of this nature cannot be other than it proves to be. Januarius has proposed from the first to use his wife; May has married him for convenience, to enjoy his property,[43] and has no intention, or even possibility, of denying her nature. By placing the act of betrayal in a spring-time garden which carries echoes of the original Earthly Paradise, and on a blossoming 'tree' at its centre that recalls the deception (also under a tree) that befel Adam through Eve, and which led to the loss of their original innocence, the Merchant finally incorporates the references to 'paradise', to a lost state of happiness, that he has scattered through his narrative. Faced by his consort's defence of her sex, Pluto in effect surrenders:

> 'Dame', quod this Pluto, 'be no lenger wrooth;
> I yeve it up!   (IV. 2311–12)

Nevertheless, to maintain the oath he has sworn to defend his sex, he opens the eyes of the victim, only to find that Proserpina too will maintain her promise to inspire May with an answer. They return to the garden where Januarius is singing to his love, 'murier than the papejay', like any romantic hero created in a poet's imagination. All this takes place under the eyes of Damian, sitting

> ful *myrie*
> An heigh among the fresshe leves grene,   (IV. 2326–7)

and preparing to receive the reward for his devotion. His 'merriment' reflects ironically on that of the 'lord' he is about to betray, and even the leaves of the tree share the epithet – 'fresh' – which has so obsessively been showered on the Merchant's dubious 'heroine'. Indeed, as though to emphasize the point, the adjective is applied once more to May in a context that stresses the note of 'romantic' and 'ideal' remoteness – 'This *fresshe* May, that is so bright and sheene' (IV. 2328) – whilst pointing to the reality, as it may seem to be, of her already pregnant condition.[44]

By the end of the tale Januarius, like so many men before him, is ready to see the illusion which has been practised upon him as 'truth', and to be argued into the belief that the evidence of his eyès is not what it seems to be. Once more, the conclusion points to a theme variously present in the tales. As May puts it,

> Beth war, I prey yow; for, by hevene kyng,
> Ful many a man weneth to seen a thyng,
> And it is al another than it semeth.
> He that mysconceyveth, he mysdemeth.   (IV. 2407–10)

May, no doubt, has her own reasons for giving this warning, but the words have an application that extends beyond the story to which they belong. The pilgrimage abounds in men and women who believe that they 'see' what they want to see, and who conduct their lives accordingly. Contrasted visions of marriage, in particular, have engaged our attention since the intervention of the Wife of Bath, and we have just been given one of the most disconcerting of them all. By bringing the 'gods' of myth and folklore into the picture, the conclusion confers upon the tale a dimension which extends beyond the Merchant's immediate purpose. If Pluto, as a male, tries to help Januarius see the bare, unwelcome 'truth' by restoring the use of his eyes, his consort inspires May with a ready answer which allows the victim of the deception to continue in his illusion of 'seeing'. Januarius, ready to be deceived so as to go on living in the world of 'fantasy' to which he committed himself when he so unseasonably married his 'fresh' May, is willing at the last to accept her reproof of him for his ingratitude: 'This thank have I for I have maad yow see' (IV. 2388).

III
'EARNEST' AND 'GAME': OR, THE TRUTH OF TALE-TELLING

VIII

THE PARDONER:
INTRODUCTION, PROLOGUE,
TALE AND EPILOGUE

The tales we have so far considered exhibit, in the main, the signs of a firm if loosely developed plan. Structured round certain nodal points – *The Knight's Tale* and the Wife of Bath's intervention, outstandingly – they have been designed to throw light from a variety of standpoints, all relevant and none final, upon fundamental aspects of the human 'pilgrimage'. It is always necessary to remember, however, that the plan as we have it remains incomplete: indeed, it is possible to argue that the incompleteness, far from being accidental, answers to the poet's conception and is an essential part of his design.

Under these circumstances it seems desirable, and indeed inevitable, in dealing with the tales printed in the latter part of the collection, to abandon the attempt to establish firm linkings between the stories and to consider those of them which seem to bring out separate, but fundamentally important, aspects of the human condition. It may even be that separation, the inability to participate in the ongoing pilgrimage, is in itself an important part of the complete plan.

Two of these later tales, which turn in different ways upon lives notably lacking in 'patience', impose themselves powerfully upon our attention. They are, respectively, *The Pardoner's Tale* and *The Canon's Yeoman's Tale*. Both illustrate perverse, or thwarted human drives which prevent their subjects from fulfilling the essential purpose of their 'pilgrimage'; and both are indicative of the obstacles which isolate men from 'fellowship' and so make them incapable of attaining the full expression of their possibilities as human beings. If there is a sense in which the conception of *damnation* has a place in Chaucer's scheme – and it would be as imprudent to overestimate the extent to which this is so as to deny the notion all relevance – it is in these tales that we shall find it exemplified.

It is notable that the introduction of both *The Pardoner's Tale* and that told by the Canon's Yeoman are given an elaboration which is only paralleled by the case of the Wife of Bath, suggesting that we are meant to see in each of these pilgrims centrally problematic features of human nature. It is essential to Chaucer's project that certain impulses, and the variously thwarted human beings who represent them, seem to be debarred – or to debar themselves – from any possibility of attaining the end which the very concept of pilgrimage posits. To recognize this is to throw a disturbing light upon the concept itself; but not to do so is to turn it into an abstraction, doubtfully relevant to the realities of human existence.

It is important, in trying to assess the uneasy effect which his tale makes upon us, to define the full implications of the Pardoner's presence among the pilgrims. Most obviously, he is a scoundrel who makes his living by the sale of the gift of forgiveness which belongs finally to God alone. From this point of view his presence affects the other pilgrims – and more especially those who are held, or consider themselves, to be 'gentil', right-minded and respectable members of society – as a living affront to themselves and their undertaking. It is also insinuated in the General Prologue[1] that the Pardoner is sexually deficient – in terms of medieval science a 'eunuch' – and, as such, cut off from the normal fulfilment of his sexuality. In a poem which is set from the opening lines under the sign of generation, of the revived fertility of the spring season, this exclusion amounts to the thwarting of a fundamental human instinct. From the first, the presence of the Pardoner is presented as a manifestation of death: so that, when death becomes the theme of his sermon, he is seen to be fulfilling with rare power and beyond any conscious intention which can be ascribed to him, the place assigned to him in the complete plan.

It is necessary in this connection to consider the full implications, as Chaucer is likely to have intended us to see them, of the Pardoner's deficient sexuality:[2] for the theme of 'eunuchry' had, for a medieval reader, reverberations which affect our understanding of the Pardoner in various ways. Just as the Wife of Bath attempted to turn aside the plain sense of the words spoken by Christ to the woman of Samaria,[3] only to find these words turning into a condemnation of her own way of life, so here we are meant to recall, no doubt, the words of the Gospel concerning those who have made themselves 'eunuchs' for the sake of the kingdom of heaven.[4] These are the eunuchs for the sake of God whose sacrifice can be expected to bear fruit in the form of spiritual treasure: and from their number the Pardoner is certainly excluded. For while it may be argued – and indeed there is a fundamental problem here, and one basic to the deeper senses of the episode – that he cannot be held responsible for his physical deficiency, it is clear that his sterility is, in a more general sense, self-willed, the product of his own deliberate rejection of grace. If he is indeed physically a eunuch he will produce no fruit in the order of 'generation'; but this sterility, however we are to understand it in the flesh, is the sign of a deeper fruitlessness which pertains to him in the spirit. Even the 'fruits' he promises as a result of his preaching are deceptive, present themselves as the opposite of the 'multiplying' which the new, spiritual man is privileged to achieve in the order of grace. The Pardoner, in other but not unrelated terms, is an exemplification of the 'old man' who has been rejected, or been unable, to accept the life offered him in the 'new' order of the spirit and who is, as a consequence of his rejection, dedicated to the opposite of life.[5] In this respect his preaching is diametrically contrary to that of the Parson who will point in his final sermon to the way in which the pilgrim can form himself through penance in the image of the 'new', redeemed man and so attain the 'heavenly Jerusalem' from which the Pardoner's nature and actions must exclude him.

This situation affects the relationship of the Pardoner to those who refuse, for a variety of reasons, respectable and otherwise, to see themselves as his fellows in pilgrimage. There is a strong sense that the Pardoner is – and *knows* himself to be – excluded from the 'fellowship' of those who look upon him with a mixture of social superiority, moral rejection, and deep-seated uneasiness. It is noteworthy that he is thrown together in a final list of characters –

> Ther was also a Reve, and a Millere,
> A Somnour, and a Pardoner also,
> A Maunciple, and myself – ther were namo –
>   (I. 542–4)

at the end of the General Prologue who seem to have in common only a sense of being in various ways suspect in the eyes of the more right-thinking pilgrims who make up the rest of the group: noteworthy too, as an example of Chaucer's question-insinuating ambivalence, that the poet-narrator includes himself in this unappreciated company. It is also significant that the Pardoner's close companion, the only person with whom he seems to have established anything that can be called a relationship, is the equally grotesque and equally corrupt Summoner. If the pilgrims are set on their way to the tune of the Miller's bag-pipe – apt symbol of sensuality and the folly of the world[6] – their rearguard is brought up by the duet with which these two recognized rascals animate the route. The result is at once wildly, crazily funny and sinister in a way that is surely true to the intentions of the poet.

The association between the Pardoner and the Summoner is of particular relevance for any assessment of the place of the former in the general scheme. The Summoner represents the corruption of God's *justice*, much as the Pardoner's occupation relates to that of his *mercy*. Upon the balance between these two principles depends the very prospect of attaining the end proposed in the pilgrimage; for without *justice* there can be no separation between 'good' and 'evil', that which, when chosen, makes for human fulfilment and that which thwarts it; and without the tempering of justice by *mercy* no man is capable of attaining the 'salvation' which is the goal of the journey.

For this reason both of these figures are excluded from the *love* which is the ruling force of the entire undertaking. When the Pardoner, to the accompaniment of the Summoner's 'stif burdoun', sings in the General Prologue his ditty 'ful loude' – 'Com hider, love, to me' (I. 672) – the effect is at once comic and something more – sharply and terribly incongruous; for the words of the popular song in this singer's mouth imply more than he is ready to recognize, indicate the need in which he and his companion both stand for the love from which their choices – and, in the case of the Pardoner, his circumstance – have excluded them. It is this sense of an exclusion from love – love both natural and supernatural, love of nature and love of God, the two levels of 'love' which are the theme of the whole pilgrimage – that gives the character of the Pardoner its final dimension.

It is interesting to see how the full implications of all this are brought out in Chaucer's handling of the Pardoner. His tale is given an introduction, in which the Host calls upon him to contribute his story, as he finally agrees to do. This is followed by a long prologue, placed in the mouth of the Pardoner himself; it is here that we are most expressly reminded of the Wife of Bath. These two characters are the only ones who are given the opportunity to explain at such length, and with such disconcerting candour, the motives which condition the telling of their tales; and in both we may feel ourselves in the presence of fundamental human attributes, attitudes with which the very concept of life as a 'pilgrimage' directed to an end, a justifying and reconciling conclusion, has in one way or another to come to terms. There follows after this elaborate preparation, the tale itself, which can be divided into two parts: a sermon against the sins of gluttony, blasphemy, and 'coveitise' which leads into an 'exemplifying' story which constitutes, for most readers, the heart of the tale. Finally, we are given a direct confrontation between the Pardoner and the Host, brought to an uneasy end by the Knight's conciliating intervention.

A. The Introduction

We begin, then, with the relatively short introduction. The Physician has just ended his story of the trials of the virtuous Virginia,[7] which is as unsatisfactory a tale as Chaucer ever wrote. Written in all probability prior to the conception of *The Canterbury Tales*, the story derives ultimately from Livy,[8] though Chaucer is also likely to have been familiar with the version included in the *Roman de la Rose*.[9] Whatever its origin the tale is poorly told and morally repugnant, or at least confused. Chaucer's inclusion of it suggests a self-critical attitude to his own past performances which is not out of line with the concern which he shows elsewhere for the implications of his art. The story tells of a Roman named Virginius, whose daughter attracts the lustful desires of a corrupt judge named Apius. Apius suborns a 'churl' to declare that far from being her father's daughter, Virginia is a servant who was stolen from him by stealth – 'my thral by right' – and demands that she be returned to his charge. Having heard the plea, Apius gives judgement in favour of the 'churl'. The 'worthy knight' strikes off his daughter's head at her request to save her from shame; and the daughter accepts her fate with proper resignation:

> Blissed be God, that I shal dye a mayde!
> Yif me my deeth, er that I have a shame;
> Dooth with youre child youre wyl, a Goddes name!
>   (VI. 248–50)

The tale seems to have all the disadvantages of the Clerk's story of the 'patient' Griselda without any of the art, the stressed pathos and the redeeming moral application that makes the latter, on its own terms and in spite of all the difficulties, acceptable.

The Physician, unlike the Clerk, is an indifferent narrator and an unconvincing moralist. We have been told in the General Prologue that he 'lovede gold in special' (I. 444): a fact which the narrator takes to be connected with the medieval use of the precious metal as a cordial, but which we, as readers, interpret as an indication of ethical outlook. We have also been told that he 'wan in pestilence' (I. 442): in other words, that he profited from a disease he was unable to cure and which will play an important part in the Pardoner's following sermon. A large part of his not very long story is taken up with discursive matter – a pedantic discourse attributed to 'Nature' on the excellence of her handiwork as 'vicaire general' (VI. 20) of God in creating Virginius' daughter, coupled with familiar advice to parents on how they should bring up their children:

> Beth war, that by ensample of youre lyvynge,
> Or by youre necligence in chastisynge,
> That they ne perisse; for I dar wel seye,
> If that they doon, ye shul it deere abeye: (VI. 97–100)

matter that neither advances the tale nor strikes us as offering any valid insight. The culminating point is reached when we are told, after Virginius

has killed his daughter, that the people intervened to save him from
execution, because they 'anon had suspect in this thyng' (VI. 263) – but in
that case why did they not declare their suspicions before? – and to cause
the unjust judge to be imprisoned, 'ther as he slow hymself' (VI. 269). The
'churl' is condemned to be hanged, but is saved, and his sentence
commuted to exile, by Virginius' intervention.

For the Physician this farrago of unpleasing inconsistencies has a moral
which he is happy to declare:

> Heere may men seen how synne hath his merite.
> Beth war, for no man woot whom God wol smyte
> In no degree, ne in which manere wyse
> The worm of conscience may agryse
> Of wikked lyf, though it so pryvee be
> That no man woot therof but God and he.
> For be he lewed man, or ellis lered,
> He noot how soone that he shal been afered.
> Therfore I rede yow this conseil take:
> Forsaketh synne, er synne yow forsake.   (VI. 277–86)

The most interesting thing about this conclusion is that it could be applied
almost exactly to the immensely more impressive tale which the Pardoner
is about to tell. In fact, when the latter finds himself called upon by the
same audience to tell 'som moral thyng',[10] also leading to the 'forsaking' of
sin, his not inconsiderable intelligence has no doubt led him to see in all
this a perfect example of what he should not do. Furthermore, he can
hardly avoid seeing the contrast between his own situation and that of the
Physician. The Physician – whom the more respectable pilgrims are ready
to recognize as one of themselves – has found easy acceptance for a tale
deficient in art and, to say the least, question-begging in its moral
assumptions; whereas he, who is well aware of his situation as an outcast
in the present company, knows himself to be capable of telling a tale which
shall be both impressive as a narrative and thoroughly effective in
conveying the moral which it is designed to illustrate.

The Host's reaction to the affecting story he has just heard is the point of
departure for the Pardoner's intervention. Swearing violently,

> as he were wood;
> 'Harrow!' quod he, 'by nayles and by blood!',
>   (VI. 287–8)

and so falling into the very sin which the Pardoner will denounce, Harry
Bailey reacts to Virginia's sad fate with the sentimental effusion of a
self-confessed plain man – 'Allas, so pitously as she was slayn!' (VI. 298) –
and makes his comment in the name of the 'philosophy' of downright

commonsense on which he so confidently, and sometimes so insensitively, prides himself:

> Wherfore I seye al day that men may see
> That yiftes of Fortune and of Nature
> Been cause of deeth to many a creature.   (VI. 294–6)

We remember the words spoken at the beginning of his tale by the Physician on the creative action of Nature,[11] who acted as God's 'vicaire' to bring into being the same Virginia whose perfection was later destroyed by Fortune; and we may think that the Host's reaction implies, beyond his understanding of it, a sense of the insufficiency of the optimistic views so glibly stated. Of 'bothe yiftes' – of Fortune and of Nature – men seem to have, according to the Host's experience, 'ful ofte moore for harm than prow' (VI. 300); but, having raised in this way questions that he is disinclined to probe further, but which the Pardoner may be in a position to appreciate, he retreats into a plain man's jest at the expense of learning – 'I kan nat speke in terme' (VI. 311) – before turning to the Pardoner and asking him for relief – 'triacle' – in the form of 'som myrthe or japes': in other words, for a 'myrie tale' as the only acceptable alternative for that other proven remedy for sorely tried sentiments, 'a draughte of moyste and corny ale' (VI. 315).

The request, and the manner of putting it, tell us something of the way in which the Pardoner is considered in this company, and still more so does the fact that the Host addresses him in French as 'Thou beel amy' (VI. 318): a phrase which carries, in the mouth of this most English of speakers, a belittling sexual innuendo. We may assume that the Pardoner, who is certainly one of the most intelligent of the pilgrims, is quick to respond to the implications of this phrase. His immediate reaction is to take up the Host's challenge, echoing the latter's dubious oath 'by Seint Ronyan!' with his own ' "It shal be doon," quod he, "by Seint Ronyon!" ' (VI. 320). 'Saint Ronyan' is no doubt the Host's mispronunciation of the name of the Scottish saint Ronan; but 'Ronyon' is also the English version of the French *rognon* and, by extension of the *double entendre*, of the male sexual organ. All this means that, far from accepting the exclusion from the company of right-thinking men which is generally forced upon him, the Pardoner makes a deliberate show of meeting his enemy on his own chosen level of manly conviviality in order, by so doing, to show him and the rest of the company that he is perfectly capable of playing the 'pilgrimage' game and of turning it, beyond their expectations, to his own finally disruptive ends.

Scarcely less significant than the attitude of the Host is that of the 'gentils', the socially respectable members of the group, towards the request of a tale from the Pardoner:

But right anon thise gentils gonne to crye,
'Nay lat hym telle us of no ribaudye!
Telle us som moral thyng, that we may leere
Som wit, and thanne wol we gladly heere.'   (VI. 323–6)

The 'gentils', forewarned no doubt by the references to 'Saint Ronyan', are afraid that after the Pardoner has refreshed himself in the way in which (once again reflecting the Host) he has just announced –

'heere at this alestake
I wol bothe drynke, and eten of a cake' –
(VI. 321–2)

some unacceptable and vaguely challenging 'ribaudye' will emerge. Who knows what kind of subversive monstrosity may come from the mouth of this uncouth, this socially unacceptable outcast? The question comes from those who, no doubt, would prefer to rest with the comfortable high-mindedness which has just been so reassuringly exemplified in the Physician's story; and it provokes an uneasy reaction in relation to what the monstrously inconvenient Pardoner may be likely to say. Let him, they demand, not without an implied sneer, tell us 'som moral thyng' which they can 'gladly' – that is, without undue challenge to their own cherished assumptions – comfortably and self-approvingly hear.

At this point we begin to see some of the deeper issues set in motion by the inadequacy of *The Physician's Tale*. The Pardoner, rogue that he may be, is certainly no fool. A challenge has been thrown to him in the name of the right-thinking society which (as he very well knows) will never accept him for what he is. Precisely because he recognizes this situation, he proposes to take up the challenge to tell 'som moral thyng', and in so doing to throw down what amounts to a counter-challenge of his own. This is implied both in his ironic echoing of the Host's words, and in his typical glance at the 'honesty' which is so prized by the world that refuses to accept him:

I moot thynke
Upon som honest thyng while that I drynke.
(VI. 327–8)

Some 'honest thing', we may reflect, which will at once outdo the facile 'honesty' just exemplified by the Physician and raise, in the process, disturbing questions about 'honesty' itself. He will preach, as he well can, a truly impressive sermon against greed, *Cupiditas*: a sermon dealing with a sin which he shares with more of his fellow-pilgrims than they would be ready to recognize, and one which – by a supreme stroke of irony – is part of the stock-in-trade by which he advances his own greed. In other words,

taking at their own estimate the 'gentils' who so obviously regard him
with a mixture of contempt and fear, he will turn their most cherished
values upside-down, throwing his unacceptable immorality into their
faces in the form of a sermon as 'moral' in its effect as it is powerful in its
expression and disturbing, for many if not most of them, in its theme.

B. The Prologue

To set the stage for his reply the Pardoner begins by offering a candid,
even shocking, account of the methods and aims which inspire his
preaching:

> 'Lordynges,' quod he, 'in chirches whan I preche,
> I peyne me to han an hauteyn speche,
> And rynge it out as round as'gooth a belle,
> For I kan al by rote that I telle.
> My theme is alwey oon, and evere was –
> *Radix malorum est Cupiditas.*   (VI. 329–34)

This candour has presented something of a puzzle to critics, who have
found it implausible in terms of 'character', but in fact it answers
admirably to Chaucer's intention. Once again, as in the case of the Wife of
Bath, it is useful to see the Pardoner as deriving in part from, and in part
profoundly modifying the established conventions of allegorical personification. To a certain extent he can be thought of as a 'type', who has
been given generalizing attributes to make him representative of recurring
patterns in human behaviour and who is permitted by an accepted
convention to declare these in his own words. In this respect his function
is exemplifying rather than characterizing, and to this extent he resembles
the figure of *Faux-Semblant* (Hypocrisy) in the *Roman de la Rose*[12] who in a
rather similar way states openly, with candour and a certain pride, the
'truth' of his hypocrisy. Chaucer, however, goes decisively beyond Jean
de Meun in moving far along the road which turns an allegorical,
exemplary conception into a richly conceived and complex character.
Faux-Semblant, rather like the Pardoner, embarks upon a long self-
revelation to *Amors*; but, unlike the Pardoner, this self-revelation turns at
times into a sermon directed against the vices represented in his person.
When *Faux-Semblant* attacks the Church for its corruption, or castigates the
sins of its representatives, he speaks less in character than as a mouthpiece
of moral denunciation; and when he lectures against begging it seems to
be forgotten that he is himself a mendicant. He is, in other words,
conceived less as a character than as a vehicle for the points of view which

his creator is interested to advance. Chaucer, drawing strength from this apparent contradiction, turns it into a revelation of character. The Pardoner's candour answers to a definite purpose, which springs from deficiencies in his own nature and from the reality of his relationship – or lack of relationship – to a society which repudiates and, in a certain sense, fears him.

Addressing his audience with the suave and deceptive deference implied in his first word – 'Lordynges' – the Pardoner declares the theme to which his sermon is to be directed: the theme of Greed, *Cupiditas*. The irony lies, of course, in the fact that, far from being the 'ribaudry', the display of crude and vulgar indecency which the 'gentils' expect of him, his discourse will take the form of a tremendously effective warning against the spiritual death which his own consuming passion implies. Since the Pardoner is well aware that, before *this* audience, he cannot hope to sell his stock-in-trade or exploit the dignified self-image which his 'hauteyn speche' is designed to project for the benefit of less sophisticated audiences, and since, moreover, it is his purpose to *shock* his hearers and so to assert his indifference to what he knows to be their judgement of him – as perhaps he needs to do, to make the terms on which he lives acceptable to himself – he allows himself to be disconcertingly frank about the motives which inspire his preaching.

It is not long before these subversive motives begin to surface in the Pardoner's discourse. He reveals himself, in the first place, as something more than his title might imply. Besides selling false relics and pardons, genuine and forged, he has some of the attributes of a 'quack' doctor or cure-all: among the goods he has to offer are cures for sick animals, remedies against jealousy, 'spells' for increasing the crops and – indeed – every kind of superstitious remedy for the prevailing ills of a primitive agricultural community. Effective, no doubt, when addressed to impoverished peasants or their 'parsons', 'dwellyng upon lond',[13] these things can hardly appear as other than repulsive or ridiculous to most of his present audience. Perhaps that is why he chooses to stress them with the deliberate intent of defying, flouting their cherished, self-bolstering standards. Particularly outrageous is his claim to be able to undo the effects of jealousy:

> And, sires, also it heeleth jalousie;
> For though a man be falle in jalous rage,
> Lat maken with this water his potage,
> And nevere shal he moore his wyf mystriste,
> Though he the soothe of hir defaute wiste,
> Al had she taken prestes two or thre.   (VI. 366–71)

It will not do, of course, to neglect the richly comic aspect of this, which is never far from the surface in the Pardoner's many-sided and elusive presentation; but we shall do well to recognize at the same time that he is touching closely – more closely, perhaps, than may be comfortable to some members of his audience – on matters that concern them more nearly than the sale of trumpery relics or the exploitation of ignorance and superstition. These things the relatively sophisticated 'gentils' might well take in their stride, as being unrelated to any perception they may have of their own weaknesses. That the remedy for the pains of jealousy, however, which some of them at least may be presumed to feel or to have felt, should consist (as the Pardoner proposes, with an effrontery as brazen as it is grotesque) in the victim's ability to blind himself to the truth of his situation[14] even when that truth implies the palpable outrage of a wife having 'taken prestes two or thre' – this has the effect of bringing the satire uncomfortably nearer home. By turning himself into a purveyor of the illusions upon which, in one form or another, most men rely to make their lives tolerable, the Pardoner contrives to undermine the complaisant sensibilities of those who presume to sneer at him, revealing to them the brittle foundations of self-deception on which they rest their acceptance of their situation.

After this retailing of the 'gaude', or trickery, by which he claims to have profited to the tune of 'an hundred mark . . . yeer by yeer' (VI. 389–90), the Pardoner passes to a portrayal of himself as a preacher. His words are as vivid as they are 'shockingly' candid:

> I stonde lyk a clerk in my pulpet,
> And whan the lewed peple is doun yset,
> I preche so as ye han herd bifoore,
> And telle an hundred false japes moore.
> Thanne peyne I me to strecche forth the nekke,
> And est and west upon the peple I bekke,
> As dooth a dowve sittynge on a berne.
> Myne handes and my tonge goon so yerne
> That it is joye to se my bisynesse.
> Of avarice and of swich cursednesse
> Is al my prechyng, for to make hem free
> To yeven hir pens, and namely unto me.
> For myn entente is nat but for to wynne,
> And nothyng for correccioun of synne.
> I rekke nevere, whan that they been beryed,
> Though that hir soules goon a-blakeberyed!
>   (VI. 391–406)

This brutal confession of indifference for the spiritual welfare of the people whom he openly, even proudly, acknowledges that he deceives is further calculated to shock the sensibility of the 'gentils'. The Pardoner presents himself in the pulpit as a counterfeit, an upside-down image of his fellow-pilgrim, the Parson, towards whom, it is relevant to consider, some of the pilgrims have already expressed their disapproval in rejection of his almost equally uncomfortable presence.[15] The Host, too, has already suggested the comparison of the Pardoner to a respectable church dignitary when he saluted him as being '*lyk a prelat*, by Seint Ronyan!' (VI. 310). The Parson is manifestly *not* 'like a prelate' of this or any other kind, as Chaucer has already gone out of his way to suggest in the General Prologue.[16] In fact his virtue, the moral consistency of his attitudes, may be said to depend on this unlikeness. The Pardoner, on the other hand, though certainly nothing like what a prelate should be, is capable of counterfeiting effectively some of the external attributes of such a one in the pulpit. To the poet-narrator, indeed, he has already appeared as 'in chirche a noble ecclesiaste' (I. 708). The 'values' he represents amount to an inversion of those which a churchman should uphold, but which tend in fact to be conspicuously absent in high places. They are inspired by *Cupidity*, in basic opposition to the love, or *Charity*, upon which the life of a real society rests, but which societies, as we commonly know them, prefer to evade. That this does not reduce the attraction of worldliness for many of those engaged in the human pilgrimage is one of the paradoxes with which any honest presentation of that pilgrimage is required to deal.

Having reached this point in his self-revelation, the Pardoner feels sufficiently confident to embark upon a challenge to his audience. My preaching, he says, consists of nothing but 'japes'; and he drives home his point by a brilliantly drawn picture of himself in the pulpit, 'bekking' upon his audience like a 'dove sitting on a barn', his hands and tongue moving rapidly – 'yerne' – and 'busily' – always one of Chaucer's favourite words, with its implication of officious self-assertion – in support of the points he is making. It is at least possible that, as we read the Pardoner's comparison of himself in the pulpit to a 'dove', we are meant to remember that this bird is the symbol of the Holy Spirit which should inspire valid preaching and against which the Pardoner, by declaring openly the end of his exhortations, recognizes that he is sinning. The self-portrait is unmistakably Chaucerian, combining humour, even a certain fascinated appreciation, with a notable detachment of presentation. We shall not be inclined to underestimate the intelligence which inspires this admirably controlled self-portrayal and which is, as we may well think, superior to that of most of his fellow-pilgrims; but we shall recognize that the Pardoner can allow himself to be so candid because he has accepted his exclusion from the human fellowship and is determined to do his best to turn to his advantage the reality of his situation.

The emphasis, indeed, lies throughout on a deliberate flouting of the moral values which the Pardoner's audience may be expected to hold, if by no means always to practise. The exploitation of this palpable, if unacknowledged, gap between principle and practice is fundamental to his plan. '*I* at least', he implies, 'am ready to recognize the reality of what I am and what I do'; it is by no means certain that the same can be said of those who reject him as a fellow-pilgrim. The Pardoner can preach, he says, continuing on the note of implicit defiance,

> agayn that same vice
> Which that I use, and that is avarice; (VI. 427–8)

for equivocation of this kind is the essence of the evil which springs from Cupidity, from the denial of love. That he himself can be said to be 'guilty of that sin' does not alter the fact that he can induce true repentance in others, making

> oother folk to twynne
> From avarice, and soore to repente. (VI. 430–1)

As always, the motives which underlie this assertion are various and revealing. Satisfaction in his ability to control the reactions of his normal congregation – those whom he despises as the 'lewd' people – is reflected strongly in the Pardoner's words, but so is the sense that he is powerfully challenging the assumptions of moral propriety which prevail in his present audience, saying in effect to the 'gentils' that he – a self-confessed, indeed self-displaying rogue – can induce deep – 'soore' – repentance in those whom he recognizes that it has been his consistent intention to deceive. The assertion carries with it disturbing implications, not only for those who are apt to assume their moral superiority to him, but for those who like to believe in a world of clearly defined moral alternatives, in which good and evil can be perceived as self-evident and easily distinguished opposites.

Even more disturbing, perhaps, is the fact that the Pardoner can assert – and assert truly, as his tale will show – that he, a man 'guilty', by his own confession, of sin, can preach effectively to induce repentance in those who hear him whilst he is concerning himself only with his own gain. For, having thus, as it were, paradoxically asserted his power to do what his hearers are bound to agree with him in thinking of as good, the Pardoner once again stresses with brutal, even outrageous directness, the *un*spiritual motives of his preaching:

> But that is nat my principal entente:
> I preche nothyng but for coveitise. (VI. 432–3)

It is important to see that, throughout the course of his 'sermon', the Pardoner plays effectively upon his sense of *two* audiences: the congregation of unlettered peasants who are the victims of his efforts to win 'gold' and the present company of 'gentils' and others from whom no gain can reasonably be expected, but whom he has deeper, more personal, and even imperfectly conscious reasons for impressing. The continual and remarkably effective shifting from one of these audiences to the other provides the tale with no small part of its subtlety and power.

The bluntness of the Pardoner's statement is calculated to act as a challenge, a kind of moral slap in the face, directed at the complacency which his audience shares with the generality of men. This is the declaration to which he has been moving since his opening exchange with the Host and to which he is now ready, after his careful preparation of the ground, to give open and scandalous expression: the act of confrontation by which he intends to turn his exclusion, his unsurmountable social and moral disadvantage, into an assertion of defiant and compensating self-affirmation.

Having dramatically unfolded his strategy the Pardoner is ready to embark upon an uncompromising and even scornful declaration of the motives which inspire his preaching:

> What, trowe ye, that whiles I may preche,
> And wynne gold and silver for I teche,
> That I wol lyve in poverte wilfully?
> Nay, nay, I thoghte it nevere, trewely!
> For I wol preche and begge in sondry landes;
> I wol nat do no labour with myne handes,
> Ne make baskettes, and lyve therby,
> By cause I wol nat beggen ydelly.
> I wol noon of the apostles countrefete;
> I wol have moneie, wolle, chese, and whete,
> Al were it yeven of the povereste page,
> Or of the povereste wydwe in a village,
> Al sholde hir children sterve for famyne.
> Nay, I wol drynke licour of the vyne,
> And have a joly wenche in every toun.   (VI. 439–53)

Once again, it is impossible to read this self-presentation without sensing that a challenge is being thrown down to everything that the Pardoner's fellow-pilgrims, and especially those who most keenly disapprove of him, regard – rightly, no doubt, but also a little too easily – as the foundation of right living. The emphasis laid upon will – 'I wol' is repeated no less than seven times in the fourteen lines quoted – is a confirmation of the speaker's determination to assert himself in the face of a world that he knows will never accept him. 'What, trowe ye?' – 'are you so naive as to expect?' – 'that I am going to live in the "poverty" which our common religion enjoins, but which nearly all of you are busily, in one way or another, engaged in rejecting?' 'Nay, nay, I thoghte it nevere trewely'. When the Pardoner stresses so emphatically his rejection of 'poverte' – he uses the word three times in the same space – and his refusal to 'counterfeit' the example of the Apostles – he who is himself by his own confession the 'counterfeit' of a preacher – he is delving rather more deeply into their motives than his audience may care to consider. He is both asserting the power of money – 'an hundred mark' won through his efforts 'year by year' – for affecting entry into respectable society and challenging, by implication, what we know from the General Prologue to be the values sustained by the Parson and his brother the Plowman: values rejected or ignored, less outrageously but hardly less definitely, by most if not all of the 'better class' pilgrims.

'I', the Pardoner seems to be saying, 'have no intention of living in accordance with the ideals of evangelical poverty; but neither – if we are to be honest – have most of you any *real*, as distinct from verbal, intention of following the apostolic precept. I have made no pretence of imitating the example of Christ's first followers, as perhaps some of you claim to do' – there is a wealth of meaning in the implications of the word 'counterfeit' – 'but I have done what I can to use my gift of preaching to obtain the means required to sustain life in the way that the "gentils" of this world – people such as some of you like to consider yourselves – regard as natural and proper: enjoying the comforts of respectable living – "money, wool, cheese, and wheat", even' (and here, given the speaker's already stressed sexual disability, the irony touches further depth) ' "a joly wench in every town" to be my support. I have, moreover, obtained all these desirable things by deliberately outraging what most of you, entrenched in the respectable values of your society, have accepted as the unquestioned foundation of a moral life'.

Then, having made his gesture of defiance in the face of the uneasiness which his presence provokes, the Pardoner declares his readiness to take up the challenge which has been put before him:

> But herkneth, lordynges, in conclusioun:
> Youre likyng is that I shal telle a tale.
> Now have I dronke a draughte of corny ale,
> By God, I hope I shal yow telle a thyng
> That shal by reson been at youre likyng. (VI. 454–8)

Not accidentally, he addresses himself once more to the 'lordynges' among his fellow-pilgrims: those who either have some claim to a superior social status or who would like to feel themselves flattered, supported in their various pretensions, by being so addressed. It is evidently not the 'rejected', or at best marginal members of the group, such as the

Summoner, the Miller, the Reeve, or the self-effacing poet who has so inscrutably aligned himself with these, that he has in mind, but those who lay claim to superior social standing and who use it to justify the contempt which they manifest towards him and what he stands for. To *them* above all, the Pardoner says that he has been called upon to tell a tale, a *moral* tale, moreover, by the very people who believe – indeed they *know*, and he has just gone out of his way to confirm them in their knowledge – that he is a man incapable of the most elementary moral reaction. Well, he concludes, they shall have their tale, and 'By God' – the emphasis is surely significant – what they are to hear will be even more 'moral' than they can have bargained for: certainly more seriously moral than the farrago of inconsequent barbarities that they have just heard, with apparent approval, from the Physician, and perhaps more moral, more deeply probing in its relation to their own assumed values, than they may be ready to consider. As soon as he has refreshed himself with 'a draught of corny ale' (the echo of the Host's recent words is also deliberate), he will show them what a man who just made an open confession of immorality can do in the way of producing what has been asked of him.

> For though myself be a ful vicious man,

(and it continues to be the Pardoner's strategy to stress what he knows to be beyond concealing)

> A moral tale yet I yow telle kan.   (VI. 459–60)

'Now hoold youre pees!'. Let his audience only be silent, like those who habitually receive his message from the pulpit and who are the deluded supporters of his 'coveitise', and they shall hear – what they are to hear: 'my tale I wol bygynne'. The foundations have been laid, the Pardoner has manoeuvred his audience into the mood he requires of them, and the tale can begin.

The implications of the Pardoner's self-presentation are various, disturbing, and such as to affect, finally, the sense of the whole pilgrimage project. Ultimately in question is a theme that has been raised more than once in the interludes between the tales: the theme of the motive that governs tale-telling and its relation to the 'truth' which the poet, following the specific conditions of his art, is concerned to explore. The Physician has contributed a story deficient in art and pointing a moral which we can hardly fail to question. The Host has expressed the discomfort with which it has left him, but in a way which seems to set aside the real difficulties. He has further ignored the whole problem of moral justification by calling upon the Pardoner, of all people, to present in reaction a 'merry tale'. His manner of rejecting the Physician's contribution and of calling upon the Pardoner has shown by his crude oaths and semi-blasphemous observations, added to his jeer at the Pardoner's expense, an insensitivity which he shares with not a few of the company and which is associated with his ale-house function.

The Pardoner, however, whilst seeming to follow the Host and to defer to the expressed will of the more respectable pilgrims, has chosen to go his own way. Whereas the Physician, whom most of the pilgrims accept as a 'moral' man, and who no doubt thinks of himself as such, has told a tale both morally and artistically deficient, he – the Pardoner – in the act of confessing openly that he is what the company already assumes him to be, sets out to tell a tale which shall answer to the demands placed upon him: a tale the moral of which is both artistically worked out in terms of 'tale-telling' and relevant to the pilgrims in the light of what we have seen to be their behaviour on the road. In the process, he raises fundamental questions about the relation between tale and teller, between fiction and truth, between moral precept and the observed realities of human nature: questions which affect the very substance of 'pilgrimage'. At the end of the journey, as the pilgrims are on the point of entering Canterbury, we shall be given another, less 'artistic' sermon, and – as we follow it through its long and often prosy development – be struck by the fact that the Pardoner can be seen as an upside-down version, a kind of parody, of the Parson. Whereas the Parson deliberately rejects 'art'[17] in the name of the 'truth' which he represents in his office and embodies in his life, the Pardoner reveals himself as consciously and triumphantly 'artful', after having declared, with open and defiant effrontery, that his 'art' is at the service of his greed.

The dilemma is one which affects the poet and his conception of his art, as it has been developed through the *Tales*. The success of the Pardoner's sermon is such as to leave us with doubt concerning the effectiveness of the Parson's preaching. Even more important, perhaps, it is apt to inspire in us a certain uneasiness concerning the moral implications of a pilgrimage which began in a tavern, under the patronage of a Host who is both careful of his own profit and not altogether above exhibiting the sins of the 'flesh' against which the tale of the three 'rioters' and their sorry end effectively warns: a pilgrimage, moreover, which set out to the tune of the bag-pipe and which has shown personal rivalries, such as those of the Miller and the Reeve, the Friar and the Summoner, side by side with the Wife of Bath's misplaced but human exuberance, and which will present – as a kind of final *reductio ad absurdum* of the very concept of 'pilgrimage' – the Cook incapacitated by drink and unable to mount his horse.[18] It is small wonder that the author is moved, through the presentation of his characters, to declare a doubt which has been unobtrusively present from the first: a doubt concerning the end and justification of 'fiction' in its relation to 'truth'.

It would seem, indeed, that there are *two* kinds of truth which the plan of the *Tales* seeks to hold together. There is the 'truth' that imposes upon the poet the obligation to be faithful to his experience as it presents itself to him and wherever it may lead;[19] and there is the other 'truth' which inspires men to set out on their 'pilgrimage' towards a goal which is of its nature beyond, and which yet justifies the present. Given the nature of the preacher, the effect of the Pardoner's sermon is to cast a measure of doubt on the efficacy of the testimony to the truth which the Parson will finally advance; for, in terms of the 'truth' of art, the Pardoner, a self-confessed purveyor of deceptions, is more convincing than the Parson either wishes to be or succeeds in being. In view of the Parson's deliberate rejection of 'art', of 'tale-telling', there is no reason why this should affect him, and indeed it does not; but equally, given that Chaucer is a poet addressing an audience which expects to be entertained, and given that the 'truth' of his art is central to his concern, he cannot fail to be moved – and we with him – to uneasy consideration.

It is this, indeed, that finally produces the famous 'retraction':[20] the 'retraction' which the Pardoner neither wishes nor is able to make, which seems to be involved in any serious 'moral' reading of life, but which also seems to lead to a final rejection of tale-telling in the interests of a 'truth' which lies outside and beyond the tale itself. This 'truth' the Parson will declare after a deliberate rejection of fiction, but at the expense perhaps of leaving his audience dissatisfied and disappointed. The Parson's teachings may be, indeed no doubt are, *true* in terms of the overriding conception, whereas those contained in many of the tales are at best shadows and, may be, deceptions; but they are deceptions to which we respond where the 'truth' can leave us cold and in a sense discontented. It may be that the tension so revealed between 'truth' and 'fiction', and the impossibility of bringing it to a clear resolution, is the ultimate sense of Chaucer's creative effort.

C. The Tale

Having set the stage to his satisfaction, the Pardoner is ready to embark upon the tale that has been required of him. This divides into two parts: the first inserted – in a way that is typical of some of Chaucer's more complex creations[21] – as a parenthesis (ls. 485–660) interrupting the development of the second. The first part, consisting of a denunciation of the sins of Avarice and Gluttony, makes effective use of rhetorical devices familiar in the contemporary pulpit: the second covers the *exemplum*, or dramatic 'example' designed to bring home the reality of death as the wages of sin. The sermon depends largely for its effect on the contrast between a 'morality' which not a few of the pilgrims may find uneasily relevant to their own conduct, and the perception of the preacher generally current among them. The 'tale' into which it leads derives equally from familiar material. It has been shown to have a great many analogues, both Eastern and Western,[22] and it has not been possible to determine exactly which version Chaucer may have taken as his source.

The general effect of the more explicitly hortatory part of the sermon is at once comic and something more. It is certainly funny – almost desperately so – to think of these exhortations proceeding from the mouth of *this* preacher and directed at pilgrims whose behaviour on the road can be thought of as exemplifying many of the aberrations and excesses so strikingly condemned; but humour of this kind does not exhaust the impression which this preaching makes upon us. There is a very special tone in the indignant, or – as it almost seems – mock-indignant apostrophes with which the sermon is so abundantly interspersed:

> Allas! the shorte throte, the tendre mouth,
> Maketh that est and west and north and south,
> In erthe, in eir, in water, men to swynke
> To gete a glotoun deyntee mete and drynke!;
> (VI. 517–20)

or, again,

> O wombe! O bely! O stynkyng cod,
> Fulfilled of dong and of corrupcioun!
> At either ende of thee foul is the soun.
> How greet labour and cost is thee to fynde!
> Thise cookes, how they stampe, and streyne, and grynde,
> And turnen substaunce into accident,
> To fulfille al thy likerous talent!
> Out of the harde bones knokke they
> The mary, for they caste noghte awey
> That may go thurgh the golet softe and swoote.
> (VI. 534–43)

Throughout this part of the sermon the devices at the disposition of the preacher are used to intensely visual and sensible ends. The picture of the drunkard stands out with powerful, and no doubt disturbing familiarity:

> O dronke man, disfigured is thy face,
> Sour is they breeth, foul artow to embrace,
> And thurgh thy dronke nose semeth the soun
> As though thou seydest ay 'Sampsoun, Sampsoun!'
> (VI. 551–4)

The abstract sin is rendered graphic in personification, placed before us in the manner of what must be called moralizing farce; and the final effect is achieved when the Pardoner, pausing to comment on the picture he has placed before his audience – the reality of which has been present before them all in the person of the Cook – adds his ironic gloss: 'And yet, God woot, Sampsoun drank nevere no wyn' (VI. 555), before returning to the drunkard whom he shows – again like the Cook – falling to the ground in dumb stupour, 'as it were a styked swyn' (VI. 556). The effect is to strengthen the dramatic immediacy upon which preaching of this kind depends; and, in the process, to expose to an essentially comic revaluation the 'moral' attitudes which make it possible. We can hardly fail to have in our minds the memory of the Pardoner's appearance as given in the General Prologue, and see in our imagination those mad, hare's eyes[23] glaring from the pulpit as he conjures up these sensational impressions of the sins of the flesh. The Pardoner is working a vein which exercises upon him an appeal of fascination. The Parson, when his turn comes to deliver his message, will deliberately renounce these devices, which he no doubt finds repulsive and unworthy of his purpose; but he will run the risk, in the process, of alienating the attention of his audience and so of failing in his aim.

The comedy of these exhortations, real as it is, is qualified by intimations of a more serious order. There is something more than merely farcical, more particularly, in the adoption by the Pardoner of the language developed by scholastic theologians to clarify the central Christian mystery of the Eucharist. Where the priest by his act of consecration turns 'accident' into 'substance', bread and wine into the body and blood of the Redeemer, the cooks, 'stamping', 'striving', and 'grinding' in frenzied activity, reverse the process to satisfy the unspiritual appetites of their masters. In his use of this supremely inappropriate language[24] we may sense the Pardoner considering just how far he may go in outraging the sensibilities of his audience, and then, as though confident of being able to carry off his gesture, deciding to continue. Moreover, in invoking so insistently these figures of gluttony, swearing, and avarice, he is involving his pilgrim audience more closely than may be comfortable for them in his denunciations. Although he has begun by telling them that the words he speaks are memorized material – 'For I kan al by rote that I telle' (VI. 332) – it is clear from the way in which he addresses himself to the company – 'herkneth, lordynges, o word, I yow preye' (VI. 573) – that he is pointing to sins of which a number at least of them – not excluding the Franklin, whose table was described in the General Prologue as being so impressively weighed down with good things to eat and drink[25] – may reasonably stand convicted. Throughout, all true uses of the 'word' are rendered suspect by the Pardoner's procedures. It almost seems that the pilgrims themselves, the 'lordynges' addressed with a revealing mixture of surface flattery and subsistent irony, have been reduced to the status of the 'lewd' people whom the Pardoner habitually manipulates in the act of promoting the specious security of his wares. Well aware as Chaucer no doubt was of the element of the ridiculous, the fundamentally and unnaturally absurd, involved in this kind of moralizing rhetoric, he must have been equally sensitive to the reality of sin, a reality which is not made less but perhaps more vivid by coming from the mouth of the self-confessed sinner who delivers these denunciations and by the obsessive tone in which they are delivered. By having recourse to these preaching devices the Pardoner contrives simultaneously to stimulate and to undercut the sense of sin which we, as readers, may be presumed to share with his audience. The difficulty of pinning him down, or confining him to a single, uncomplicated effect, constitutes a large part of the fascination of his performance.

The other side of the contrast is underlined, still in the theatrical, sensational idiom appropriate to the sermon, by the medley of brutal curses and hysterical religious exhortations which constitute one of the Pardoner's chief devices and which are taken up, against an explicit background of death, in the tale which follows. When the Pardoner says

> That it is grisly for to heere hem swere.
> Oure blissed Lordes body they totere, –
> Hem thoughte that Jewes rente hym noght ynough,
>   (VI. 473–5)

or when he quotes Paul as saying:

> 'Ther walken manye of whiche yow toold have I –
> I seye it now wepyng, with pitous voys –
> That they been enemys of Cristes croys,
> Of whiche the ende is deeth, wombe is hir god!'
>   (VI. 530–3)

he is at once anticipating and turning to rhetorical effect the 'moral' which his 'example' is designed to enforce. Such devices belong to comedy, but to comedy of a special kind. Uniquely adapted to the speaker in whose mouth they are placed, the effect of these denunciations is at once grotesque and horrifying, absurd and – in their macabre way – serious to the point of disquiet. The resulting impression is not one which can easily be defined without reducing the real measure of its complexity. The Pardoner is without doubt engaged in exploiting his audience emotionally in the process of bringing out the repugnant tricks of his trade. These in turn imply a comment, of a kind which is likely to have been close to Chaucer's heart, on so much misanthropic and finally self-satisfied clerical or 'scholarly' moralizing; but beyond this, qualifying the comic effect, there is the question of the Pardoner's true motives, the uneasy sense that this grotesque and self-confessed exploiter is capable, on occasions and in the very act of preaching, of finding himself carried away, subdued to the fascination of his own eloquence.

All this, however, is no more than a parenthesis inserted into the real 'drama' of the tale. This gets under way with the introduction of the plague: the 'Death', as it is menacingly personified:

> Thise riotoures thre of whiche I telle,
> Longe erst er prime rong of any belle,
> Were set hem in a taverne for to drynke,
> And as they sat, they herde a belle clynke
> Biforn a cors, was caried to his grave.   (VI. 661–5)

As they ask the tavern boy for information about the dead man, the unexpected but universally present visitant is given the full force of dramatic personification:

> He was, pardee, an old felawe of youres;
> And sodeynly he was yslayn to-nyght,
> Fordronke, as he sat on his bench upright.
> Ther cam a privee theef men clepeth Deeth,
> That in this contree al the peple sleeth,
> And with his spere he smoot his herte atwo,
> And wente his wey withouten wordes mo.   (VI. 672–8)

The Pardoner, by thus dramatizing his story, is making it live through images familiar to his audience and calculated to obtain from them a response in which fear and fascination are powerfully mingled. When he identifies the personified Death, through the boy's words, with 'this pestilence', and warns that those who hear him would do well at all times – 'everemoore' – to be 'redy for to meete' such an 'adversary', he is relating his tale to familiar realities in a way calculated to strike home to the intimate experience of his hearers.

The advice which the boy gives for dealing with this dread enemy is sound. He says that he has learned it from his mother – 'Thus taughte me my dame; I sey namoore' (VI. 684) – and thereby lends to what he says the force of universal human experience, perhaps even that of the teachings of the Church – often described as the 'mother' of all believers – made available to men. All men are called upon to remember that death is an inescapable part of life, and that after physical death they will be called to judgement. This truth is brought home to them in a variety of ways during their pilgrimage, and they forget or evade it at their peril. The story which follows rests on the consequences of misinterpreting this advice by following, or trying to follow it, in a literal rather than in a spiritual sense.

This error is first made by the 'taverner', who – rather like the Host, whom the Pardoner is likely to have in mind – is inclined to take the warning at its face value:

> 'By seinte Marie!' seyde this taverner,
> 'The child seith sooth, for he hath slayn this yeer,
> Henne over a mile, withinne a greet village,
> Bothe man and womman, child, and hyne, and page;
> I trowe his habitacioun be there.
> To been avysed greet wysdom it were,
> Er that he dide a man a dishonour.'   (VI. 685–91)

By suggesting that men may avoid by foreknowledge the 'dishonour' which death does them – indeed, by thinking in terms of 'dishonour' at all – the taverner is contributing to the wrong path which the rioters will take; and they, in their literal-minded blindness, are only too ready to follow it.

The rioters, then, set out to discover death in the form of a literally conceived 'traitor'. By meeting and 'slaying' this figment of their imagination they hope to achieve what is, for all men, impossible: in other words, to escape the reality of their own mortality. They will – they say, with the absurd confidence born of illusion – 'make death dead': but all they achieve by the end of their story is their own subjection to the meaningless play of fortuity – 'cas', or blind chance – by which their lives are governed and which will cause them to 'die' in a sense deeper than any they can understand. In this sense the 'gold' which destroys them is a parody of the 'treasure' which the Gospel exhorts men to seek beyond the order of the merely temporal,[26] and their own search for it a symbol of their rejection of the true life of the spirit.

The rioters embark on their quest in a spirit of rash defiance rather than in one of salutory and reasoned fear:

> 'Ye, Goddes armes!' quod this riotour,
> 'Is it swich peril with hym for to meete?
> I shal hym seke by way and eek by strete,
> I make avow to Goddes digne bones!
> Herkneth, felawes, we thre been al ones;
> Lat ech of us holde up his hand til oother,
> And ech of us bicomen otheres brother,
> And we wol sleen this false traytour Deeth.
> He shal be slayn, he that so manye sleeth,
> By Goddes dignitee, er it be nyght!'   (VI. 692–701)

Several aspects of this speech are notable for the contribution they make to the complete intention of the tale. The misplaced oaths are, of course, one of the preacher's principal objects of attack, and this is brought home by the double reference to God's 'dignity' which the rioters – and not a few of the pilgrims, including very notably the Pardoner's arch-enemy, the Host – have been habitually engaged in setting at nought. More significant, perhaps, is the emphasis on fellowship and brotherhood – 'herkneth, *felawes*', 'ech of us bicomen *otheres brother*' – as though we were witnessing the grim parody of an essential affirmation of humanity; for we shall soon see that the tale ends not in 'fellowship', but in an act of betrayal. To be noted in this connection is the association of death and treachery: 'this false traytour Deeth'; for the point of the following story is that betrayal will bring the rioters to the end – the death – which answers to the manner in which their lives have been conceived.

The point upon which the situation turns is more variously subtle than these considerations may indicate. The misconceived course upon which the rioters propose to embark represents a danger which is very close to all 'pilgrims', and indeed to human life as such. The child spoke truly when he advised them to place themselves in a state of readiness to meet the 'death' which derives inescapably from the reality of the human condition. This is a truth to be accepted in a proper spirit of what, following Chaucer, we have learned to call 'patience'. That saving virtue is far from being present in the minds of the dissolute trio. For them, the matter presents itself in a different, indeed an opposite light from that which the boy's inherited realism implied. They set out to meet death not in order to evaluate their lives in the light of that universal presence, but to evade the reality which it represents: in other words, to 'slay' him as a feared and repudiated adversary. It is their desire to avoid their own subjection to their mortal condition, a thing that no human being can realistically hope to do without incurring in spiritual terms the very fate which he is concerned to avoid.

The *real* way is that in which the pilgrims will in due course be instructed, however abstractly, by the Parson, who stands in relation to the Pardoner as a true as opposed to a false preacher. It consists in accepting the reality of death as a factor inescapably woven into human life, and in achieving in the course of their pilgrimage the death of their own sinful natures in order to arrive, through that death – manifested in a saving action for all mankind in the death of Christ – at the 'treasure', the true immortality which is offered to men, after they have passed through physical death, in the order of the spirit. The truth is that all men are required to 'meet' death by virtue of their share in the sin by which Adam originally brought death into the world by an act committed, not without significance in relation to this story, in the shadow of a 'tree'. As a result of their share in the primal transgression all men are required to 'slay' death by dying to their unregenerate natures, consciously and deliberately 'killing' in themselves the manifestations of the original 'Adam'. To do this

is an indispensable condition of entering into the 'new' life in which the
end of the human pilgrimage is made manifest.

In other words, it is not required of men that they should seek to evade
the present reality of the death implicit in their lives, as the rioters propose
to do when they set out on their absurd adventure. Rather they are called
upon to accept the fact of their mortality in the spirit of 'dying' to the self
which is their share in man's burden of sin, and to achieve thereby the
possibility of being 'resurrected', reborn in the 'new' life of the spirit.
Perverse as his intentions are, the Pardoner's 'example' cuts very deep:
deeper, perhaps, than his immediate rival, the Host, or indeed the greater
part of the pilgrims are prepared to recognize. We begin to see how not a
few aspects of this sermon – the denunciation of drunkenness which, as
we remember from *The Knight's Tale*,[27] prevents a man from following the
path which leads to his 'house': the condemnation of cursing as offensive
to God's 'dignity' and that of his created image: the emphasis on the
gluttony which has played no inconsiderable part in the pilgrimage – are
in the process of coming together in a tale in which all but a few of the
pilgrims – the Parson and his brother, the Plowman, certainly, perhaps
the Knight – are likely, if they are capable of reflecting so deeply, to feel
themselves very uncomfortably implicated. That the call to sober reality
should come to them, not through the exemplary preaching of the Parson,
but through the most questionable of all the company, is a fact which cuts
across the entire concept of 'pilgrimage' and affects the declared purpose
of the author in 'making' his poem.

All these aspects of the tale converge on its most impressive moment:
that which confronts the three young dissolutes with the mysterious old
man whom they treat with brutal contempt and who directs them
enigmatically to their doom. The passage has a quality of mystery which
seems designed to evade exact definition:

> Whan they han goon nat fully half a mile,
> Right as they wolde han troden over a stile,
> An oold man and a povre with hem mette.
> This olde man ful mekely hem grette,
> And seyde thus, 'Now, lordes, God yow see!'
> The proudeste of thise riotoures three
> Answerde agayn, 'What, carl, with sory grace!
> Why artow al forwrapped save thy face?
> Why lyvestow so longe in so greet age?'
> This olde man gan looke in his visage,
> And seyde thus: 'For I ne kan nat fynde
> A man, though that I walked into Ynde,
> Neither in citee ne in no village,

> That wolde chaunge his youthe for myn age;
> And therfore moot I han myn age stille,
> As longe tyme as it is Goddes wille.
> Ne Deeth, allas! ne wol nat han my lyf
> Thus walke I, lyk a restelees kaityf,
> And on the ground, which is my moodres gate,
> I knokke with my staf, bothe erly and late,
> And seye "Leeve mooder, leet me in!
> Lo how I vanysshe, flessh, and blood, and skyn!
> Allas! whan shul my bones been at reste?
> Mooder, with yow wolde I chaunge my cheste
> That in my chambre longe tyme hath be,
> Ye, for an heyre clowt to wrappe in me!"
> But yet to me she wol nat do that grace,
> For which ful pale and welked is my face.'   (VI. 711–38)

To bring out the full implications of this tremendously impressive presence is a matter of no small difficulty. Some have seen in the figure of the old man nothing less than a personification of the 'Death' itself. According to this view,[28] the old man would not only point to, but actually *be* the 'Death' which the rioters are so rashly seeking. This, perhaps, is to go farther than the text will take us, if only because of the obvious fact that the old man wishes to die, but is unable to do so, and that his function in the tale is to tell others where Death is to be found. It has been pointed out that he appears to have traceable literary antecedents, more especially in the writings of a certain Maximianus, in his *First Elegy;*[29] and this would make him, in the first instance, what he appears to be – a very old man, one not far from, and therefore bitterly conscious of, the fact of his own death. Beyond this, we may feel at this point the presence of the medieval tendency to generalize from the particular, to see the individual case as exemplifying a more universal reality. This would make of the figure something which answers well to the impression of mystery, of unrevealed but suggested meanings, which it gives us: the sense not merely of a particular old man, but of the *senex*, a figure of age personified. The 'old man' is not, on balance, a sinister figure, in the sense of one who deliberately points the arrogant young men to their doom, or who in any way misleads or deceives them. He is rather an aspect of life with which, in one way or another, all human beings are required to come to terms.

It is interesting in this respect to note that the old man's inability to die is one of several traits which are reflected in various passages of the Parson's concluding discourse.[30] This suggests that we are meant to see him as standing in some relationship to the 'old man' in *all* human beings: the 'old man' whom we are all required to 'slay' in ourselves as a condition of entering into the 'new life' of the spirit, and whose advice stands in ironic juxtaposition to that given to the tavern boy by his 'dame' at the beginning of the tale.[31] The 'dame' advised her son to be at all times ready to face the reality of his own death; whereas the burden of the old man's lament is that he searches for the death which would be for him a release, but that he has been unable, in spite of his desire, to find it. The 'old man' is *unable* to die. In other words, like all men unredeemed by the 'truth', he seeks for release from his burden, but seeks it in death, in a return to his 'mother' the earth, and is unable to partake of the life which only death *in the spirit* could give. His lack of success in finding the death he craves is reflected in the living burden to which he feels himself condemned and which he desires, in vain, to shake off. This is not to make him into a figure of evil. The old man is tired of life, and wishes to die; but he does not seek death in the form of self-destruction and, although he knows that death is what the rioters will find under the tree to which he directs them, it cannot be said that he encourages them to meet their fate. It is *they* who choose, not the old man who pushes, or deceives them, into choosing. Moreover, he does not seek death in the spirit of the rioters, whose search is inspired by their misconceived desire not to be subject to physical extinction. Their desire is a vain one, and the old man explicitly states that he does not share it. He is resigned to the burden of his age, prepared to

> han myn age stille,
> As longe tyme as it is Goddes wille.

But he is ready, and even anxious, to accept his death when it comes to him, and in this his attitude is the opposite to that of those whose aim is the unnatural and impossible one of escaping man's universal fate. To the extent that it is 'patient' the old man's attitude to the death he craves is realistic and even positive; but it is also limited, in as much as it reflects the way which men, in their fallen state, choose to follow, craving release from the living 'death' of their lives in ignorance of the 'straight', the narrow way which alone leads to the renewed life of the spirit.

We may reasonably feel, then, that we are dealing in this figure with something more than the old man under whose form it is presented. He seems to have something of the force of a personification of age, and as such he naturally knows – is, if we will, intimately connected with – the reality of death itself. Being so closely related to it, he knows where this dreaded presence is to be found: at the end of the 'crooked way' which seems, like the 'stile' already mentioned, to have about it something of a fairy-tale quality. This is a landscape of legend, almost of dream, at once concrete in its simplicity and pointing to meanings beyond itself. There is a suggestion – it is no more: here, as throughout, the tale achieves its effects by avoiding the explicit – that the 'crooked way' may be a representation of human life as unredeemed and subject to meaningless vicissitude, set in opposition to the 'straight way' of redemption, and leading to the dark presence which, in one or other of its forms, awaits all men at the conclusion of their journey in time. The old man is mysteriously 'al forwrapped', muffled, except for the face. We need not go so far as to allegorize him – to do this would be to take from him something of his overriding quality of mystery – and yet we may reasonably see in him an aspect of the universal, more than merely individual significance which seems to be implied in his poignant relationship to the death he cannot find.

What the old man tells the rioters is where death is to be found. He does *not* tell them how this forbidding presence can be 'slain'. Indeed, he does not know how to 'slay' it: for, if he did, he would not be craving for the release he says he cannot obtain. Once again, we note that the heart of a Chaucerian tale concerns a 'tree': a tree which stands at the centre of a 'grove' (VI. 762) and which can be connected with that which bore the occasion for Adam's loss of Paradise. Under this tree there is to be found 'gold': a material treasure which is the limit of the rioters' aspiration and which becomes the symbol of their misconceived quest; for what they find is earthly treasure which gives no lasting satisfaction and which is not the 'treasure' which the Gospel urges men to seek: the treasure 'in heaven' which is not subject to fading and corruption.[32] To put the matter in yet another way the rioters, in following their drunken inclinations (which the Pardoner has eloquently shown to be the cause of death), surrender themselves to Fortune – 'cas', blind chance – and meet the real death which such a surrender entails:

> 'Now lat us sitte and drynke, and make us merie,
> And afterward we wol his body berie.'
> And with that word it happed hym, par cas,
> To take the botel ther the poyson was,
> And drank, and yaf his felawe drynke also,
> For which anon they storven bothe two.   (VI. 883–8)

The irony of the situation is, once again, varied and complex. Having arrived at the tree and uncovered the gold at its foot, the rioters desist from their original intention of finding Death and 'slaying' him; we have been told somewhat earlier 'No lenger thanne after Deeth they soughte' (VI. 772). The irony consists in the fact that it is just at this moment – when they have given up the search for the imaginary enemy whom they were confident of overcoming – that they find the reality and succumb to it. The irony is related to the significance given to the 'tree' in the symbolism which underlies the tale. By the fact of his death on Calvary Christ truly 'slew' death, overcame it upon the 'tree' which was, in familiar liturgical terms, the symbol of the Cross. By so doing, he undid the inheritance of sin which Adam bequeathed to following mankind. In the same way his followers are required not to seek to evade the reality of their individual deaths, which the nature of their fallen condition requires, but rather to accept death as the fruit of their inheritance of sin; for this acceptance is a condition of 'slaying' the *true* death, which is that of the spirit, and of entering upon the 'new' life which Christ's 'victory' offers to all mankind.

This is the thrust of the irony as it operates *within* the sermon; but beyond it, there is a further irony which concerns the Pardoner as preacher, as a 'counterfeit' of the Parson, and which affects both his 'tale' and the attitude which has gone to the telling of it. For him, his sermon has been an occasion for winning the 'gold' which – as he has openly confessed – is his object in preaching; but, by implication and in order to achieve effectively this corrupt, indeed sacrilegious end, he has pointed eloquently to the *real* death which his own activities and the exclusion from love – and so from life – which they imply, must involve. In this sense, for him as for the rioters, the 'tree' with the gold at its foot is nothing less than a parody of the Cross, the 'tree' of life for all humanity: the 'tree' which is often depicted with the skull, the symbol of death, at its foot. Furthermore, in the final and fatal feast, in which the rioters partake of 'bread and wine' under the tree, we may see, without overly stressing the point, a parody of the Eucharistic communion, seen as a sacrament of unity – 'fellowship' – and a source of life. The rioters have seen themselves as 'brothers' in their misplaced endeavour;[33] but their 'brotherhood' is revealed in its true light when it ends in treachery, in the sin of Cain which was the fruit of Adam's fall. These self-styled 'brothers' have coveted, not the true 'treasure' of the spirit, which is to be sought in 'heaven', after and beyond accepted mortality, but its delusive shadow, the cause of 'cupidity' – the sin against which the Pardoner preaches – and of final death. What the rioters have found at the foot of the tree is the root of evil and the occasion (or the fruit?) of the Pardoner's own exclusion from grace: for the root of all evil, *radix malorum*, is indeed *Cupiditas*.[34]

D. The Epilogue

In this way we are brought to the aftermath of the tale, which has also occasioned a good deal of perplexity. For some readers,[35] the Pardoner at the end of his sermon seems to show an unexpected glimpse of sincerity when he admits that true repentance is worth more than any relic or pardon he can offer:

> And lo, sires, thus I preche.
> And Jhesu Crist, that is oure soules leche,
> So graunte yow his pardoun to receyve,
> For that is best; I wol yow nat deceyve.   (VI. 915–18)

On this reading, it might be possible to see the Pardoner as in some sense, and as it were in spite of himself, 'redeemable'; but it seems difficult, in view of the lack of support from the rest of the tale, to push the point so far. The reality is likely to be more complex. The Pardoner's words answer to the kind of conclusion which the 'gentils' required of him when they enjoined upon him the obligation to tell 'som moral thyng'. They amount to a reminder, of the type which orthodox doctrine would demand, of the fact that only sincere repentance can finally obtain pardon, and that the 'heigh power' (VI. 913) which the Pardoner has taken it upon himself to 'assoile' those who make the required offering to him, leaving them

> as clene and eek as cleer
> As ye were born,   (VI. 914–15)

is inoperative where this is absent.

By making this reservation, the Pardoner draws attention to the real efficacy of the sermon he has preached and requires his audience, however unwillingly, to recognize that he has provided what they originally demanded of him beyond any expectation that they are likely to have had. Beyond this, again, the words have a special propriety in relation to the wider design of the *Tales*, serving to remind *us*, the poet's audience, that penitence and pardon are, after all, the substance of 'pilgrimage' – as the Parson will confirm at the end, when he steps out of the framework of story-telling to give his final address – and that the functions which the Pardoner has misused to the ends of death belong, when properly exercised, to the purposes of creative love. The Pardoner's success in exploiting his victims depends on their sense of the reality of the forgiveness which he so speciously holds up to them. If they did not share the natural human craving for pardon, and believe that it was possible to obtain it, the very ground of his activities would be cut from under him. He too, accordingly, in his own way and for his own purposes, implicitly confirms the reality of the pilgrimage *motif* upon which his activities shed such a strange and distorting light. This admission on the part of the Pardoner, which has often been seen as a sign of inconsistency on the part of his creator, is an indication that this character too, however far he may be from recognizing a positive and living order by which the whole design is animated, is in fact conditioned by the truth which he is engaged in rejecting: he recognizes – in spite of himself, as it were – the reality which he needs must pride himself in denying.

This, however, is not the end of the episode, but rather a transition to what follows. Having taken the calculated risk of going for a moment beyond his deception, the Pardoner returns to what he has already declared to be the real end of all his preaching, and asks the pilgrims to participate in that deception by purchasing the relics and pardons which he offers them. In this way, he confirms that the 'art' he has displayed has been an instrument of deceit, and raises in the process questions which must affect us as readers and, finally, the poet as author. 'I wol yow nat deceyve', the Pardoner has just said, only to proceed immediately afterwards to try to do just that: in effect, to practise upon the audience which is so patently inclined to repudiate him the very deception he has flaunted before them as the sign of his monstrous, stressed perversity. Striking home while the effect of his sermon is fresh in the minds of his audience, and confident in the effect that he has produced in them, the Pardoner is incautiously moved to test the power he wishes to exercise over those who have listened to him by moving a step further: 'But, sires, o word forgat I in my tale' (VI. 919). Then, repeating the stock warning against unforseen calamities which is, no doubt, one of his favourite gambits in addressing his habitual audiences and which he adapts to the present circumstances –

Paraventure ther may fallen oon or two
Doun of his hors, and breke his nekke atwo –
(VI. 935–6)

he presents himself and his goods as 'a seuretee to yow alle' against the operation of that same 'blind' chance which has played so large a part in his tale and offers his relics, not without a kind of witty effrontery, to the very Host who, not so long ago, sneered at him and whom he now singles out, in return, as 'moost envoluped in synne' (VI. 942). For a moment the Pardoner seems to have been so far carried away by his exercise in tale-telling as to believe that he has established control over his hearers and can lead them – and more particularly the Host – in the direction which will confirm him in his sense of mastery over them.

Here, however, the Pardoner has gone too far. Up to now, he has been able to feel himself the master of the situations he has deliberately provoked. He has done this by maintaining the illusion – upon which a teller of tales relies – that he is in control of the audience which he has carried with him in the course of his performance. Now, however, the performance is over, and a return to the 'real' world is imposing itself upon illusion. When his confidence in himself and his art pushes him so far as to force a confrontation which, if it could be carried through, would confirm him in his sense of triumphant 'art', the reality emerges as one which is finally and irremediably beyond any control that he might conceivably exercise. The fact of his isolation – if we will, of his 'damnation' – is there for all to see. It was there at the beginning, and not all the Pardoner's eloquence, the mastery over his audience which his sermon may seem, while it lasted, to have given him, can alter the reality of his position. The Host's brutally direct replay – it is in its own way the most openly offensive passage in the whole of the *Tales* – reminds us that the Pardoner is still an outcast among the pilgrims and that the love for which he unconsciously expressed his need – 'Com hider, love, to me' – can never be his lot among men.

Not unnaturally, the violence of this rejection leaves the Pardoner speechless:

> This Pardoner answerde nat a word;
> So wrooth he was, no word ne wolde he seye.
>   (VI. 956–7)

Indeed, it would not be easy to think of words adequate to the situation. A moment of deep and barely resolvable tension has come upon the 'fellowship': so much so that the Host, perhaps sensing that he has roused a response beyond any humanly acceptable, draws back from his line of retort and allows himself to be persuaded by the Knight to a show of reconciliation:

> I prey yow that ye kisse the Pardoner.
> And Pardoner, I prey thee, drawe thee neer,
> And, *as we diden*, lat us laughe and pleye.   (VI. 965–7)

'As we diden': the words seem to contain a plea for a return to the former area of safety within which the pilgrimage has so far operated. It is not fanciful, perhaps, to see the Knight making an appeal in the name of the 'fellowship' which should inspire the journey to a common end, and which needs to be maintained if our faith in the possibilities of human life, and in our own motives, are to remain valid. It is an appeal, perhaps, which fails at this point – under the uneasy impression of what we have just heard – completely to impose itself, which may even leave the uncomfortable reality of the Pardoner very much where it has always been. It is, at any rate, as near as he gets to finding the measure of acceptance, incorporation into the pattern of 'pilgrimage' upon which, for all human beings *in via*, life finally depends.

Uneasiness, indeed, has been a marked feature of the episode from the start, and it affects not only the Pardoner in relation to the rest of the company, but – finally – our whole conception of the human 'pilgrimage' and its relation to the 'reality' which it is supposed to serve. As we reached the end of the Pardoner's tale it became clear that there is a relation between what has just been said and the story previously told by the Physician. The latter has been a tale poorly told to declare what the teller unimaginatively believed to be a valid moral; and the point was that it left us dissatisfied and with a sense that the real problem raised had not been answered. To put the matter in another way, the 'moral' advanced in what normally passes for sincerity by the Physician seems to any sensitive reader suspect, or at least inadequate; whereas that put forward by the Pardoner with open and confessed dishonesty strikes us with the force of truth to experience: a truth moreover which stands in uneasy relationship to the behaviour of many of the pilgrims (not excluding the Host, for all his pride in his plain-speaking integrity) in respect of drunkenness, blasphemy, and fundamental lack of fellowship.

Yet the moral of the tale, superbly conveyed as it is in the telling, is invalidated by the self-confessed perversity of the teller. When the Pardoner, apparently carried away by the success of his own perfor-mance, is moved to tempt fate by offering his relics to the company he is, in fact, offering a 'gift' of the same order as his tale. The tale, which has seemed to convey a true moral lesson, has been told for ends of personal gain; and the sale of relics which it is intended to promote answers to the same purpose. At the end the Host, as spokesman for his fellow pilgrim, is unable to reject the tale, because the Pardoner has told it in a way designed to forestall any objections that might be raised on moral grounds. It has been, though not quite in the way that they anticipated, the 'moral thyng' for which the more 'gentil' among them incautiously asked; and if its relation to the teller raises questions more unsettling than many of them would willingly consider, there is no valid reason, within the tale itself, for repudiating it. The relics, however, are another matter. The Host *can* reasonably reject these as false; and in doing so he rejects the falseness which is an aspect of the tale in the mouth of this particular teller, and which has been openly, even defiantly stated as its *raison d'être*. The rejection is expressed with a vehemence which suggests that the whole incident has gone beyond surface hostility to point to tensions almost beyond reasonable resolution which affect the very heart of the conception of 'pilgrimage'.

The issues raised, indeed, point beyond the incident to affect the poet's attitude to his conception. The Pardoner has been, in a very special and disturbing way, at once a liar and a teller of truths. His intervention has raised questions which involve not only the conduct of the pilgrims, their motives in undertaking the journey and the adequacy or otherwise of the ways in which they perceive themselves and their participation in it, but – beyond this – the very nature of the poet's art as a maker of fictions and the effect of these fictions upon the audience. If the Pardoner's tale is read as an independent unit standing in its own right – read for what it *says*, and without relation to the motives of the teller – it may be held to promote a true 'moral', applicable to the 'real' world and exhorting those who hear it to live more 'truly' in that world; but if we have regard to the teller, and the motives which inspire him to such convincing eloquence, what we contemplate is a deception, a deliberate and confessed *un*truth, the sense that a notable imaginative effort has been directed only to a shabby and inhuman purpose. We find ourselves asking, in other words, whether the 'truth' of the story lies in the effect which the tale makes in its own right or in its relation to the purposes which inspired the telling of it; and, faced with this question, which seems to require us to separate the inseparable, we come up with no easy or reassuring answer.

It seems that the power of the telling, and our sense of the essential 'truth' advanced by the tale may have no relationship to anything beyond the tale itself. The Pardoner has declared that he is not concerned with its 'moral' effects, and none of his audience, presumably, has been persuaded by it to amend his life. The fact that it has been so effectively told by a self-defined scoundrel, who has presented himself as a conscious manipulator of moral 'truths' for ends of personal gain, challenges us to examine our acceptance of the 'truths' contained in it, and makes us consider whether such acceptance can only rest on an act of faith of the kind to which the Pardoner himself, for whatever motive, seems to have pointed by implication when he concluded his sermon by recognizing – 'I wol nat yow deceyve' – that his shoddy wares are no substitute for genuine and reasoned acceptance of the need for pardon. Whether that faith is justified by its 'truth' – whether, indeed, the 'reality' by which we live is not, in a very necessary sense, the creation of our 'faith' – is the question that Chaucer's art, and perhaps all great art, ultimately poses. What disturbs us, as we look back on our reading of *The Canterbury Tales*, is that the Pardoner's sermon, delivered for unworthy motives, has given us a sense of imaginative truth such as we do not derive either from the Physician's 'moral' story or even from the Parson's final, and *true* exposition of sin. The Parson, indeed, explicitly refuses to enter the game of tale-telling, and this may – as we now begin to see – be prudent on his part. He would say, no doubt rightly from his standpoint, that *truth* lies of its nature outside and beyond fiction, and that fiction cannot, in the final analysis, advance it; but the question remains as to what validity fiction, the imaginative process, can properly be said to embody, and – further – how far, in its absence, the 'truth' itself can be so presented as to be *humanly* acceptable.

IX

THE
CANON'S YEOMAN'S TALE

Less well known than *The Pardoner's Tale*, but hardly less powerful in its different way, is the tale told by the Canon's Yeoman. Although it is separated from the earlier episode, in as much as it seems to belong more definitely to the approaching end of the pilgrimage, it deals with aspects of human nature not entirely dissimilar. Once again, we are made aware of the way in which man's misdirected or inordinate appetites (those summed up in the word *cupidity*, which embraces greed but covers all forms of wrongly directed 'desire') lead to delusion, enslavement, and finally to self-destruction. If we were to look for an equivalent in Chaucer's very different world to Dante's hell, it is in this underworld of twisted motives, manipulation, and willed self-deception, among those of whom it could be said that they have 'submitted their reason to their will',[1] that we might seek it.

Several unusual features distinguish Chaucer's handling of this tale. In the first place, as though to emphasize the entry of a new element into the pilgrimage, the narrator is – uniquely – not of the original company. He and the Canon, his master, *erupt* into the action from outside, and there is an element of mystery in their arrival on the scene:

> At Boghtoun under Blee us gan atake
> A man that clothed was in clothes blake,
> And under-nethe he hadde a whyt surplys.
> His hakeney, that was al pomely grys,
> So swatte that it wonder was to see;
> It semed as he had priked miles three.
> The hors eek that his yeman rood upon
> So swatte that unnethe myghte it gon.
> Aboute the peytrel stood the foom ful hye;
> He was of foom al flekked as a pye.   (VIII. 556–65)

From the first it is clear that these newcomers are not part of the pilgrim group, not engaged in the common enterprise that constitutes for the rest, howbeit with widely varying degrees of awareness, the reason and justification of their presence.

The extent of this separation does not make itself felt at once. Although Chaucer, as pilgrim-narrator, is initially puzzled to define the status of the newcomer, he is predictably ready to see him as a 'worthy man' (VIII. 568); and both master and servant show themselves at first profusely anxious to be taken into the company. The Canon, hasty and travel-worn in appearance ('it was joye for to seen hym swete!': VIII. 579), is urgent in his expressions of sociability:

> 'God save,' quod he, 'this joly compaignye!
> Faste have I priked,' quod he, 'for youre sake,
> By cause that I wolde yow atake,
> To riden in this myrie compaignye';   (VIII. 583–6)

and the Yeoman, 'ful of curteisye' (VIII. 587), stresses that his master, as one that 'loveth daliaunce' (VIII. 592), is 'ful fayn' to join the pilgrims for his 'desport'. Thus far, it seems, we have a man after the Host's heart, who can very plausibly be invited to 'glad' the company by contributing 'a myrie tale or tweye' (VIII. 597) to relieve the tedium of the route.

Closer consideration suggests that there is more beneath this initial exchange than may meet the eye. The Yeoman's anxiety to stress his master's unique but still undefined powers ends by raising questions as to his own motives and attitudes. He calls the Canon 'my lord and my soverayn' (VIII. 590), and says, with a deliberate affectation of mystery, that he is 'gretter than a clerk, ywis' (VIII. 617): how much greater he insinuates when he presents him as one who can work 'wel and craftily' to bring into being

> many a greet emprise,
> Which were ful hard for any that is heere
> To brynge aboute, but they of hym it leere.   (VIII. 605–7)

The effect is to convey, by almost imperceptible stages, the sense of a peculiar tension beneath the convivial surface. Before long, the Yeoman is stressing an element of 'supernatural' power which emanates from his master, a spell from which it seems that he is unable to free himself:

> I seye, my lord kan swich subtilitee –
> But al his craft ye may hat wite at me,
> And somwhat helpe I yet to his wirkyng –
> That al this ground on which we been ridyng,
> Til that we come to Caunterbury toun,

> He koude al clene turne it up-so-doun,
> And pave it al of silver and of gold.   (VIII. 620–6)

The Yeoman sees the Canon as by now he *needs* to see him, as a magician engaged in activities that separate him from the rest of men: activities to which he has been granted the privilege of access. The element of evident unreality in these claims is stressed by the Yeoman precisely because he is aware, in spite of himself, of the deception on which he has built his life and from which, as it seems, he can no longer afford to disengage himself.

Once again it is the Host's function to reduce these magniloquent 'fantasies' to the level of plain fact. Ready as ever to expose the unnatural, the 'up-so-doun' view of life, he points to the threadbare appearance which this 'magician' presents to the world and which stands in such incongruous contrast to the claims made on his behalf:

> This thyng is wonder merveillous to me,
> Syn that thy lord is of so heigh prudence,
> By cause of which men sholde hym reverence,
> That of his worshipe rekketh he so lite.
> His overslope nys nat worth a myte,
> As in effect, to hym, so moot I go!
> It is al baudy and totore also.
> Why is thy lord so sluttissh, I the preye,
> And is of power bettre clooth to beye,
> If that his dede accorde with thy speche?
> Telle me that, and that I thee biseche.   (VIII. 629–39)

The Host is exercising one of his principal functions in the *Tales*: that of the child in the fairy-tale who, faced with the claim of the emperor to be marvellously clothed, can only see the visible reality of his nakedness. The Host may not be a man of imaginative subtlety or spiritual depth. His is emphatically not the Parson's view of the world, nor even that of the Knight, though we may think that he is capable on occasions of exercising a salutory realism in relation to the interventions of both. He shows consistently the capacity, which can also reflect a limitation, to return to what the common run of mankind accepts as the *real*; and if this means that important aspects of life are apt to escape his understanding, it nevertheless enables him, in the process of keeping his feet firmly on the ground, to affirm the plain 'truth' of things in opposition to the elaborations of 'fantasy' and the 'upside-down' distortion of them which the human tendency to indulge misdirected or unnatural desire fosters in not a few of the pilgrim company.

Pressed in this way, led back to the reality he has been brought to the point of needing to deny, the Yeoman begins the painful process of detaching himself from his misplaced dream. When the Host puts the direct question 'Where dwelle ye, if it to telle be?' (VIII. 656), his reply amounts to a capitulation of the fevered imagination before the plain truth of things:

> 'In the suburbes of a toun,' quod he,
> 'Lurkynge in hernes and in lanes blynde,
> Whereas thise robbours and thise theves by kynde
> Holden hir pryvee fereful residence,
> As they that dar nat shewen hir presence;
> So faren we, if I shal seye the sothe.'   (VIII. 657–62)

Under the pressure of the Host's blunt realism, the Yeoman is driven to recognize the element of secrecy and stealth which has constituted, for himself and his master, their separation from the shared, common, daylight world of men. Here, as often throughout the *Tales*, the urge to 'privacy' and concealment is the sign of a fundamental defect, a failure in humanizing sociability which expresses itself in the will, the misplaced need, to cling to illusion at the expense of common reality.[2] Something of the same kind, though in a very different order, motivated the Pardoner to embark, with his repeated and obsessive 'I wol',[3] on his flouting of the accepted values of his audience. The Pardoner differs from the Yeoman in clinging, apparently beyond redemption or correction, to the position which he has both chosen and, in some sense, had imposed upon him; and this makes him at once a more powerful and a more enigmatic figure. The Yeoman's final words – 'if I shal seye the sothe' – point in a different direction. They come out with a sense of compulsive relief, the awakening from a protracted nightmare, as a recognition of the truth that he has been unwilling or – so far – simply unable to contemplate: the reality hidden in the dark and precarious environment – 'lurkynge', 'blynde', 'fereful' – in which these conspirators against nature and daylight 'truth' have for so long carried on their 'pryvee', secret operations.

The realism of the Host, backed by the presence of the listening company, finally precipitates in the Yeoman an embittered release of pent-up resentment:

> I am so used in the fyr to blowe
> That it hath chaunged my colour, I trowe.
> I am not wont in no mirour to prie,
> But swynke soore and lerne multiplie.
> We blondren evere and pouren in the fir,
> And for al that we faille of oure desir,
> For evere we lakken oure conclusioun.
> To muchel folk we doon illusioun,
> And borwe gold, be it a pound or two,

> Or ten, or twelve, or manye sommes mo,
> And make hem wenen, at the leeste weye,
> That of a pound we koude make tweye.
> Yet is it fals, but ay we han good hope
> It for to doon, and after it we grope.
> But that science is so fer us biforn,
> We mowen nat, although we hadden it sworn,
> It overtake, it slit awey so faste.
> It wole us maken beggers atte laste.   (VIII. 666–83)

In all this there is more at stake than a confession on the Yeoman's side that he has taken part in a deception at the expense of his fellow-men. What he is bringing painfully to the surface is a process of 'blundering' and 'groping' – the latter word is used elsewhere by Chaucer in connection with the fumbling deception of others and of self – a pursuit of vanity in self-imposed darkness, the obstinate following of a 'desire' which is known, in terms of reason and common-sense, to be 'illusion': the pursuit of a mirage that 'slides away' as it is 'chased', that remains always so far 'before' its victims that it leaves them finally the 'beggars' they are driven at the last to recognize in themselves.

Throughout the exchange between the Yeoman and the Host the Canon, after his initial outburst of sociability, has maintained silence. We have been aware of his increasingly suspicious presence and – as the narrative has proceeded – of a sense of unspoken guilt emanating from his person: aware, above all, of his secretive ('privee') nature and of an uneasy sensitivity to the situation in which he embarrassingly finds himself. As the spell under which his servant has so far lived is broken, and as he begins to speak out, the Canon can only make his escape 'for verray sorwe and shame' (VIII. 702). Relieved of the presence of the incubus that has weighed for so long upon him, the Yeoman is free to give expression to the resentment he harbours against the man who, as he is at last ready to recognize, has perpetrated nothing less than his moral and material ruin:

> He that me broghte first unto that game,
> Er that he dye, sorwe have he and shame!
> For it is ernest to me, by my feith;
> That feele I wel, what so any man seith.
> And yet, for al my smert and al my grief,
> For al my sorwe, labour, and meschief,
> I koude nevere leve it in no wise.
> Now wolde God my wit myghte suffise
> To tellen al that longeth to that art!
> But nathelees yow wol I tellen part.
> Syn that my lord is goon, I wol nat spare.   (VIII. 708–18)

In this way, he declares his readiness to contribute, after his own fashion and in the light of his awakening from his nightmare, to the series of 'merry' tales which are designed to lighten the tedium of the route.

Given this state of mind, it is not surprising that the Yeoman feels the compulsive urge to expose the truth of his relationship to his departed master. It is interesting that he chooses to divide his tale into two parts, in a way which may remind us of the procedure followed in the case of the Wife of Bath.[4] On that occasion, we remember, the first part of the Wife's story consisted in her version of her life with her successive husbands, and was followed by the 'tale', properly so called, in which she revealed more of the truth concerning herself and these realities than she is likely to have realized. Rather similarly, the Yeoman begins by speaking of his experience with his late master and follows this by describing the machinations of another clerical alchemist, whom he insists in presenting as an entirely different person from the first Canon. It would seem that, by introducing this second alchemist, the Yeoman feels able to generalize from his own case by giving expression to what he feels to be a 'demonic' element in the quest for unlimited wealth and the power over nature by which the alchemist hopes to achieve it. By suggesting that there was something 'diabolic' in his late master's actions, the Yeoman may hope to salvage something of his self-respect, in as much as it may seem to him more dignified to present himself as the victim of a 'devil' rather than as the easy dupe of a human trickster. Beyond this, and looking further than the Yeoman's situation as he may perceive it, the second part of the story may answer to a desire on the part of the poet to isolate the essential meaning of the first by concentrating on the elements of perversity, unnatural and willed dedication to ends of deception and death, which the Yeoman's sorry history has implied. The effect is to show a penetrating, if disillusioned insight into the extremes into which deception, and the will to be deceived, can lead its human victims. No tale of Chaucer's, perhaps, seems to stand so far removed as this from the tolerant and urbane humanity which we normally associate with his genius.

The first part of the Yeoman's tale, then, directly reflects his own experience and is a revealing compound of resentment and continued weakness. He is conscious, on the one hand, of having been rudely awakened from his dream; but, on the other, at least a part of his mind remains under the spell of the 'mystery', and clings to the sense of superior power which the years of dedication to it fostered in him. His attitude is a compound of bitterness and contradiction which prepares the ground, in the first part of the story, for what will emerge in the underlying sense of the second. Something of this is indicated in the Yeoman's recognition, as he recreates his own experience, that those who have become aware of the deception practised upon them find pleasure, a sort of compensation, in furthering the ruin of others. He acknowledges that the kind of man who follows the paths of deception he is describing will awake at the last to the realization that, through his 'madness' and his 'folly', he has lost 'his owene good' in the most extensive sense of the word; but, having become aware of the pit into which he has allowed himself to fall, he is so far from desiring to see others escape his fate that

> he exciteth oother folk therto,
> To lesen hir good, as he hymself hath do.
> For unto shrewes joye it is and ese
> To have hir felawes in peyne and disese.   (VIII. 744–7)

The recognition goes far beyond the exposure of a fraud to touch the roots of man's situation as a 'pilgrim' in search of the 'good'. It is the essence of hell that the damned, in their awareness of the irretrievable loss of the 'good' which is the object of their quest, should find satisfaction in contemplating the ruin of their fellow-creatures.

Side by side with this negation of common humanity the Yeoman's attitude to the 'illusion' from which he claims to have awakened covers a strange mixture of motives. In part, he is moved to express his bitter resentment against the man who manipulated his greed and abused his confidence; but when he bursts into a long recital (VIII. 784–829) of the pseudo-scientific terms used by practitioners of the 'elvissh craft', the broad comedy which is always a part of the tale's effect combines with a sense of powerful, if misplaced, creative energy which is very close to its deeper intention.

There is at least a suggestion that the Yeoman is still not beyond feeling the fascination of his murky past, not above seeking to indulge his vanity by impressing an audience composed of those who have not been privileged to share the revelations granted to him with his mastery of the recondite terms of his 'mystery'. The process of escaping from 'hell' is not, on the best of terms, easy or smooth to those who suffer it. The secret of the Canon's hold over the Yeoman has lain in his appeal to one of the most persistent and ineradicable illusions to which men and women are subject: the conviction that – once a decision has been taken, a commitment made, in the name of a man's most deeply engaged hopes – the future will bring what has been lost, or found to be beyond possible attainment, in the present:

> I warne yow wel, it is to seken evere.
> That futur temps hath maad men to dissevere,
> In trust therof, from al that evere they hadde.
> Yet of that art they kan nat wexen sadde,
> For unto hem it is a bitter sweete.   (VIII. 874–8)

The propensity for willed delusion, for following the mirage that is *not*, but always *will be*, turns these conspirators against reason and the light of day into grotesque caricatures of reasoning human beings:

>   for nadde they but a sheete,
> Which that they myghte wrappe hem inne a-nyght,
> And a brat to walken inne by daylyght,
> They wolde hem selle and spenden on this craft.
> They kan nat stynte til no thyng be laft.
> And everemoore, where that evere they goon,
> Men may hem knowe by smel of brymstoon.
> For al the world they stynken as a goot;
> Hir savour is so rammyssh and so hoot
> That though a man from hem a mile be,
> The savour wole infecte hym, trusteth me,
> And thus by smel, and by threedbare array,
> If that men liste, this folk they knowe may.
>
>   (VIII. 879–91)

Few panoramas in Chaucer remind us more closely of those contemplated by Dante in his downward journey through the infernal regions. The Yeoman, of course, follows another inveterate human tendency in his effort to present his misplaced actions under the best possible light. He claims to find a bitter satisfaction in his own reflections; but we are not allowed to forget that his is a voice of disappointment, and compounded as such with resentment.

Persecution mania, as we should now call it, is yet another effect which the pursuit of this 'science' imposes upon its followers. It was the belief of these men, born of the mistrust which their secret activities inspire in their fellows,

>   if that they espied were,
> Men wolde hem slee by cause of hir science.
>
>   (VIII. 895–6)

Most significant of all, in relation to the ultimate sense of this sorry tale, is the vivid exchange between the 'scientists' after an explosion which has brought their latest experiment to an inglorious end. Far from submitting to the evidence of failure before their eyes, they exhort one another – besmirched and scorched as they are, surrounded by the shattered evidence of their latest failure – to be 'glad and blithe' (VIII. 937), and set out once more in obstinate pursuit of the dream from which, it seems, they can no longer afford to awaken. The comedy, for all its aspects of absurdity, is of the kind that is compatible with a serious, even a sombre

awareness of what it implies for an understanding of the darker crevices of
human nature.

Throughout this first part of the tale there has been a sense that the
Yeoman is deeply involved – more deeply, perhaps, than he can afford to
recognize – in the compulsive urge to recreate the miseries of his past. This
may be why he feels the need, in the sequel, to make the effort to detach
himself from these memories by dwelling on the activities of a second
alchemist-cleric who is *not*, he insists, to be taken for his former master.
The key to this otherwise puzzling repetition is likely to lie in the
Yeoman's insistence that the new Canon has at least some of the attributes
of a 'fiend', a denizen of 'hell':

> Ther is a chanoun of religioun
> Amonges us, wolde infecte al a toun,
> Thogh it as greet were as was Nynyvee,
> Rome, Alisaundre, Troye, and othere three.
> His sleightes and his infinite falsnesse
> Ther koude no man writen, as I gesse,
> Though that he myghte lyve a thousand yeer.
> In al this world of falshede nis his peer;
> For in his termes he wol hym so wynde,
> And speke his wordes in so sly a kynde,
> Whanne he commune shal with any wight,
> That he wol make hym doten anonright,
> But it a feend be, as hymselven is.
> Ful many a man hath he begiled er this,
> And wole, if that he lyve may a while;
> And yet men ride and goon ful many a mile
> Hym for to seke and have his aqueyntaunce,
> Noght knowynge of his false governaunce.
>
>   (VIII. 972–89)

The 'demonic' attributes of the master-alchemist, which the preceding
narrative has insinuated, are now more insistently presented. The new
Canon is something more than a shabby artist in deception. He is said to
move 'among us', carrying out his work of 'infection' in the midst of all
mankind, much as Satan is present in the 'world', penetrating every
aspect of human society. His power is as great as that which, in former
ages, undermined the great cities of antiquity; and he is ready, no doubt,
to undo as many more in the present, and at all future times. His cunning
and his 'falseness' are said to be 'infinite', as though extending beyond the
limits of any single human life-time: 'a thousand years' would not suffice
to chronicle his sinister activity or to do justice to the cunning by which he
induces his human dupes to 'dote' in the prospect of their own deception.

The Yeoman, indeed, explicitly calls the new Canon a 'fiend', a devil who covers his true nature under a human aspect and who exercises – now as at all times – a fascination over those who actively seek his 'acquaintance' in the hope of attaining their illusion of wealth and power, only to end by co-operating effectively in their own ruin.

The new Canon, then, though connected with his late master in the Yeoman's mind, goes well beyond him to touch on more general attributes, or perversions, of human nature. Chaucer's intention in extending the scope of his story is evidently double. In the process of showing the Yeoman seeking to come to terms with his own situation by distancing himself from it and by presenting himself as a victim of more than merely human deceptions, he is concerned to relate the alchemist's activities to underlying motives of the 'pilgrimage' as a reflection of human life. The emphasis now rests on the element of betrayal, on the absence of 'truth', or saving human trust. When the unsuspecting priest-victim greets the new Canon's return of the scraps of silver he gave him as an earnest of good faith – 'To swich a man I kan never seye nay' (VIII. 1041) – the 'demon'-alchemist's reply is 'satanic' in its inversion of positive truth:

> 'What!' quod this chanoun, 'sholde I be untrewe?
> Nay, that were thyng yfallen al of newe.
> Trouthe is a thyng that I wol evere kepe
> Unto that day in which that I shal crepe
> Into my grave, and ellis God forbede.
> Bileveth this as siker as your Crede.   (VIII. 1042–7)

It may be no accident that the lines include a close echo of those in *The Franklin's Tale* in which Arveragus affirmed to Dorigen the central value of 'truth' as 'the hyeste thynge that man may kepe'.[5] In the present context, the protestation of good faith put into the 'demon's' mouth is given an extra dimension by being related to man's common mortality and by the irony which enables him to point to the 'truth' of the Christian creed, which he is supposed by his office to represent, in the very act of betraying the 'trust' – that other face of 'truth', the expression of its human aspect – which he is inducing his victim to place in his operations. It is relevant for the sense of the tale that the new Canon and his victim are both priests: men who should represent in their lives what the 'pilgrimage' motive presents as the *truth*, the saving reality of things, but who are turned aside from the human way by greed and weakness, to find themselves involved in a community of 'damnation'.

The new Canon's activities, like those of the Yeoman's master, involve the extinction of light, both in its physical and its symbolic aspects. Before he embarks on his operations, he stresses the secrecy of a 'trade' that purports to make of his victim a 'philosopher', offering him access to a unique revelation –

> Ther been ful fewe to whiche I wolde profre
> To shewen hem thus muche of my science –
> (VIII. 1123–4)

in the act of insisting on the need for concealment:

> Voyde youre man, and lat hym be theroute,
> And shette the dore, whils we been aboute
> Oure pryvetee, that no man us espie,
> Whils that we werke in this philosophie.   (VIII. 1136–9)

'Science' and 'philosophy' are terms which claim much and which read strangely in connection with so much emphasis on 'pryvetee' and closed doors: the exclusion of common daylight which goes together with that of reason, the twin attributes on which 'philosophy' and 'science' properly rest and by which any distinctively 'human' conception of life must be governed.

The priest-victim, moved by his own compelling cupidity, and blinded to the obvious truth, places himself willingly, even exultantly, in the hands of his deceiver. Indeed, he goes so far as to invoke the sanctions of his religion in support of his greed:

> He putte his hand in and took up a teyne
> Of silver fyn, and glad in every veyne
> Was this preest, whan he saugh that it was so.
> 'Goddes blessyng, and his moodres also,
> And alle halwes, have ye, sire chanoun,'
> Seyde the preest, 'and I hir malisoun,
> But, and ye vouche-sauf to techen me
> This noble craft and this subtilitee,
> I wol be youre in al that evere I may.'   (VIII. 1240–8)

It is clear at this point that Chaucer is not concerned with the claim of the alchemists to be serious scientific investigators – a claim with regard to which he is likely to have preserved something of an open mind – but with what he presents as a 'demonic' aberration fundamental to human nature and affecting the very substance of 'pilgrimage'. As practised in both parts of the tale, this is a 'science' which proceeds, not from a reverence for the workings of nature or from a confident trust in man's relation to it, but from a desire to manipulate nature itself, to ends which are in medieval terms (and perhaps not in those alone) perverse and finally blasphemous. It has been argued that the alchemist's quest, as the tale presents it, is a perverted manifestation of man's search for truth, and that the frequent

medieval association of the 'philosopher's stone', the object of the
alchemist's not necessarily fraudulent search, with the Saviour confers
upon the Yeoman's 'demonic' Canon some of the attributes of an
'anti-Christ'.[6] Whether or not this is so, the implications of the tale
evidently go beyond the comic exposure of picaresque roguery: though,
indeed, it would be rash to exclude this element which serves, in a very
Chaucerian way, to dissuade us from any one-sidedly 'serious' or
moralizing reading of the tale. There is, beyond the comedy and without
in any way replacing it, a 'serious' content of the tale which relates it to
some of the deeper senses of the 'pilgrimage' theme. To pursue the
alchemist's 'mystery' by seeking to impose human will, inspired by greed
and the urge to dominate nature, on the creative purpose manifested in
the natural order, wresting what is generous and life-dispensing to ends
of self-affirmation and cupidity, is to embark upon a misplaced effort
which passes through willed self-deception and the pursuit of 'illusion'
into a form of 'damnation'.

There is meaning, in this connection, in the fact that the victim
expresses his enthusiasm in terms that amount to a grotesque caricature of
the 'love' by which men express in a variety of ways, some more adequate
than others, but all of them recognizably human, their sense of
participation in the creative processes of life. The lines which convey his
joy at having attained, as he believes, the end placed before him, are
revealing:

> This sotted preest, who was gladder than he?
> Was nevere brid gladder agayn the day,
> Ne nyghtyngale, in the sesoun of May,
> Was nevere noon that luste bet to synge;
> Ne lady lustier in carolynge,
> Or for to speke of love and wommanhede,
> Ne knyght in armes to doon an hardy dede,
> To stonden in grace of his lady deere,
> Than hadde this preest this soory craft to leere.
> And to the chanoun thus he spak and seyde:
> 'For love of God, that for us alle deyde,
> And as I may deserve it unto yow,
> What shal this receite coste? telleth now!'   (VIII. 1341–53)

Here, given in the light of the sharply disillusioned vision which prevails
in so much of this tale, we see what, in this priest's following of his greed,
has replaced the natural instincts of life and the sense of the creed he
professes. We see what it is that renders his besotted enthusiasm a
caricature of all the 'romantic' commonplaces, and that finds grotesque
issue in his readiness to invoke the sacrifice of his God's love, 'that for us

alle deyde' – even in the act of avidly questioning the cost, asking what he will have to *pay*, to become 'rich: 'What shal this receite coste? telleth now!'

The answer is, certainly, more than this fictional victim can have bargained for when he delivered himself, as the Yeoman himself had done, into the hands of the deceiver who recommends him to secrecy. The Canon makes his plea rest, once more, on the allure of 'mystery' implied in the hermetical nature of his craft; and once again the victim, moved by his own naive but consuming greed, falls into the trap laid for him:

> 'God it forbeede,' quod the preest, 'what sey ye?
> Yet hadde I levere spenden al the good
> Which that I have, and elles wexe I wood,
> Than that ye sholden falle in swich mescheef.'
>
> (VIII. 1375–8)

The point of the comedy, of course, is that just this – the sacrifice of his *real* 'good', spiritual and moral not less than material – is the end to which this self-blinded victim finally arrives.

At the conclusion of this exposure of one of the ways in which men effectively will their own 'hell' the true nature of the 'philosophy', the 'sliding science' which has led its devotees to self-destruction and abasement is bluntly stated:

> Philosophres speken so mystily
> In this craft that men kan nat come therby,
> For any wit that men han now-a-dayes.
> They mowe wel chiteren as doon thise jayes,
> And in hir termes sette hir lust and peyne,
> But to hir purpos shul they nevere atteyne.
> A man may lightly lerne, if he have aught,
> To multiplie, and brynge his good to naught!
>
> (VIII. 1394–1401)

That this is the result of the alchemist's activities has been made abundantly clear in the course of the Yeoman's story and confirmed in the sequel; but, once we have responded to the tale's most obvious thrust, certain questions remain disturbingly posed. More is involved than the comic exposure of superstition and greed as they work on what is for us – as it may have been, in part, for Chaucer – the exploitation of a pseudo-science by a rapacious charlatan. The question which remains is one which affects the very substance of the human pilgrimage. What is it in man's nature that drives him, in the way that the tale has so powerfully shown and in so many others, to follow the mirage of future profit, the delusion of what is always to be attained 'to-morrow' and never 'to-day', to the ruin of his natural happiness and the undoing of what he flatters himself by calling his 'soul'? What, in other words, is the nature of the misplaced 'love' which men so obstinately elect to follow: the 'love' which presents itself to them in the forms of restless curiosity and the prospect of limitless achievement, only to lead them, in the course of seeking to satisfy this innate compulsion of their natures, to ends of self-destruction and death?[7]

Nor do the implications of the tale end here. Some of them extend beyond an exposure of false 'science' and mean 'cupidity' to cover the poet's own pursuit of his artistic purpose. The motive which moves him to his creative effort is no doubt different from, more positive than that of his alchemists, but the end attained may be more similar than he might wish to think. The alchemist is, after his own fashion, an aspiring 'creator', who works upon his chosen material with the intention of producing what he conceives imaginatively as a transformation of the stuff of common reality: an effect not altogether unlike that which the 'magician' of *The Franklin's Tale* – who was also a practitioner of 'illusion' – claimed to exercise upon the 'rocks' which so troubled the heroine in her husband's absence.[8] The passionate commitment with which the alchemist and his dupes pursue their own 'illusions', and the grandiose prospects they envisage for their 'science' find a certain ironic parallel in the artist's claim to exercise upon the 'real' his transforming imaginative action. The artist, like the alchemist, requires his audience to believe that he can effect the transformation at which – perhaps not without an arrogance of his own – he aims and to accept his claim that the ability to do this contributes to the understanding of 'real' life. In each case the possibility exists, and is at least insinuated by the poet, that the pursuit of this aim – which answers to a natural and distinctively human craving – may involve an element of presumption and imply a commitment to 'illusion'. The 'truth' which the artist, for his own ends, presumes to explore and to make available to others through his creative action, may prove – like the alchemist's coveted 'gold' – to be, realistically considered, beyond the range of his achievement: and to recognize this, if not as a fact at least as a possibility, may prove to be in the end a salutory recognition of human limitation. 'Men shal nat maken ernest of game'.[9] More is involved in that injunction, placed at the outset of the pilgrimage, than a warning against the confusion of genres or the misreading of artistic intent. The telling of tales has its own purposes and is its own justification: nothing is gained, and much may be lost, by pretending to find in it a significance, a meaning, that ignores its limits and that it will not bear. As in so much of Chaucer's work, we may find involved in it the recommendation to a proper sense of proportion. The tale, so curiously unlike most of what surrounds it, is designed to raise questions which are not often asked so directly in the course of Chaucer's great poem, but which it is part of the richness, the inclusive variety of the 'pilgrimage' scheme to pose in this masterpiece of obsessive and disillusioned comedy.[10]

X

THE
NUN'S PRIEST'S TALE

For all their undoubted fascination, and although they provide the Chaucerian pilgrimage with motives essential to its completeness, *The Pardoner's Tale* and *The Canon's Yeoman's Tale* are not the stories we should choose to characterize his genius. That genius was essentially comic in kind, though in affirming this we are certainly not implying that it was less serious than that which expresses itself through tragedy.[1] The 'comic' has no exclusive connection with what we like to think of as 'funny' or ridiculous, though it certainly rejects the solemn and the pretentious in arriving at its own reflection of life. If we are looking for a tale to serve as a distillation of the distinctively Chaucerian spirit we can hardly do better than turn to *The Nun's Priest's Tale*, which takes up many of the themes, serious and comic alike, which we have found in the other stories and brings them together in a remarkable play of mature comic invention.

It is not an accident that the tale follows immediately on that told by the Monk: for a good deal in the second tale implies a comment on the inadequacy of the first. We are reminded of the juxtaposition of *The Physician's Tale* and that told by the Pardoner, and indeed the situation is in certain respects not dissimilar, as a reading of the prologue which precedes *The Monk's Tale* will show. As in so many other instances, this prologue begins with a forthright comment by the Host, referring to the prose 'tale' of Melibeus which the poet himself has just told. The comment is strictly limited by the point of view, bluntly self-centred and self-assertive, that we have learnt to associate with his interventions as arbiter and moving spirit of the pilgrimage. He sees the Dame Prudence of the tale as a contrast to his own wife, of whom he has already spoken, briefly but ruefully, in the epilogue to *The Merchant's Tale*.[2] Now he

expresses himself more forcibly, but not less absurdly or irrelevantly to the
intention of the tale we have heard:

> As I am feithful man,
> And by that precious corpus Madrian,
> I hadde levere than a barel ale
> That Goodelief, my wyf, hadde herd this tale!
> (VII. 1891–4)

for she is, he goes on to say, entirely without the 'patience' so exhaustively
(in every sense of the word) exhibited by Dame Prudence. The remark,
typically, cuts several ways. It serves to remind us, through one man's
blunt assertion of his immediate concerns, of the gap that separates theory
from practice, allegorical 'doctrine' from real life, and moralizing
discourse from tale-telling; but at the same time it reminds us, by the
manner of its expression, its crude and misplaced oaths, together with the
repeated references to the comforting properties of 'ale', that the Host is
not immune from the sins – those of gluttony and thoughtless blasphemy
– attacked by the Pardoner. The question is whether, and at what point,
these things can properly be called 'sins', and whether the moral
repudiation of them in the name of the 'higher' abstractions is compatible
with a recognition of human life as it is actually lived. The 'story' of
Melibeus no doubt conveys important 'truths', and its lesson of the need
for 'patience' can be seen as central to the entire 'pilgrimage' conception;
but, equally, the statement of it is long-winded and abstract, remote from
the reality of life as most of the pilgrims must conceive it.

At all events the picture of the Host in his domesticity, beating his
'knaves' with 'the grete clobbed staves' which Goodelief provides for the
purpose in the act of urging him on with shrill vituperation –

> Slee the dogges everichoon,
> And brek hem, bothe bak and every boon! –
> (VII. 1899–1900)

is at once brutal and ridiculous, as is the tone of the unquiet exchanges
which, still on Harry Bailey's account, follow these exploits:

> By corpus bones, I wol have thy knyf,
> And thou shalt have my distaf and go spynne!
> (VII. 1906–7)

Here, and in the lines which follow, we may surely sense an indirect
comment on the reality that underlies the Wife of Bath's claim to exercise
'maistrie' over her men. The plain-speaking Host, who is so ostentatiously
proud of his masculinity, is capable of pleading for the sympathy of his
audience. 'This is my lif, but if that I wol fighte' (VII. 1913); and, if he does

resist his wife, there is the danger of what the violent end of their quarrel
may irreparably bring:

> For I am perilous with knyf in honde,
> Al be it that I dar nat hire withstonde.   (VII. 1919–20)

All this paves the way for the Host to address that worldly celibate, the
Monk, calling upon him to contribute his tale and addressing him with a
bluff carelessness that is both habitual in him and somewhat belittling in
its implications:

> Wher shal I calle yow my lord daun John,
> Or daun Thomas, or elles daun Albon?:   (VII. 1929–30)

where the title 'daun' seems to show a respect for status which, however,
the following uncertainty about names – 'John', 'Thomas', 'Albon', or
whatever – to some extent qualifies.[3] After this unceremonious opening
the Host goes on to make clear his own limited conception of the religious
vocation:

> I pray to God, yeve hym confusioun
> That first thee broghte unto religioun!
> Thou woldest han been a tredefowel aright.
> (VII. 1943–5)

We can hardly help recalling this when the 'hero' of the tale which follows
The Monk's Tale turns out to be a spectacularly endowed cock, and a
'tredefowel' of no common capacity. This leads the Host to develop his
own view of priestly celibacy in terms which reflect his particular blend of
insensitive aggression and worldly common-sense:

> God yeve me sorwe, but, and I were a pope,
> Nat oonly thou, but every myghty man,
> Though he were shorn ful hye upon his pan,
> Sholde have a wyf; for al the world is lorn!
> Religioun hath take up al the corn
> Of tredyng, and we borel men been shrympes.
> (VII. 1950–5)

The comment on the Monk, and on what we must suspect to be his
misplaced vocation, is valid, and so is the light thrown by implication on
the limitation of the Host's own values. It is easy to imagine how the
Parson, who has heard himself dismissed, again by the Host, as a heretical
and sanctimonious moralizing 'Lollard',[4] must have reacted to the view of
the religious vocation which is here implied.

The Monk, at all events, can be presumed to be uncomfortable, aware of
the way in which his celibacy is regarded by his fellow-pilgrims, and

affected, beneath and beyond his show of congenial worldliness, by the Host's words. Though he makes no direct protest – he 'took al in pacience', we are told – he makes a point of reserving, somewhat self-consciously, the 'honesty' appropriate to his status.[5] He also remembers that he has 'in his cell' numerous examples of 'tragedy' – a 'hundred' or more in number – which can suitably be used to point a moral and to support his claim to learning. In introduction of these, he feels prompted to declare the definition of tragedy which, at some relatively remote time past, he learnt in his frequentation of the schools. The definition is wooden enough to serve as a target for the Nun's Priest's satire in the tale which will follow the Monk's series of edifying 'examples':

> Tragedie is to seyn a certeyn storie,
> As olde bookes maken us memorie,
> Of hym that stood in greet prosperitee,
> And is yfallen out of heigh degree
> Into myserie, and endeth wrecchedly.
> And they ben versified communely
> Of six feet, which men clepen *exametron*.
> In prose eek been endited many oon,
> And eek in meetre, in many a sondry wyse.
> Lo, this declaryng oghte ynogh suffise.   (VII. 1973–82)

The Monk, we may feel, is drawing on the scraps of his half-forgotten learning. Indeed, the long sequence of monotonous rhymes in the lines just quoted suggests a mnemonic device, of the type dear to scholastic pedagogues, to facilitate the memorizing of definitions and similar matter. As the Monk himself goes on to say,[6] he realizes that his memory of his studies may have been rendered less than perfect by the passage of time and the following of other, less scholarly interests; for he foresees the possibility that he will relate his exemplary 'tragedies' out of their proper order, 'som bifore and som bihynde',

> As it now comth unto my remembraunce, (VII. 1989)

in the sequence of ill-digested matter that turns out to constitute the body of his intervention. It seems to be a sense of this probability and the embarrassment that he anticipates from it, that leads him to beg, not without a certain engaging candour, for indulgence on the part of his audience: 'Have me excused of myn ignoraunce' (VII. 1990).

The implications of this confession may go some way towards redeeming the Monk as he takes his place among the ecclesiastical misfits of the pilgrimage. His definition of tragedy, however, is more closely related to Chaucer's conception. The relation of tale-telling to truth, of imaginative art to exemplifying moral precept, is a question that runs through the entire work, and is set up as a dichotomy that has no easy or obvious resolution. It is noteworthy that, more particularly in this part of the *Tales*, we are given a series of 'stories' – *The Tale of Melibeus*, *The Physician's Tale*, *The Monk's Tale* – all of which aim at pointing a moral, and all of which are – considered in terms of the 'art' they fail to display – variously inadequate; whereas the one tale – the Pardoner's – that is both 'moral' in content and 'artistic' in the manner of its telling, has been given to the pilgrim who can be seen – and *is* seen by the whole 'fellowship' – to stand outside the redeeming framework of the common journey. When we add to these complexities the obvious insufficiency of the Host's attitudes, both moral and artistic, and recognize that these incongruities proceed from human reactions that simply refuse to be fitted into the 'pilgrimage' scheme, we begin to obtain an insight into the scope and subtlety of Chaucer's conception. The Parson bears this out, for instance, in another 'tale' that fails, deliberately in his case, to aspire to or to achieve the status of a work of art. To explore the various implications of the 'truth' which may be presumed to animate an imaginative creation, the work of an artist conscious both of the claims and the limitations of his 'art', and to relate these to the more ample conception of 'truth' which inspires and sustains the embracing image of 'pilgrimage' is, perhaps, the justifying principle which Chaucer came finally to see as the concern of *The Canterbury Tales*.

The Nun's Priest's Tale, following on the Monk's painstaking but heavy-handed attempt at edification, includes in its many-sided content a satire on the conception of 'tragedy' so wearisomely illustrated by the Monk; for Chauntecler, like the classical notabilities listed, allowed himself to become subject to the operations of blind Fortune and fell from prosperity to low estate. What the Monk took seriously, however, the Nun's Priest treats with ironic detachment; and what emerges in his telling as a splendid piece of varied art is, in the Monk's treatment, pedantic and dead. The Monk is sure of his morals and repetitiously ponderous in his pointing of them; the Nun's Priest is ready to recognize that tale-telling has a moral aspect, but is also aware that in human life as it is lived in time only one thing is permanent and that is change. At the end of *The Monk's Tale* it is left to the Knight to protest in the name of common sense against so much heavy edification. The Monk, he observes, has said 'ryght ynogh' on the theme of his choice; indeed, he has said 'muchel moore' than is either necessary or appropriate in the essentially 'merry', sociable and recreative undertaking to which all the members of the company are, by their own free decision, committed.

The Knight then proceeds to make his own comment on what the pilgrims have heard. If it is indeed sad – 'a greet disese' (VII. 2771) – to consider the 'sodeyn fal' of great men from a state of 'welthe and ese', there is a corresponding satisfaction to be gained from the contemplation of the opposite process:

> As whan a man hath been in povre estaat,
> And clymbeth up and wexeth fortunat,
> And there abideth in prosperitee.   (VII. 2775–7)

Commonsense tells us that this aspect of the operations of 'Fortune' is as much in accordance with the observed facts as its opposite, and it is no more than human to find satisfaction in being reminded of it:

> Swich thyng is gladsom, as it thynketh me,
> And of swich thyng were goodly for to telle.
>   (VII. 2778–9)

What the Knight expresses in terms of his tolerant and balanced view of human existence is supported by the Host on more elemental grounds. In the process of giving this support he renders his own position a little suspect; for he has to a powerful degree the almost universal desire, and need, to reshape 'reality' according to his own comfortable, and comforting image of it. His reaction is nothing if not forthright in its rejection:

> Ye seye right sooth; this Monk he clappeth lowde.
> He spak how Fortune covered with a clowde
> I noot nevere what; and als of a tragedie
> Right now ye herde, and, pardee, no remedie
> It is for to biwaille ne compleyne
> That that is doon, and als it is a peyne,
> As ye han seyd, to heere of hevynesse.   (VII. 2781–7)

We may find the Host's reaction human and, as far as it goes, reasonable; though it is based less on reason than on the desire to hear only what can be thought of as convenient and soothing. The problem of 'Fortune', and of the way in which men should react to her operations remains, and there is truth – as well, no doubt, as an element of pedantry – in the treatment of it developed in *The Tale of Melibeus*. When the Host brusquely tells the Monk 'namoore of this', and dismisses his contribution as 'nat worth a boterflye' (VII. 2790), he is exhibiting, beyond his claim to represent the natural reaction of the ordinary, plain-spoken man he prides himself on being, his own kind of bluff and insensitive arrogance. The reason of his reaction, moreover, is declared when he goes on to say that there is 'no desport ne game' in what he has just heard. The same attitude prompts him to require the Monk to tell a tale of hunting, taking as his pretext the

> clynkyng of youre belles,
> That on youre bridel hange on every syde.
> (VII. 2794–5)

Here, indeed, he is touching on a sensitive point in the Monk who, though he is no doubt aware of the extent to which he is uncomfortable in his 'vocation', is not prepared to disown it in public: hence the marked note of reluctance in which he phrases his refusal to follow the Host in this matter: ' "Nay," quod this Monk, "I have no lust to pleye" ' (VII. 2806).

The Host's comments, however, penetrate rather more deeply than he may realize. He points out, not unreasonably, that the Monk has told his tale in such a way as to induce sleep in himself and in the audience; and this, he argues, implies that whatever moral purpose the teller may have had in mind has been rendered vain by the manner of the telling:

> For certeinly, as that thise clerkes seyn,
> Whereas a man may have noon audience,
> Noght helpeth it to tellen his sentence.
> (VII. 2799–2801)

The point is obvious enough – so obvious that the reference to 'thise clerkes' no doubt carries its usual satirical implication – but it is none the less true; for a tale told for moral ends without a measure of art will, in the process of failing *as a tale*, fail to persuade those who hear or read it of the validity of the 'lesson' it is designed to convey. We have seen, from the example offered by the Pardoner, that a confessedly *un*moral man can tell a 'ful moral tale' in such a way as to obtain the involvement of his audience. Finally, as the Host concludes, any tale is what its hearers choose to make of it: as he puts it, with unusual and presumably unconscious subtlety,

> wel I woot the substance is in me,
> If any thyng shal wel reported be. (VII. 2803–4)

This seems to involve the poet-pilgrim as 'reporter' of *all* the tales told on the way, and finally the poet himself in his capacity as creator. The telling of a tale, like any reporting of 'realities', human or other, is inevitably conditioned by the particular vision of the teller. Beyond this, the proof of the narrative lies ultimately in the reaction which it provokes in the hearer, and any teller of tales who ignores this reality is both acting contrary to the nature of tale-telling, which implies communication to an audience, and running the risk of rendering his effort vain: which is perhaps what has been done, in their very different ways, by the teller of the *Melibeus* tale, by the Physician, who has shown moral insensitivity and artistic ineptitude, and by the Monk, who has tried to tell a series of tales that stand in almost grotesque contrast to what presents itself, visibly and palpably to every pilgrim, as his real nature.

With all this behind us, the Host turns to the Nun's Priest, addressing him with his usual blunt and slightly belittling familiarity – 'Com neer, thou preest, com hyder, thou sir John!' (VII. 2810) – and asks for a tale which shall be 'swich thyng as may oure hertes glade' (VII. 2811). Let his sober appearance, he says, not prevent him from telling the happy story for which his audience is waiting and which the Monk has so notably failed to provide. 'What thogh thyn hors be bothe foul and lene?'

> Looke that thyn herte be murie everemo.   (VII. 2815)

It should be noted in this connection that the Nun's Priest was not given a description in the General Prologue. We only know of him through the Host's words, and there is a moment in the so-called Epilogue to the tale[7] when it looks as if, at some stage, Chaucer intended to establish a parallel of some kind with the Monk. If so, the intention seems to have been dropped or forgotten when the time came for the Nun's Priest to tell his tale. His is, it would seem, a markedly unobtrusive presence which is – as it turns out – not the less powerful on that account; for the tale takes up some of the deepest themes of the pilgrimage and exposes them to a subtle comic scrutiny which is perhaps as near to Chaucer's final intention as we are likely to get. The full sense of the tale emerges, as it no doubt should, in the course of the telling. The Nun's Priest will, so to speak, *be* his tale, and he will have little or no separate existence apart from it. That is, perhaps, his strength as compared with the Monk, of whose character we are made sharply aware, but in a way which fails to reflect itself in his tale or to answer to his audience's perception of him: a way, in short, that points to the discrepancy between what the man is and what he tries to say. The Nun's Priest, on the other hand, who enters the picture without any clearly defined characteristic, and whose status among the pilgrims is conditioned to a certain degree by the fact that he is there in a subsidiary capacity, as part of the Prioress' entourage,[8] accepts the Host's request for a 'merry' tale because he is aware that acceptance of this is a condition of his success in making his point. He accepts it, however, in his own way, one which takes him a good deal beyond the Host's peremptory demand for 'merriment': a way which will allow him to penetrate, at least as much as any other participant, to the underlying themes of the pilgrimage. The tale offers a comic comment on the human condition: a comment which is many-sided, incapable of being pinned down to any definite and correspondingly limited meaning or 'lesson' of the kind so heavily presented by the Monk. In this protean quality, this rich and deliberate elusiveness, it is close to the poet's final intention as the whole work conveys it.

The tale begins with a description – direct and simple, as befits the theme, but remarkably vivid and realized in its effect – of the setting in which the action will take place:

> A povre wydwe, somdeel stape in age
> Was whilom dwellyng in a narwe cotage,
> Biside a grove, stondynge in a dale.
> This wydwe, of which I telle yow my tale,
> Syn thilke day that she was last a wyf,
> In pacience ladde a ful symple lyf,
> For litel was hir catel and hir rente.
> By housbondrie of swich as God hire sente
> She foond hirself and eek hir doghtren two.
> Thre large sowes hadde she, and namo,
> Three keen, and eek a sheep that highte Malle.
> Ful sooty was hire bour and eek hir halle,
> In which she eet ful many a sklendre meel.
> Of poynaunt sauce hir neded never a deel.
> No deyntee morsel passed thurgh hir throte;
> Hir diete was accordant to hir cote.
> Repleccioun ne made hire nevere sik;
> Attempree diete was al hir phisik,
> And exercise, and hertes suffisaunce.
> The goute lette hire nothyng for to daunce,
> N' apoplexie shente nat hir heed.
> No wyn ne drank she, neither whit ne reed;
> Hir bord was served moost with whit and blak, –
> Milk and broun breed, in which she foond no lak,
> Seynd bacoun, and somtyme an ey or tweye;
> For she was, as it were, a maner deye.   (VII. 2821–46)

The description is admirably, and most precisely, pointed to an evocation of the widow's situation in her world. This is medieval agriculture on what an economist would to-day call a subsistence level, basically poor but with a certain implication of honest independence. The widow's life is one of recognized if relative poverty, and Chaucer, for all that his own position in life was very different, is able to write of it as one possessing direct knowledge: one, moreover, who, precisely because this knowledge comes naturally to him, is in no way inclined to sentimentalize his subject. The description, indeed, is not without relevant social implications. It postulates the existence of a society whose members, though differing from one another very widely in social status, are – like the pilgrims – still in touch with one another, still able at least to envisage the situation of those whose lives differ widely from their own. Chaucer, it is clear, knew a great deal more about the lives of peasants in his relatively simple, undifferentiated society than the average middle-class Marxist of the twentieth century knows about those whom he chooses to call the 'working-class': although this is not said with implications of criticism – we are all in the same situation, and nothing is here implied concerning the validity or otherwise of the Marxian analysis, either in history or in the present – but simply as the statement of a reality, a relevant fact.

Another aspect of this opening description of the setting of the tale connects it with a main theme of the pilgrimage. It is stressed that the widow's 'symple lyf' is lived in a spirit of 'pacience', an unassuming acceptance of the inescapable reality of things. Knowing that she is 'poor', and recognizing the limitation of her resources, she is ready to accept what she cannot change. Content with what she has, she is ready to build on it a life free from the pressures of illusory and transitory desires – the kind of life represented by the 'poynaunt sauce' and the 'deyntee' morsels to which, as we have seen, not a few of the pilgrims are addicted[9] – and a life free from the ailments and useless discontents to which these indulgences lead.[10] It is hardly necessary to say that this injunction to 'patience' has nothing to do with the tendency, continually to be observed in those favoured by fortune with wealth or social standing, to require those less fortunate to be content with their less happy lot. The tale concerns the universal human condition, not any single manifestation of it; and the 'patience' that it advocates is that which is required of *all* men in recognition of the limits which their common humanity realistically imposes.

The widow's yard, then, properly considered, becomes nothing less than a kind of 'symbol' – the word is much too abstract for what it is intended to convey, but, given our understanding of this, it may serve – of the normal, the *real* world, with its privations and compensations. It is the place where life has, for most human beings, to be lived, and any departure from it is likely to be both attractive and perilous. In contrast to the widow, who lives 'patiently' within her circumstances, the cock Chauntecler and his leading hen Pertelote (for he has others, who minister effectively to the male self-esteem which is so tellingly satirized in this tale), live in the same yard a life of elaborate, decorative pretence: a sort of unending colourful fantasy. We shall not, indeed, simplify the judgement which this situation invites. To live is in some measure to indulge one's fantasies, and not to do so is a kind of death to that human quality which calls for, indeed demands, the superfluous as a condition of continuing to be in any significant sense alive; but, as this story is designed to make clear, the process has its limits. If Chauntecler is in a position to indulge in his colourful fantasy of a life of courtly elegance and social grace, it is because he and his hens are securely enclosed, isolated from the dangers of the outside world, by the protecting boundaries of the widow's domain.

All this answers to Chaucer's purpose which is to be set up, under the deceptively simple form of his fable, something like a penetrating comic image of the ways in which men and women respond to the reality of their situation. The aim is to give their story a human dimension, not merely in terms of a moral to be extracted from it, but by ironically humanizing the behaviour and attitudes of the birds and beasts with which it deals. In the passage which immediately follows the description of the widow the balance is finely struck between a beauty which is real, but also – when contrasted with the way of life just presented – superfluous and precarious, and what is seen to be, in human terms, 'courtly' pretentiousness. The bird protagonists of the tale are set firmly in the limiting circumstances which govern and safeguard the existence they have chosen to lead:

> A yeerd she hadde, enclosed al aboute
> With stikkes, and a drye dych withoute,
> In which she hadde a cok, hight Chauntecleer.
> (VII. 2847–9)

This, and nowhere else, is the place where life has to be lived, and these the limits which its inhabitants will do well to accept in a spirit of 'patience' that recognizes both the advantages and the limitations offered by their abode: a place 'enclosed al aboute' by a fence of 'stikkes' and the dry 'dych' beyond it, limits within which there is security – hum-drum, unpretentious, perhaps, but within its limits *safe* – and outside, the fascination, again perhaps, of the adventurous unknown, but also all the unforeseeable dangers that go with it.

Within this fence, protected by it and taking the protection for granted, there lives a cock: a cock whose splendour has rarely been equalled, whose glory may be, or seem to be, more than merely gallinaceous, but who is none the less neither more nor less than a domestic fowl. It is true that 'In al the land, of crowyng nas his peer' (VII. 2850); but 'crowing', even of this superlative kind, is after all a cock's attribute, and to say that

> His voys was murier than the murie orgon
> On messe-dayes that in the chirche gon,   (VII. 2851–2)

or to compare its reliability in time-keeping to 'a clokke or an abbey orlogge' (VII. 2854), may seem to insinuate a comparison with distinctively human attributes but cannot alter the facts of this cock's condition. He may know by nature or instinct.

> ech ascencioun
> Of the equynoxial in thilke toun,   (VII. 2855–6)

and so be able to crow with impressive accuracy 'whan degrees fiftene weren ascended' (VII. 2857). These are things which men have to work out by long and difficult efforts of calculation, which may make them seem laborious or pedantic in the process. Instinctive knowledge of them enables the bird to dispense with these efforts; but it is a bird, after all, that he remains, and the status of the monk singing his Office in the abbey church will always be beyond him. The description which follows is conceived as a splendid blaze of colour, and as such we can respond to it:

> His coomb was redder than the fyn coral,
> And batailled as it were a castel wal;
> His byle was blak, and as the jeet it shoon;
> Lyk asure were his legges and his toon;
> His nayles whitter than the lylye flour,
> And lyk the burned gold was his colour.   (VII. 2859–64)

A vision of splendour, indeed, and one which stands out against the drab, day-to-day uniformity of the 'yard' in which, however, it is still enclosed: a vision not unrelated to other pictures, equally colourful and equally precarious, of distinctively human aristocracy, but one limited, finally placed, by the setting in which its magnificence is revealed.

The full implications of the human parallel only emerge when the hen, the other protagonist of the story, is brought into the picture. Chauntecler – this 'gentil' cock, as he is called, with an epithet that points to a parallel with the aristocratic love poetry of Chaucer's own age – has in his male and self-satisfied 'governaunce'

> Sevene hennes for to doon al his plesaunce,
> Whiche were his sustres and his paramours;
>   (VII. 2866–7)

the sense of a harem, with the females of exceptional quality ready to minister to their master's 'plesaunce', is essential to what is to follow. All the hens were 'wonder lyk to hym, as of colours' (VII. 2868), worthy mates to satisfy such a 'lord's' appetites; but outstanding among them, 'the faireste hewed on hir throte', was the one named – 'cleped': the verb has about it a flavour of aristocratic convention – 'faire damoysele Pertelote' (VII. 2870). As befits one so named, and dedicated to such a lord, Pertelote is no common hen, but one who can only be described in terms of elaborate and decorative courtliness:

> Curteys she was, discreet, and debonaire,
> And compaignable, and bar hyrself so faire,
> Syn thilke day that she was seven nyght oold,

(and the detail, of course, serves to recall us to reality, to awareness that the object of this description is not a court lady but a domestic fowl)

> That trewely she hath the herte in hoold
> Of Chauntecleer, loken in every lith.   (VII. 2871-5)

Chauntecler is devoted, enslaved – as a courtly lover should be, according to the poets – to the 'service' of this vision of gracious and decorative urbanity. Pertelote has his heart entirely 'in hoold', 'loken in every lith', like the heroines of so many romances in alliterative verse; and the result is that they form a pair such as any poet might fittingly celebrate.

The cock's attitude is an appropriate extension from this situation. A sense of complacent gratification exudes from him in the form of male self-esteem – 'He loved hire so that wel was hym therwith' (VII. 2876) – and so far imposes itself that the narrator is moved to transports of admiration –

> But swich a joye was it to here hem synge,
> Whan that the brighte sonne gan to sprynge,
> In sweete accord, 'My lief is faren in londe!' –
> (VII. 2877-9)

before he adds, with yet another of his disingenuous, and placing, returns to the order of common reality:

> For thilke tyme, as I have understonde,
> Beestes and briddes koude speke and synge.
> (VII. 2880-1)

In 'thilke tyme', perhaps, but no longer: for reality has the power to impose itself on even the most delicate of fictions, and the contrast so insinuated is fundamental to the story we are about to hear. In the enthusiastic, and apparently simple-minded comments offered by the teller of the tale we sense the presence of something not altogether unlike the naively approving judgements advanced throughout the pilgrimage by the poet narrator. The tone is similar, with the essential difference that what is offered by the narrator, within the framework of the tale, as direct, spontaneous, and undiscriminating enthusiasm is now distanced, subdued to the ironic detachment of the telling.

The equilibrium so finely struck combines intelligence of a high order, unemphatically displayed, with a keen appreciation of man's ability to enhance his life by the exercise of his transforming imagination. The balance is held between a beauty which is real, capable of exercising a genuine transforming effect upon the humdrum circumstances of living, and the down-to-earth realities of the widow's way of life. Plain human fact becomes, in this way, a reflection upon 'courtly' artifice and

pretension: a reflection which receives its exquisite comic projection in the
gap which separates our sense of the 'poor' widow, who is – within stated
and objectively recognized limits – in some measure mistress of her
circumstance, from '*demoiselle* Pertelote', who was 'curteis', 'discreet', and
'debonaire'. The hen's splendour is celebrated in courtly terms derived
from French sophistication, terms which are, as such, certainly not devoid
of the real attractions of 'civilization', but which are simultaneously
'shown up' in their essential limitation through the irony of their
attribution to what after all remains a farmyard situation.

It is possible, indeed, and perhaps useful to see in this situation the
reflection of something more universal than its immediate surface
meaning. There is throughout the tale a suggestion – it is no more than
that and we should be quite wrong to press any detailed parallel – that the
widow's yard represents in some sense a kind of rustic Eden where the
Adam and Eve of the story (the cock and hen) live in precarious confidence
before a Fall. This would give meaning to Chauntecler's dream of the fox,
which introduces a note of foreboding into the story:

> Me mette how that I romed up and doun
> Withinne our yeerd, wheer as I saugh a beest
> Was lyk an hound, and wolde han maad areest
> Upon my body, and wolde han had me deed.
> His colour was bitwixe yelow and reed,
> And tipped was his tayl and bothe his eeris
> With blak, unlyk the remenant of his heeris;
> His snowte smal, with glowynge eyen tweye.
> Yet of his look for feere almoost I deye.   (VII. 2898–2906)

The dream could be seen as prefiguring the entry of Satan, in the form of
flattery, deception, evil, into the rural Eden, which is at the same time and
before anything else the real, concrete farmyard.[11] It would certainly be
wrong to press this point so far as to make a detailed parallel of it. Chaucer
does not work in quite that kind of way, and the bare 'subsistence' setting
of the yard is as different as may be from what we normally think of as the
luxuriant superabundance of mankind's lost dwelling-place. On the other
hand, and once this has been recognized, it can hardly be doubted that
awareness of the Fall as a basic myth, an archetype of human experience,
is so close to the imagination of medieval man that it is likely to find echoes
in the most diverse places. To say this is not to undercut the essentially
comic effect of Chauntecler's dream, which contains a gently ironic
deflation of the place occupied by dreams in the sententious catalogue of
'tragedies' so recently and monotonously offered by the Monk.[12] It is
simply to suggest that where a pattern of universal human experience is as
generally available as that of the Fall was to Chaucer's contemporaries, it is

capable of finding 'comic' as well as 'tragic' reflections and of losing nothing of its fundamental, unpretentious 'seriousness' in the process of being so transformed.

What, at any rate, most immediately matters is that the fox, with his small 'snoute' and his 'glowynge eyen tweye', is beautifully realized in strictly visual terms. Both the cock's premonitory fear and Pertelote's 'womanly' reproof of her husband's 'cowardice' are essential factors in the situation. The latter in particular is full of implied meaning:

> 'Avoy!' quod she, 'fy on yow, herteless!
> Allas!' quod she, 'for, by that God above,
> Now han ye lost myn herte and al my love.
> I kan nat love a coward, by my feith!
> For certes, what so any womman seith,
> We alle desiren, if it myghte bee,
> To han housbondes hardy, wise, and free,
> And secree, and no nygard, ne no fool,
> Ne hym that is agast of every tool,
> Ne noon avauntour, by that God above!
> How dorste ye seyn, for shame, unto youre love
> That any thyng myghte make yow aferd?
> Have ye no mannes herte, and han a berd?
>
> (VII. 2908–20)

Throughout this part of the story the Nun's Priest seems to be considering the kind of issue concerning the relationship between the sexes that so exercised the Wife of Bath. Indeed, if we choose to develop the point just made concerning the Fall, we can find an implied, though deliberately unstated, point of reference applicable both to 'Dame' Pertelote and to Alice of Bath: for it is hard not to feel that the tone of the former's argument answers, in the story's free, essentially unpedantic way, to a situation that might well have been that of Adam and Eve at the time of the original Fall. Considered not as a Biblical or theological 'event', but as a *fact* of human experience, the sense of a 'fall' is present in every human relationship and every human situation. That is why its presentation cannot be limited to, even evades, the sententious and the 'tragic', and why its reflection in the story of a cock and hen whose reactions are those familiar in the everyday life of ordinary human beings is an appropriate and ultimately 'serious' part of Chaucer's comic design.

The long discussion on dreams, to which this initial exchange leads, shifts the attention to another target, which has also appeared in a number of ways in the course of the *Tales*. This time the object of deflation is provided by certain aspects of contemporary science – reflected in the talk of 'humours', 'complexions', and the like – and above all by attempts to

establish a scientific basis for the interpretation of dreams. The tone is
struck in Pertelot's appeal to authority –

> Lo Catoun, which that was so wys a man,
> Seyde he nat thus? –   (VII. 2940-1)

and in the deliberate bathos of her conclusion: 'For Goddes love, as taak
som laxatyf' (VII. 2943). What must strike us is the long-windedness of
this display of academic learning: we could, indeed, compare the effect of
Troilus' discourse on free will in Book IV of *Troilus and Criseyde*:[13] a theme
which will also be touched upon in the course of the tale. The comparison
is not without relevance, in as much as Troilus, Chauntecler, and the
'scientists' who are here subjected to the Nun's Priest's probing irony are
all engaged in the universal human pursuit of comforting illusion: the
illusion which supports them in their effort – which reflects their *need* – to
see life as accommodated to their desires and to their wish to think well
and comfortably of themselves, to see life as in fact *other* than what it really
is.

The cock responds to his wife's dismissal of his fears with a deliberate
assumption of superior politeness, standing on his dignity after the
affront offered to his masculine self-esteem in the contemptuous reference
to his 'beard'. Beyond that, he is ready – as a male conscious of his
intellectual superiority – with his counter-appeal to 'authority':

> By God, men may in olde bookes rede
> Of many a man moore of auctorite
> Than evere Caton was, so moot I thee,
> That al the revers seyn of this sentence. . . .
> Ther nedeth make of this noon argument;
> The verray preeve sheweth it in dede.
>   (VII. 2974-7, 2982-3)

Once again, it is natural to feel that there is a reference here to the display
of half-remembered 'learning' so recently advanced by the Monk, not to
mention other members of the pilgrim company who have prided
themselves on using their intellectual endowments to advance their own
reading of life. When it comes to 'authority' and to the 'preeve' which life
may be held to provide in support of it, Chauntecler is not less able than
any human scholar to lay hands on the arguments which support what he
finds it convenient to believe; for there are plenty of texts at his disposal,
and any of them will serve to enforce the position which he is concerned,
for reasons which have less to do with truth than with self-approval, to
defend. Chaucer is concentrating his satire at this point on one of his
favourite themes: the way in which 'authority', divorced from a healthy
respect for what presents itself as 'real', intractable to subjective and

self-serving (or at least self-deceiving) manipulation, can be found to support *any* conclusion. Only, in this particular case, an added thrust is given to the irony by the fact that Chauntecler's arguments will turn out to be confirmed by the event and so, in relation to the tale, to be *true*; but only after he has been led astray by the particularly uxorious brand of self-importance which so largely prevails in what he says and does and persuaded to set them aside to his own downfall.

Having touched on this line of satiric comment the Nun's Priest is skilled enough as story-teller to vary it with other matter germane to his purpose, which we may believe to have been that of drawing into one urbane comic vision some of the principal motives he has heard introduced by other speakers into the pattern of 'pilgrimage'. At this point, accordingly, he switches from the satire of intellectual pretensions to return to very concrete and indeed violent reality in the two *exempla* which Chauntecler advances in support of his argument. They are, we might say, stories inserted into the greater story; and they are, not by accident, evocations of murder, sudden death, and retribution which remind us of *The Pardoner's Tale*[14] in their brutality and in their emphasis on the part played by *cas*, chance, in human life. The spirit behind them emerges in the reference, in the first story, to the 'dung-cart'[15] in which the body of a murdered man was hidden: in the realistic and unflinching contemplation, in both incidents, of the bloody wounds and of the ignominy of death in a society which tended to hold life cheaply and thought of its violent termination as horrible indeed, but also as a matter of daily experience: the whole leading to the moral conclusion, at once realistic and thoroughly medieval, that 'mordre wol out' (VII. 3052),[16] and that the destiny of the killer is to be, quite inexorably, 'anhanged by the nekke-bon' (VII. 3062).

The second 'example' is equally realistic in its recognition of the intervention of chance as an element affecting the best planned of human affairs: chance as an essential agent in the process of living: 'But *casuelly*' – by an unforeseeable, but never impossible coincidence – 'the shippes botme rente' (VII. 3101). Men are characteristically and short-sightedly 'jolif and glad' in conducting their affairs on the optimistic assumption that their present good fortune will hold indefinitely, even as an obscure fate is preparing the condition of their downfall. This short-sighted optimism can be seen as absurd on their part; but so is the readiness to make it the object of sententious moral comment which is rendered ridiculous by proceeding from the mouth of a scholarly and self-infatuated fowl. Having been effectively exposed to the 'sentence', we are reminded that the reality of this story is that of a cock and a hen living in their farmyard situation. Accordingly these tragic or 'realistic' examples are undermined by the operation of an unobtrusive irony tending – once again – to the exposure of 'authority' and of all forms of self-bolstering pretension. The 'kyng of Egypt', 'daun Pharao' and 'His bakere and his butiller also' (VII. 3133) are there, present in Chauntecler's mind, to remind him by living or by dying that dreams are indeed to be taken (or are they?) seriously: and so, for that matter, are the great pagan figures, Scipio Africanus,[17] Croesus, 'which that was of Lyde kyng', and 'Andromacha, Ectores wyf' (VII. 3141). The weight of testimony is, one might think, solemn enough to impose itself: and indeed the irony of the tale, which glances here upon the Monk's tedious narration, operates in a typically complex way, side by side with the recognized seriousness of moral example.

For, after all, the examples are 'true', and Chauntecler recognizes their lesson, which is not one that can be conjured away by following Pertelote's advice – reflective as it may be of a compensating common-sense – to take 'laxatives':

Shortly I seye, as for conclusioun,

(and it is, of course, relevant that he has been delivering himself of 'wisdom' at no small length)

That I shal han of this avisioun
Adversitee: and I seye forthermoor,
That I ne telle of laxatyves no stoor,
For they been venymous, I woot it weel;
I hem diffye, I love hem never a deel! (VII. 3151–6)

Chauntecler himself will soon be brought to disaster by neglecting the warning offered him in dream; and he will neglect it for the universal human reasons that have applied since the beginning of man's history, because 'thilke tale is al to longe to telle' (VII. 3149) – and because, since the time of Adam, man has felt compelled, against his better judgement, to follow the advice of Eve to his own undoing. The fault, however, is clearly *his*, the product of his own masculine vanity, not in any primary sense that of his hen. Since he is a male, with his full share of masculine presumption, he turns away from the depressing considerations which his own reading of the 'authorities' has put into his mind, to seek solace where uxorious and self-satisfied males have been inclined, since the days of Adam, to seek it, in his relations with Pertelote.

'Now let us speke of myrthe, and stynte all this' (VII. 3157), he concludes; and 'mirth', of an accessibly engaging kind, is there in the shape of the fairest of companions:

Madame Pertelote, so have I blis,
Of o thyng God hath sent me large grace.
(VII. 3158–9)

We can sense the note of pretentiousness in the courtly opening – '*Madame Pertelote*' and respond to the intimations of bliss, warm and gratifyingly sensual beatitude, to which it leads, and which Chauntecler is presumptuous enough to see as a gift of 'large grace' provided for his enjoyment. In this mood, he rejects the dream warnings for the authenticity of which he has just argued on the most respected 'authority', and abandons himself to the beatific contemplation of his beloved:

> For whan I se the beautee of youre face,
> Ye been so scarlet reed aboute youre yen,
> It maketh al my drede for to dyen;
> For al so siker as *In principio*,
> *Mulier est hominis confusio*, –
> Madame, the sentence of this Latin is,
> 'Womman is mannes joye and al his blis.'
>
> (VII. 3160–6)

On the last point we might properly ask the opinion of Alice of Bath, who would have been able – and ready – to make her own comment.[18] Just so – observing a necessary distinction in proportions – might Adam have explained things to Eve, listening to the gratifying sound of his own voice mistranslating his chosen 'authority', before agreeing to share a bite of the apple. For Pertelote, of course, has just played the role of Eve in the garden. She has used his susceptibility to the 'beauty' of her face, the 'scarlet red' about her eyes, to induce Chauntecler to set aside the true warnings which his dreams have given him, and he has not only accepted her point of view – whilst recognizing that he really knows better – but has shown that his motive in this surrender is an impulse of sensual self-indulgence, typically and avowedly masculine in kind. 'He for God only, she for God in him':[19] we can imagine Chaucer, who would no doubt have accepted the essential orthodoxy of Milton's statement, none the less raising a mildly deprecating eyebrow at the element of vanity, typically male self-importance, conveyed in its rotund magnificence.

Yet this, important as it is, is only one side of the story, and Chauntecler's 'translation' of his Latin tag offers us the other. It indicates, although the speaker cannot know it, that there are two attitudes to human and sexual love which are apt to present themselves as in contradiction, but which a balanced view will seek to hold in relationship. Eve's counsel led to Adam's fall and bequeathed to all subsequent mankind a legacy of loss and disappointment; yet we have seen in the relationship between the cock and his hen an element of beauty, of imaginative transformation, which – however precarious, even absurd, it may be in its frail and vulnerable manifestations – is a transforming reality of human life. The love of woman can also be a means by which man[20] rises to the full measure of his potentiality; an important tradition available to Chaucer affirmed that this was so, and the Nun's Priest is concerned in his tale to remind us of this truth. 'Joy' and 'bliss' of no common kind are to be found in the relationship between men and women, and the fact that the Chaunteclers of this world are apt to interpret these realities in the light of their own blindly self-serving attitudes – displaying in the process a kind of complacent innocence which is rather the motive for tolerant irony than for moral condemnation – does not alter this essential fact; but confusion, leading alternately to real tragedy and to the depths of absurdity which this tale prefers to contemplate, has also shadowed the relationship from the time of Adam, and to recognize this is also to show a saving deference to the real. The ambiguity conveyed by these lines is of that creative kind which men, if they are wise, will recognize without seeking to subject it to one-sided or self assertive resolution; and it brings us very close to the heart of the vision of life reflected in the *Tales*.

This is indeed, one of Chaucer's most brilliantly effective passages, and its brilliance is confirmed and extended by what follows:

> 'For whan I feele a-nyght your softe syde,
> Al be it that I may nat on yow ryde,
> For that oure perche is maad so narwe, allas!
> I am so ful of joye and of solas,
> That I diffye bothe sweven and dreem.'
> And with that word he fley doun fro the beem,
> For it was day, and eke his hennes alle,
> And with a chuk he gan hem for to calle,
> For he hadde founde a corn, lay in the yerd.
> Real he was, he was namoore aferd.
> He fethered Pertelote twenty tyme,
> And trad hire eke as ofte, er it was pryme.
> He looketh as it were a grym leoun,
> And on his toos he rometh up and doun;
> Hym deigned nat to sette his foot to grounde.
> He chukketh whan he hat a corn yfounde,
> And to hym rennen thanne his wyves alle,
> Thus roial, as a prince is in his halle,
> Leve I this Chauntecleer in his pasture,
> And after wol I telle his aventure.   (VII. 3167–86)

What we are reminded of here, and what all the cock's 'high sentence' cannot disguise, is that he remains in the end what he has always been: a farmyard animal, whose instincts are those of his kind, but who suffers – much as his human 'betters' do – from inability to give them full satisfaction. He can 'feather' and 'tread' Pertelote in male sufficiency 'twenty times', as 'royally' satisfied with himself as 'a prince in his hall'; but, like the rest of us, he has eventually to recognize the limitations of his state – 'Oure perche is maad so narwe, allas!' – in a final reluctant salute to realism that is closely allied to the central theme of 'patience' which plays so great a part in the Chaucerian view of life. Man, when all is said and done, finds himself in a situation which limits the scope of his desires, and does well to recognize the fact. Here we have the clear voice of Chaucer's ironic realism speaking through the chosen terms of his fable.

At this point the narrator is reaching the crucial turning-point, the foreseen but not on that account avoided 'fall' in Chauntecler's story. The approach of disaster is emphasized with high sententiousness. It was the first of April, the end of the month of March, 'whan God first maked man' (VII. 3188), the month 'in which the world bigan', and also – we may believe – that of man's original fall from the state of paradise. Chauntecler, unconscious on the verge of his own comic 'fall', is presented exercising his mastery over his petty domain,

> in al his pryde,
> His sevene wyves walkynge by his syde,
> (VII. 3191–2)

daring in his satisfaction with himself to 'Caste up his eyen to the brighte sonne' (VIII. 3193). This seems to be the moment of fulfilment for him, and he salutes it ecstatically:

> 'The sonne,' he seyde, 'is clomben up on hevene
> Fourty degrees and oon, and moore ywis.
> Madame Pertelote, my worldes blis,
> Herkneth thise blisful briddes how they synge,
> And se the fresshe floures how they sprynge;
> Ful is myn herte of revel and solas!'   (VII. 3198–3203)

Chauntecler, in short, is proudly confident, full of the sense that his is the best of all possible worlds, as convinced of continued happiness as any 'romantically minded lover or poet might be.

Every preacher knows, however, – knows sometimes a little too readily – that to place one's confidence in the transitory attractions of the world is to invite disappointment. In the farmyard, as in the greater world beyond its limits, pride is apt to come before a fall, and the lines which follow make this clear. 'But *sodeynly*' – and the effect of the adverb is much like that of the 'casuelly' which introduced the earlier inset story of murder and sudden death[21] –

> hym fil a sorweful cas,
> For evere that latter ende of joye is wo.
> God woot that worldly joye is soone ago;

> And if a rethor koude faire endite,
> He in a cronycle saufly myghte it write
> As for a sovereyn notabilitee.   (VII. 3204–9)

We shall not be tempted to take this too readily or too simply at its own estimate. This 'sovereign notability' has been told too many times – most recently by the Monk in his lengthy collection of 'examples' – to be taken quite as such. The teller of the tale makes his point in a way which enables him to include a characteristic gesture at the moralist's expense. What academic clerics and scholars are apt to advance as a 'sovereign notability', worthy to be set down in the dignity of a 'chronicle', is the oldest of platitudes; although this need not mean that it does not contain a measure of truth which may be of salutory application even in the farmyard. The story – he insists – 'is also trewe, I undertake' (VII. 3211): as 'true', indeed, as the romances concerning Lancelot de Lake, which 'wommen' – not without a further sly turn of irony – 'holde in ful greet reverence' (VII. 3213), and which are in fact fictions. And, the moral point having been made, and once the underlying irony has been allowed to play glancingly, but with the effect of qualifying rather than of demolishing them, on various of the tale's central themes, the speaker deliberately resumes his habitual stance of neutrality in returning to his matter: 'Now wol I torne agayn to my sentence' (VII. 3214).

The 'cole-fox' – the real one this time – accordingly penetrates the rural Eden 'ful of sly iniquitee', to Chauntecler's downfall. The parallel between the intruder and a human murderer –

> Waitynge his tyme on Chauntecleer to falle,
> As gladly doon thise homycides alle –   (VII. 3223–4)

leads to satire on yet another of Chaucer's favourite themes, which he treated seriously in *Troilus and Criseyde*,[22] but which he is here ready to expose to ironic treatment – the scholastic discussions on free will and predestination, regarding which the narrator confesses that he is in the same position as the rest of men ('I ne kan nat bulte it to the bren' [VII. 3240]) – before turning from the puzzles presented by Augustine, Boethius and the rest to his more humble theme.

As usual it is important to avoid an over-simple reaction to these ironies. It is not that Chaucer does not think that these themes are serious or that they have no relation to the conduct of human life. It would even be rash to conclude that he is conveying, through the person of his elusive narrator, any sense of his own that such matters are not worth discussing, or that men should evade them because no final solution is in sight; for as much might be argued plausibly concerning most of the basic questions that men explore, and by exploration of which they express what is deepest, most germane to their humanity. Chaucer's treatment of the same subjects elsewhere, and his evident admiration for Boethius, is sufficient proof of his real concern with these questions. What is here insinuated, perhaps, is that it is always salutary for men to avoid the temptation to take themselves too seriously, and better for them to understand the real, necessary, and inescapable limits imposed upon thought by the plain realities of the human situation always avoiding any kind of 'tragic' excess, which would be *really* ridiculous, in as much as it would reflect an exaggerated sense of their own importance. Man's 'perch' – to return to the earlier farmyard image – is what it is, neither more nor less. He can aspire to recognize his errors in judgement, as Chauntecler is eventually brought to do by harsh experience, and in the process he can learn something valid about his own nature; but on such large matters as Fortune, Love or Destiny, his reflections must always end in open questions, and perhaps he does well to admit to this reality too. We may very reasonably allow ourselves to wish that the 'perch' might be bigger, more amply accommodated to our convenience and to our favourable opinion of ourselves, or that the thoughts upon which we are driven by our very human condition to embark might more adequately encompass the 'truth' of things. Indeed, it is human to do this; but, if we are wise, we shall not confuse the wish with the reality we are moved to explore. The difference between 'simple' and 'conditional' necessity may be fascinating as an object of intellectual speculation, an important theme to be discussed in the light of 'authority'; but its relation to the practice of daily life continues, on any prudent estimate, to evade us. The tale which the Nun's Priest is engaged in telling is of lesser, but more immediately practical concern: though, we must add, it would not be what it is if it were not told by one who is aware of the final relevance of these large questions and what they imply. It is the story of 'a cok, as ye may heere': a cock who was led by his vanity, and the flattery contained in his 'wife's' counsel, to a fall from his presumptuous estate. The situation, it is suggested, reflects the common lot of man since Adam; but, having made his point elegantly and without pedantry, the teller skilfully excuses himself for having seemed to speak ill of women –

> Thise been the cokkes wordes, and nat myne;
> I kan noon harm of no womman divyne –   (VII. 3265–6)

though, it should be noted, he does so in such a way as to allow his original point to stand. We may even speculate, if we will, that the Nun's Priest's position in the service of a Prioress with 'aristocratic', or at least 'ladylike' pretensions has taught him both to see feminine weaknesses with tolerant detachment and to be reasonably prudent in expressing himself in their regard.

Unaware of his approaching fate, brashly confident to the last,
Chauntecler continues his song, 'murier than the mermayde in the see'
(VII. 3270): for we have been assured by the best authorities – none other
than 'Physiologus' among them – that they do in fact sing 'wel and
myrily'. When he sees his enemy his first instinct is to escape in time, but
the fox makes a successful appeal to his vanity with fair words and
expressed admiration for his superior lineage:

> For trewely, ye have as myrie a stevene
> As any aungel hath that is in hevene.
> Therwith ye han in musyk moore feelynge
> Than hadde Boece, or any that kan synge.
> My lord youre fader – God his soule blesse! –
> And eek youre mooder, of hire gentillesse,
> Han in myn hous ybeen to my greet ese;
> And certes, sire, ful fayn wolde I yow plese.
> But, for men speke of syngyng, I wol seye, –
> So moote I brouke wel myne eyen tweye, –
> Save yow, I herde nevere man so synge
> As dide youre fader in the morwenynge.
> Certes, it was of herte, al that he song.
> And for to make his voys the moore strong,
> He wolde so peyne hym that with bothe his yen
> He moste wynke, so loude he wolde cryen,
> And stonden on his tiptoon therwithal,
> And strecche forth his nekke long and smal.
> And eek he was of swich discrecioun
> That ther nas no man in no regioun
> That hym in song or wisedome myghte passe.
>
> (VII. 3291–3311)

Once again, this is a perfect example of the effects which Chaucer is able to
obtain by the humanizing of his farmyard world. Particularly effective is
the grotesque picture of the father singing with all his might, stretched out
on tiptoe, seeking to outdo himself to sustain his very human vanity.
'Ravysshed' by the sweet words that fall so persuasively on his ears,
Chauntecler takes up the challenge and sets out to surpass his parent in
absurdity. He is, of course, duly caught, as the story tells us in lines which
lead up to and underline the moment of catastrophe (VII. 3331–5). All the
appropriate 'tragic' parallels are cited – and 'placed' in the citing – to
underline the decisive moment. 'Gaufred', who 'compleyned' for the
death of his king, the ladies recorded in the *Aeneid* as weeping for Priam's
death and the fall of Troy, 'Hasdrubales wyf' lamenting her husband's
death and the doom of Carthage, the wives of the Roman senators crying

for the loss of their husbands and Nero's burning of the city: all contribute
to the mock-heroic effect before the narrator, blandly and with devastating
effect, returns yet again to his theme: 'Now wol I turne to my tale agayn'
(VII. 3374). The satire so persistently directed in the tale against the
exercise of rhetoric is germane to its entire purpose: for rhetoric, as seen
here, is one of the devices that men most persistently use to bolster up,
even to create, the satisfying images which they set up as defences against
a reality which refuses to accommodate itself to their desire to think
consistently well of themselves.

The effect of this disaster upon the little world of the widow's yard
becomes the occasion for one of the most brilliant pieces of writing in the
tale:

> This sely wydwe and eek hir doghtres two
> Herden thise hennes crie and maken wo,
> And out at dores stirten they anon,
> And syen the fox toward the grove gon,
> And bar upon his bak the cok away,
> And cryden 'Out! harrow! and weylaway!
> Ha! ha! the fox!' and after hym they ran,
> And eek with staves many another man.
> Ran Colle oure dogge, and Talbot and Gerland,
> And Malkyn, with a dystaf in hir hand;
> Ran cow and calf, and eek the verray hogges,
> So fered for the berkyng of the dogges
> And shoutyng of the men and wommen eeke,
> They ronne so hem thoughte hir herte breeke.
> They yolleden as feendes doon in helle;
> The dokes cryden as men wolde hem quelle;
> The gees for feere flowen over the trees;
> Out of the hyve cam the swarm of bees.
> So hydous was the noyse, a, *benedicitee*!
> Certes, he Jakke Straw and his meynee
> Ne made nevere shoutes half so shrille
> Whan that they wolden any Flemyng kille,
> As thilke day was maad upon the fox.
> Of bras they broghten bemes, and of box,
> Of horn, of boon, in whiche they blewe and powped,
> And therwithal they skriked and they howped.
> It semed as that hevene sholde falle.   (VII. 3375–3401)

Once again the lines point to meanings beyond those which they bear on
the surface. The fox's entry into the 'yard' is seen as bringing *disorder* into
the fenced and protected place, which has become more than ever a mirror

of the world of men after the 'Fall'. 'It semede as that hevene sholde falle'. Yes, but – of course – the disaster, catastrophic as it may seem, is not final or beyond repair: which is a feature that it has in common with most of the blows that a compensating 'fate' seems to aim at men with the effect of undermining their excessive confidence in themselves and in their works. Even after the effect of such human calamities as Jack Straw's rebellion and the reaction against the 'Flemings' in the England of Chaucer's own day, life continues on its course, and it may be that a wise, a balanced human reaction will, without seeking to underestimate the seriousness of what has occurred, take this saving, repairing reality into account.

As though to reinforce this truth the intruding marauder is not allowed, at the last, to have his way. He is led by over-confidence, his own kind of vanity, to release his prey. Chauntecler is resourceful enough to seize the opportunity to make his escape, and the final 'moral' is pointed by each party in his own words:

> 'Nay thanne,' quod he, 'I shrewe us bothe two.
> And first I shrewe myself, bothe blood and bones,
> If thou bigyle me ofter than ones.
> Thou shalt namoore, thurgh thy flaterye,
> Do me to synge and wynke with myn ye;
> For he that wynketh, whan he sholde see,
> Al wilfully, God lat him nevere thee!'
>   'Nay,' quod the fox, 'but God yeve hym meschaunce,
> That is so undiscreet of governaunce
> That jangleth whan he sholde holde his pees.'
>   Lo, swich it is for to be recchelees
> And necligent, and truste on flaterye.   (VII. 3426–37)

The 'moral' is appropriate to the nature of the tale, carefully avoiding any excess of solemnity. Its true weight has lain in the unobtrusive mastery of the telling which has contrived to address itself to the human situation in a variety of ways without forcing the tone to convey its deeper meanings; and it is only against this beautifully controlled set of conclusions that the Nun's Priest, as though to remind us of his profession, allows himself to stress the 'serious' implications of what we have heard:

> But ye that holden this tale a folye,
> As of a fox, or of a cok and hen,
> Taketh the moralite, goode men.
> For seint Paul seith that al that writen is,
> To oure doctrine it is ywrite, ywis;
> Taketh the fruyt, and lat the chaf be stille
>   (VII. 3438–43)

The problem of conveying a necessary moral without expressing a finally inappropriate condescension, or – we might add – making oneself simply ridiculous, is one which has been considered from a variety of standpoints in the course of the tales. We have seen men and women of varying degrees of goodness tell tales which have failed to carry their audience with them; and we have seen at least one self-confessed rogue preach, for ends of gain, a 'moral' sermon which outdoes them in power and effectiveness. Now, as few tales remain to be told, and before the moment comes to put an end to tale-telling, a quiet, effective voice makes its contribution: a contribution based in no small part on unassertive attention to what has been heard on the road, attached to no very definable or individualized personality (though answering at the same time to the sense of a very definite presence, which may even be in some respects the poet's own) and yet offering what is at once a consummately told tale and a moral 'lesson' uniquely adapted to a distinctively human dimension. For, as the teller gently points out, the tale, like the pilgrimage, has a moral end, and it is right that this should be declared as we approach the goal. It has, in fact, touched in the finest spirit of Chaucerian comedy on more aspects of the complete design than perhaps any other single tale, and in the spirit which has governed the telling it is close to the heart of the whole undertaking in its humane, entirely unsolemn seriousness:

> Now, goode God, if that it be thy wille,
> As seith my lord, so make us alle goode men,
> And brynge us to his heighe blisse! Amen.   (VII. 3444–6)

It would be wrong to see in this nothing more than the conventional rounding-off of a priest's story. The 'heighe blisse' to which 'alle goode men' aspire is the end of the whole pilgrimage enterprise, and the tone in which it is evoked is that of the author who will, without seeking to evade his responsibility, append his 'retraction' to the Parson's concluding sermon. It is less 'seriously' expressed, indeed, as befits the different purpose and nature of the tale, but it is not less true to the general pilgrimage conception. It is perhaps Chaucer's supreme gift to be 'moral' without forcing his purpose, to let his final intentions emerge naturally from the free, unhampered pattern of his plan. Tale-telling is, in the long run, its own justification, most effective when unhampered by any attachment of an explicit or hortatory 'moral'; but the 'morality' *is* there, firmly if undidactically asserted, quite free of any aggressive design or compelling intention, simply the natural and spontaneous development that has made *The Canterbury Tales* the unique comic achievement, at once fully human and deeply civilized and civilizing, that they are.

NOTES

I The 'Frame' of the Tales

1. The note in F. N. Robinson's edition (to which readers are referred, p. 651) indicates possible sources in Guido delle Colonne's *Historia Troiana*, Boccaccio's *Amato, Filocolo*, and *Teseida*; Petrarch's Sonnet IX: Boethius, *De Consolatione Philosophiae*; Virgil's *Georgics*; and the *Pervigilium Veneris*. The number and variety of these possible references indicates that Chaucer was drawing upon images which were a common possession, available for any literary enterprise in his age.

2. Ls. 790–5.

3. The assumption of a *one-way* journey as Chaucer's final intention has been questioned, most notably by Charles A. Owen, Jr., who, in a number of papers and most recently in his *Pilgrimage and Story-Telling in the Canterbury Tales* argues persuasively in favour of a return to the Tabard with the supper proposed by the Host to conclude the whole work. The argument seems to rest on a degree of conjecture which makes it finally incapable of either rejection or acceptance. I prefer, on balance, to believe that Chaucer ended by following normal medieval practice in thinking of a pilgrimage as essentially a one-way journey: but I would add that Owen's thesis, which sees in the *Tales* an opposition between 'earnest' and 'game', with 'game' finally coming out on top, is deeply suggestive and not necessarily at variance with what is here proposed.

4. Robinson, in his introduction to the *Tales*, tells us (p. 16) that in calling his sermon 'a merry tale' the Parson 'was only having his little joke'. This is no doubt true, but it is reasonable to think that the 'joke' was also Chaucer's and that the Parson himself was, however respectfully, the object of it. It is also relevant, perhaps, that the purpose of the sermon was to point the way which led to the fulfilment of the pilgrimage and therefore to true, spiritual 'merriment'.

5. An 'atonement' is, literally, an 'at-onement', a bringing into unity of what was originally separate. For a use of the word in this 'literal' sense see *As You Like It*, V. iv. 113–15.

6. Compare, for example, I. 725–46: I. 3167–86: IX. 207–10.

7. It seems possible that, by calling his sermon in prose a 'merry tale' and so echoing the adjective which many of the pilgrims will use to express their sense of the fictions offered to them, the Parson is deliberately challenging, in the name of his own conception of 'truth', the 'old man' in his audience

    and the entire view of tale-telling which they, and most of us as readers,
    are likely to hold.

8. For a consideration of the Pardoner's sermon see pp. 178–89 below.

9. See X. 1–5.

10. A similar double time-scheme can be found in *Troilus and Criseyde*, where it
has been suggested that the events of the story may cover a span of as long
as three years, but where the poetry indicates a passage from the
spring-time birth of the year in Book I to the death of winter in the final
stages.

11. *Troilus and Criseyde*, V. 1786–1869.

II   The General Prologue

1. It is true that reference is made from time to time to places in the vicinity
of the pilgrimage route, or actually passed by the company in the course of
their journey. They are not, however, sufficiently frequent or systematic to
alter the general impression.

2. See pp. 11–14 above.

3. On the structure of the General Prologue and on its place in Chaucer's plan
for his work a most suggestive study is that of Ralph Baldwin in *The Unity
of the Canterbury Tales*. Some of Baldwin's points are cogently challenged, or
modified, by R. M. Jordan in *Chaucer and the Shape of Creation*.

4. We are being asked to react to this portrait in much the same way as Dante
when he requires us to respond to his narrative about Francesca in *Inferno*
V: we are both to identify with the pity which he, as narrator involved in
the journey, feels for her, and yet also to reserve the judgement which the
reality of the situation imposes.

5. *Roman de la Rose*, 13385–6, 13408–32. It is interesting to note that the lines
are given in the French poem to the character named La Vieille, and
answer there to the stratagems used by a woman to attract and hold her
lover. The origin of the lines, as used by Jean de Meun, is Ovid's *Ars
Amatoria*, III. 755–6. For the 'romance' elements in the description of the
Prioress see Muriel Bowden's *Commentary on the General Prologue*,
pp. 93–7.

6. The word 'counterfeit' occurs in *The Canterbury Tales* frequently enough,
and in contexts of sufficient significance, to suggest Chaucer's very
particular concern with the difference between what men and women are
and the appearance they choose to present to the world. For an example,
compare the Pardoner's words at VI. 447.

7. On this aspect of the monastic rule see the material brought together by
Bowden *op. cit.*, p. 98.

8. Virgil, *Eclogue X*, 69. The phrase occurs frequently in medieval writing,
where the meaning fluctuates between the secular and the sacred.

9. See *Roman de la Rose*, 21327, and D. W. Robertson's *Preface to Chaucer*,
p. 246.

10. St. Augustine, *De Doctrine Christiana*, III. 15. 23. The passage is given by Huppé and Robertson in *Fruyt and Chaf*, p. 9.
11. For Aquinas, 'matter is the principle of individuation'. Baldwin (*op. cit.*) quotes interestingly from the French neo-Thomist philosopher Jacques Maritain's *Three Reformers*: 'In so far as we are individuals we are only a fragment of matter, a part of the universe, distinct, no doubt, but a part, a point of that immense network of forces and influences, vegetative and animal, ethnic, atavistic, hereditary, economic, and historic, to whose laws we are subject. As individuals we are subject to the stars. As persons we are liberated, we rule them'.
12. For the description of the 'olde vekke', see the 'Chaucerian' *Romaunt of the Rose*, 4286–4300, and for her confession, *Roman de la Rose*, 14441–14547.
13. On the part played respectively in the Wife's character by Venus and Mars, see W. C. Curry's *Chaucer and the Medieval Sciences*, pp. 94–110. On the larger question of the pagan gods, and their survival in a Christian order, see Jean Seznec, *Survival of the Pagan Gods*.
14. *Troilus and Criseyde*, III. 694–5.
15. We are reminded of the presence of the bag-pipe in many paintings by Hieronymus Bosch.
16. VI. 323.
17. See p. 164 below.
18. More especially in the confrontation with the Host that concludes *The Pardoner's Tale*. See pp. 191–2.
19. *Convivio*, II. i. 3.
20. See Aquinas, *Summa Theologica*, Q. 1, Art. 9: 'Whether Holy Scripture should use metaphors'.
21. Dante, *Paradiso*, XIX, 45.
22. Notably in the prologue to *The Miller's Tale* and, later, in *The Manciple's Tale*.
23. See pp. 17–18 above.
24. VI. 946–55.
25. *Timaeus*, 29B: Boethius, iii, pr. 12.
26. The obvious sexual implication is also relevant here.

III   The Knight's Tale

1. The existence of an early version of Boccaccio's poem by Chaucer is confirmed by a reference in the Prologue of *The Legend of Good Women* (G. 408) to 'the love of Palamon and Arcite'.
2. This view of Theseus has behind it a long tradition in literature. That it survived long after Chaucer's time will be evident if we consider the reappearance of some of the same attributes in Shakespeare's Theseus in *A Midsummer Night's Dream*.
3. See I. 56–66.
4. Compare Dante, *Paradiso*, XXIX, 13–18.

5. Augustine, *City of God*, XI. 28.
6. Compare the use of the adjective, with a similar sense of beauty and remoteness, to describe Antigone as she sings her nostalgic song in celebration of 'romantic' love in *Troilus and Criseyde*, II. 824.
7. The comparison derives ultimately from Boethius, III. Pr. ii, 82–9.
8. See *The Wife of Bath's Prologue*, III. 246.
9. See I. 1895–1901.
10. On the transformation of the pagan gods in the Christian world, and on their relationship to astrological 'science', see Seznec, *op. cit.*
11. I. 1940.
12. F. N. Robinson, in the notes to his edition, suggests that Chaucer was drawing at this point, and in the description of Mars, upon some such theological treatise as that of Albricius Philosophus, *De Deorum Imaginibus*.
13. I am thinking, of course, of the three pictures of the battle of San Romano, painted for Cosimo de' Medici between 1456 and 1460, and now divided between the National Gallery of London, the Louvre, and the Uffizi in Florence.
14. On this, as on many points connected with Chaucer's versification, there are useful comments in Ian Robinson's *Chaucer's Prosody*.
15. On the development of the concept of the 'Chain of Being' from classical antiquity through the Middle Ages and the Renaissance, see E. O. Lovejoy's study, *The Great Chain of Being*.
16. Compare Alanus de Insulis, who says of God in his *De Planctu Naturae*, quoted by J. A. W. Bennett in a book on *The Parliament of Fowls*, that 'he wedded all things to himself in the lawful wedlock of proportion'.

IV   The Miller's Tale and The Reeve's Tale

1. The element of blasphemy in these oaths announces a theme which will be developed, to different and indeed opposed effect, in the sermons delivered by the Pardoner and the Parson.
2. Notably by the Pardoner: see VI. 439–453.
3. It is interesting to note that a number of the themes here put forward are given further expression, towards the end of the pilgrimage, in *The Manciple's Tale*.
4. I. 3454.
5. This is a belief which is shared by the 'god' Apollo in *The Manciple's Tale*; and, 'god' though he is, the conclusion to which it leads him is not very unlike that which overtakes the human carpenter in *The Miller's Tale*. For Apollo's attitude to his 'wife', see IX. 139–54.
6. For the Wife of Bath, see pp. 91–121 below; and for the Merchant, pp. 135–58
7. The presence in *The Miller's Tale* of verbal parallels linking it with *The Knight's Tale* has often been observed. Compare, for example, the statement that Nicholas the clerk lived in the carpenter's house 'Allone, withouten

any compaignye' (I. 3204) with the same phrase used of Arcite at the moment of his death (I. 2779).

8. See pp. 12–13 above.

9. The 'pere-jonette' is the tree that bears the early-ripe pear. According to Robinson's note 'jonette' is likely to be connected with 'Jean' because the fruit ripens about St. John's Day: which is June 24th, and therefore close to Midsummer Day and the occasion for many festivals and ceremonies preserved in folklore from very ancient times.

10. See III. 320.

11. See I. 2777.

12. I. 1838.

13. We are reminded, in quite another key, of the intrusion of the 'Death' at the opening of the Pardoner's sermon on the three 'rioters'. See VI. 661–84.

14. See, for example, the two exemplary stories woven into The Nun's Priest's Tale, VII. 2984–3103.

15. I. 3163–6, discussed on p. 65 above.

16. I. 550–1.

17. For a witty development of this idea see E. Talbot Donaldson's essay, Medieval Poetry and Medieval Sin, reprinted in Speaking of Chaucer, pp. 165–74.

18. I. 587–622.

19. T. S. Eliot, Little Gidding, II.

20. It may be worth noting that the Friar will in due course express his animosity against his rival, the Summoner, in very similar terms. See III. 1353–4.

21. See IV. 1–1212, and pp. 122–34 below.

22. See I. 3305–6.

23. I. 3815.

V   The Wife of Bath: Prologue and Tale

1. The tale has obvious connections with The Clerk's Tale and with the prose tale of Melibeus. It has been argued that the latter was originally intended for the Man of Law.

2. Strictly speaking, the longest 'series' of tales, as presented in its presumably final state, is that provided by Fragment I, from the General Prologue to The Cook's Prologue and Tale. The tales which derive their original impulse from the Wife of Bath's contribution are more varied, more loosely structured (at least in their present state), and less obviously cohesive in their effect; but they do seem to proceed from a unifying preoccupation which touches the pilgrimage at more points, and more extensively, than any other.

3. Most notably by G. L. Kittredge, as long ago as 1915. Kittredge's conclusions have been variously controverted, with the result of adding to our understanding of the tale, but they remain an essential point of

departure for discussion of it. More generally, the case for a 'dramatic' reading of the tales has been made persuasively by R. M. Lumiansky in *The Art of the Canterbury Tales*.

4. For a statement of the view that there is in fact, strictly speaking, no such thing as a 'marriage group' of tales, see H. B. Hinckley, *The Debate on Marriage in The Canterbury Tales*.

5. D. W. Robertson, for example, sees the tale, not as resolving the 'marriage theme', but as an 'exposure of the kind of "headless marriage" dear to Epicurean middle-class ideals' (*Preface to Chaucer*, p. 376).

6. III. 1109–1206.

7. The position can be illustrated, and related to medieval thought on the concept of 'musical' harmony as a reflection of universal order, by the following passage from St. Augustine's *De Vera Religione*: 'The harmony of the parts with the whole is called *convenientia*, and is said to involve two principles: the similarity of equal parts and the gradation of unequal parts.' See D. W. Robertson, *A Preface to Chaucer*, p. 120. As Robertson observes, 'The study of music was the study of those aesthetic principles which govern the universe and the activities of man.'

8. For this, and other aspects of *The Pardoner's Tale*, see pp. 161–94 below.

9. See pp. 195–209 below.

10. For the argument which follows I am indebted to R. A. Pratt's article on *The Development of the Wife of Bath*, printed in *Studies in Medieval Literature*, ed. M. Leach. Both Pratt and Charles A. Owen, Jr., in his essay on *The Development of The Canterbury Tales* (*Journal of English and Germanic Philology*, Vol. LVII [1958]), argue that the opening of the Wife's prologue was originally connected to the Man of Law's Epilogue, so that II. 1185–90 was directly followed by III. 1 and what follows, the whole intended to introduce what is now *The Shipman's Tale*.

11. It is reasonable to suppose that much of the material used by the Wife in support of her position derives from Jean de Meun's continuation of the *Roman de la Rose*, in which similar arguments play a prominent part.

12. See *John*, IV. 17–18.

13. A. Huppé, *A Reading of the Canterbury Tales*, p. 116.

14. See, especially, *Roman de la Rose*, 19505–19700.

15. For the 'philosophy of creation' and Jean's defence of the sexual functions, see T. M. Gunn, *The Mirror of Love*, and J. A. W. Bennett's study of *The Parliament of Fowls*. For the 'Scale of Being', and its relation to these ideas, Lovejoy's *Great Chain of Being* can also be consulted.

16. On the Pardoner's condition as a 'eunuch' see pp. 162–4 below.

17. VI. 946–55.

18. III. 9–11.

19. *Mark*, X. 38–9: *John*, XVIII. 11.

20. III. 14–20.

21. *John*, IV. 16–18.

22. I. 461.

23. They are, to a large extent, the 'sins' which we have seen exemplified in the person of the Reeve and in the tale which he tells. See p. 83 above.

24. For *The Merchant's Tale*, see pp. 135–58 below.

25. It is worth remembering that the Host too suffers, by his own account, from his wife's dominating attitudes. See p. 211.

26. The virtue of 'patience' in relation to marriage is considered in the tale of *Melibeus*, and plays an essential part in the Clerk's story of Griselda.

27. It may be worth remembering that the Clerk, in words which are evidently intended as a challenge to the Wife at the end of his tale, stresses ironically his advice to his 'archewyves' to be 'strong' and stubborn. See IV. 1195–1200 and pp. 135–6 below.

28. *Luke*, IX. 60.

29. We may recall that Theseus, the *pagan* hero of *The Knight's Tale*, shared this attitude sufficiently to turn aside from his triumph to help the sorrowing widows of Thebes to fulfil the obligation, which Creon denied them, to provide decent burial for their dead husbands. See p. 38 above.

30. IV. 1142–4: 1163–9.

31. I. 476.

32. On the 'two Venuses' Bernardus Silvestris writes as follows: 'We say that the legitimate Venus is *mundana musica*, that is, the equal proportion of worldly things, which some call 'Astraea' and others 'natural justice'. For she is in the elements, in the stars, in animate things. But the shameful Venus, the goddess of sensuality, we call concupiscence of the flesh, which is the mother of all fornication'. (Quoted by J. A. W. Bennett in *The Parliament of Fowls*.

33. See III. 1735–9.

34. By R. A. Pratt in his study, already referred to, on *The Development of the Wife of Bath*.

35. Ovid, *Metamorphoses*, XI. 174 ff. The story is there told of Midas' 'butler', not of his wife.

36. Ls. 1125 ff. refer to *Purgatorio*, VII. 121 ff., but the main argument is more closely related to *Convivio*, IV, and especially to chapters 3, 10. Parallels have also been found with the *Roman de la Rose*.

37. It is interesting to note that this same theme – that of the common tendency of men to confuse the 'word', or the name of a thing, with its effective reality – is taken up from a slightly different point of view in *The Manciple's Tale*. See IX. 209–10.

VI The Clerk's Tale

1. The argument in favour of this theory was first put forward by G. L. Kittredge in his study already referred to.

2. Charles Muscatine remarks, interestingly, that 'I am not the first whom the tale reminds of Wordsworth'.

3. It is the last tale told on the tenth day of the *Decameron*. That Boccaccio, who is not usually thought of as the author of this kind of tale, should have chosen it to wind up his collection, tells us something both about the

nature of the story and about its acceptance by a fourteenth-century audience.

4. Petrarch's *De Obedientia ac Fide Uxorie Mytologia* is a Latin version of Boccaccio's tale.

5. See I. 725–46, and pp. 32–4 above.

6. See pp. 17–18 above.

7. For the recognition in Chaucer's work of this kind of social reality, compare the description of the widow's yard at the opening of *The Nun's Priest's Tale*. See VII. 2821–46, and pp. 218–20 below.

8. Dante conveys this aspect of man's understanding of the Divine reality when he says that God is, necessarily and as it were by definition, 'in infinite excess' of any conception of him that men may have. See *Paradiso*, XIX. 45.

9. It is interesting to compare Chaucer's use of this same phrase in the early part of *The Parliament of Fowls*. See ls. 47 and 75.

10. See p. 124 above.

11. *Job*, I. 21.

12. III. 688–9.

13. III. 706.

14. *James*, I. 13.

VII   The Merchant's Tale

1. The Clerk's words, just spoken, have been

> Be ay of chiere, as light as leef on lynde,
> And lat hym care, and wepe, and wrynge, and waille.   (IV. 1211–12)

Both this and the Merchant's phrase could be seen in relation to the Wife of Bath's opening declaration in her prologue.

2. It has been pointed out that the prologue to *The Merchant's Tale* figures in only 23 of the extant Mss. No one, however, has seriously questioned that Chaucer wrote it, and it seems reasonable to suppose that it answers to his final intention in incorporating the tale into his plan.

3. See p. 83 above.

4. See p. 95 above.

5. I. 1–18. See pp. 11–14 above.

6. IV. 1284.

7. III. 671.

8. IV. 1265.

9. See p. 153 below. A stimulating discussion of this passage, and of other aspects of the tale, is offered by E. Talbot Donaldson in his study *The Effect of the Merchant's Tale*, reprinted in *Speaking of Chaucer*, pp. 30–45.

10. IV. 1341.

11. Several writers – notably T. W. Craik in *The Comic Tales of Chaucer* and

B. H. Bronson in his *Afterthoughts on the Merchant's Tale* – have argued with some force that the prevailing effect of the tale upon medieval readers would be comic in just such a direct and primary sense; but Donaldson's argument, in the study quoted above, seems to me to bring out convincingly the limitations of this point of view in relation to what the tale actually offers.

12. An outstanding example is that of the Pardoner's words concerning repentance and forgiveness at the end of his sermon. See VI. 915–18.
13. See, more particularly, IV. 1356–61.
14. *Ephesians*, V. 25: 29–31.
15. See IV. 2117.
16. It is interesting to note that in this line the Merchant echoes the Wife of Bath, in her thoughts on 'virginity'. See III. 112.
17. See p. 157 below.
18. It is worth noting that one of these names – Placebo – recurs, also in connection with advice complaisantly given, in *The Tale of Melibeus*.
19. Compare Chauntecler's neglect of his 'wife's' advice concerning dreams at VII. 2970–77.
20. *The Franklin's Tale*, which presumably follows closely on the Merchant's, deals extensively with the part played by 'illusion', in the form of 'magic' appearances, in human life. See V. 1137–61 and 1189–1204.
21. For a similar use of this theme of love's 'blindness', it may be interesting to compare the conversation between Valentine and Speed in *Two Gentlemen of Verona*, II. i. 58–66.
22. Compare the similar description of Criseyde in *Troilus and Criseyde*, III. 1247–53.
23. This may refer either to matrimony or to the taking of communion by the newly wedded pair. From the point of view of the tale, either alternative will serve.
24. E. Talbot Donaldson (*op. cit.*) has written particularly well in discussing this passage.
25. It is ascribed to May frequently in the tale (see, for example, ls. 1782, 1871, 1882, 1896, and 1932), and always with the effect of undercutting the springtime implications of her name.
26. Compare the use of the same word in IV. 1289.
27. See pp. 228 below.
28. It is interesting to find the Parson making use of this phrase to a contrary purpose in the section of his sermon devoted to Lechery (*Luxuria*): 'God woot, a man may sleen hymself with is owene knyf' (X. 859).
29. I. 100.
30. See, more particularly, the part of *The Squire's Tale* devoted to the story, told to Canacee, of the falcon and her betrayal by the false 'tercelet' (V. 409–650).
31. IV. 1955.
32. It may not be altogether fanciful to see in this a comment on the *real* obligations which marriage imposes upon women as indicated in *The Man of Law's Tale*, II. 708–14.

33. See *The Nun's Priest's Tale*, VII. 3236ff.
34. IV. 1429–30.
35. IV. 2117.
36. It would seem that Chaucer associated the transports of romantic love with the loss by the lover of his 'shirt'. See *Troilus and Criseyde*, III. 1099.
37. Compare *The Knight's Tale*, I. 1761, for one of several uses by Chaucer of this favourite phrase.
38. Compare Shakespeare, *Sonnet 70*:

> For canker vice the sweetest buds doth love,
> And thou present'st a pure unstained prime:

one of several examples of his use of this image.
39. We remember Januarius' reference to 'wax' in relation to the moulding of human character earlier in the tale.
40. See the discussion between Melibeus and his wife Prudence (VII. 1054–1114), where Solomon and *Jhesus Syriak* are also quoted as authorities and where a number of themes developed in the course of *The Merchant's Tale* are discussed.
41. Compare III. 965–8.
42. III. 35 ff.
43. References to property in relation to the marriage occur frequently in the course of the tale. Compare IV. 1696–8, among others.
44. IV. 2328–37.

VIII The Pardoner: Introduction, Prologue, Tale, and Epilogue

1. I. 688–91.
2. For a consideration of the Pardoner's 'eunuchry', see R. P. Miller, *Chaucer's Pardoner, the Scriptural Eunuch, and The Pardoner's Tale*, reprinted in *Twentieth Century Interpretations of the Pardoner's Tale*. I have also found helpful Janet Adelman's study, *'That we may heere some wit'* from the same collection.
3. *John*, IV, 7–19. See p. 96 above.
4. *Matthew*, XIX. 12.
5. The contrast between the life of the spirit and that of the flesh – between the 'old man' and the 'new man' – is one which runs through the writings ascribed to St. Paul in the New Testament. For an eloquent statement of the contrast see *Ephesians*, IV. 17–32.
6. See Note 15 on p. 239 above.
7. VI. 1–286.
8. Livy, *History of Rome*, Book III.
9. *Roman de la Rose*, 5589 ff.
10. VI. 325.
11. VI. 11–28.

12. *Romaunt of the Rose*, 6135–6218.

13. I. 702.

14. We are reminded of *The Merchant's Tale*, where the victim of May's deception is induced to deny the evidence of his own eyes in the interest of continuing to live in a comfortable state of illusion.

15. See the Epilogue of *The Man of Law's Tale*, II. 1166–1183.

16. I. 507–14.

17. X. 31.

18. IX. 46–55.

19. See I. 725–42 and p. 32 above.

20. See X. 1081–92, and pp. 17–18 above.

21. Typical in their different ways, are *The Merchant's Tale*, with its digression from IV. 1267 to 1392 (See pp. 138–43 above) and *The Canon's Yeoman's Tale*, with its division into two separate parts (See pp. 200–9 below.)

22. For a convenient summary of what is known on this subject, see F. N. Robinson's Introductory Note to the Prologue and Tale, p. 728. Chaucer seems to have been influenced, as we have indicated, by the self-confession of *Faux-Semblant* in the *Roman de la Rose*.

23. I. 684.

24. The passage from St. Paul (*Philippians*, III. 18–19) is also used by the Parson in his section on Gluttony, X. 819.

25. I. 342–54.

26. *Luke*, XII. 33.

27. I. 1260–5.

28. It has been suggested that the Old Man represents 'the Old Adam', the unregenerate man, who longs in vain for the release which is not available to him in the absence of grace.

29. See J. M. Steadman, *Old Age and 'Contemptus Mundi' in the Pardoner's Tale* (*Medium Aevum*, 33 (1964), pp. 121–30). The resemblance was previously noted by G. L. Kittredge.

30. See, for example, X. 210–17.

31. VI. 680–4. See p. 182 above.

32. See note 26 above.

33. See VI. 697–704 and p. 184 above.

34. VI. 334 and p. 169 above.

35. The first notable proponent of this view was G. L. Kittredge in his discussion of *The Pardoner's Tale* in *Chaucer and his Poetry* (1915), pp. 211–18.

IX   The Canon's Yeoman's Tale

1. *Inferno*, V, 39.

2. For other uses of the word 'privy' in the *Tales*, with similar implications of unnatural secrecy and perversity, see I. 3164 I. 3454, IV. 1879, IV. 2105, and IV. 2121.

3. VI. 439–53.

4. See p. 94 above.
5. V. 1479.
6. See Donald R. Howard, *The Idea of the Canterbury Tales*, p. 297. Professor Howard makes reference to Bruce A. Rosenberg's study, *Swindling Alchemist* (*Centennial Review* 6 [1962]), pp. 566–80. *The Canon's Yeoman's Tale* has also been seen as standing in significant opposition to that told by the Second Nun.
7. Dante's account of Ulysses' last adventure (*Inferno*, XXVI) raises similar questions in a very different spirit.
8. V. 1261–69.
9. I. 3186.
10. Robert W. Hanning, in an essay on *The themes of Art and Life in Chaucer's Poetry*, suggests an analogy between the activities of the alchemists ('literature's first depiction of the laboratory of the mad scientist') and Chaucer's own art: 'Given inspired poetry, human failure and technological jargon become both fascinating and beautiful. *The Canon's Yeoman's Tale* is a piece of self-congratulatory bravura writing that forces us to acquiesce in the poet's self-conscious assessment of its effect: "but it was joye for to seen hym swete!" '. I find myself unable to go all the way with this argument, but it would be wrong to dismiss it as irrelevant to the effect which Chaucer intended for his tale.

X   The Nun's Priest's Tale

1. Something like this, presumably, is what Matthew Arnold had in mind when he wrote of Chaucer's lack of 'high seriousness' as excluding him from the highest order of achievement in poetry. In any important sense, it is hard to see why Chaucer is less 'serious' than Milton or Wordsworth.
2. IV. 2427–40.
3. It is worth noting that the disreputable monk of *The Shipman's Tale* is referred to, on more than one occasion, as 'Daun John' (VII. 43, 68, 158 *et al.*). The fact is no doubt at the back of the pilgrim Monk's mind when he comes to tell his tale, and contributes to his self-conscious refusal to tell the kind of story which his audience evidently expects of him. Since there are also connections between *The Monk's Tale* and that told by the Nun's Priest, it is interesting that the Host, in calling upon the latter for his contribution to the pilgrimage, refers to him as 'sir John' (VII. 2810) and, in the Epilogue, offers a description of him (VII. 3447–60) which could be read as applying to the Monk himself.
4. In the Epilogue to *The Man of Law's Tale*. See II. 1173–7.
5. VII. 1965–8.
6. VII. 1984–90.
7. VII. 3447–60.
8. It has been suggested, with some measure of plausibility, that a sense of

this status also colours his ambivalent remarks on women, their character and weaknesses, in the course of the tale.

9. Compare, particularly, the picture of the Franklin and his household in the General Prologue, I. 331–54.

10. The irony, of course, points very typically in more than one direction. If the widow is, from one point of view, to be considered fortunate in having no need for the tempting refinements of sophisticated society, it is equally true that her 'freedom' in this respect springs from her poverty and that what she does not desire is what she cannot have.

11. The fox is at one point explicitly connected with Judas Iscariot and the betrayal of the Saviour (VII. 3227). Some writers have seen a parallel running through the tale between Chauntecler and Christ himself; but the support alleged for this idea seems too thin to carry much conviction.

12. Notably in the last of his 'examples', devoted to 'Cresus, kyng of Lyde' (VII. 2727–66).

13. *Troilus and Criseyde*, IV. 958–1078.

14. VI. 885. See p. 188 above.

15. VII. 3036.

16. There is a possible reference here to the moral of *The Prioress' Tale*. See VII. 576.

17. Scipio Africanus' dream, as mediated by Macrobius' commentary on Cicero, had already played a part in Chaucer's earlier *Parliament of Fowls*. See ls. 29–84 of that poem.

18. See III. 201–23.

19. *Paradise Lost*, IV. 299.

20. I write 'man' because we are speaking here of Chauntecler's male predicament; but, of course, what is said of 'man' applies equally, as a statement of general truth, to 'woman'.

21. VII. 3101.

22. There is, of course, an element of satire at the expense of academic philosophers and theologians in *Troilus and Criseyde*, more particularly in Troilus' over-long, wordy and confused reflections. These, however, are the reflection of Troilus' desire to see himself as a victim of 'Fate' and so to absolve himself from responsibility for his own tragedy. This does not alter the fact that the theme, however inadequately he and others may reflect it, is in itself serious and that it constitutes an integral part of the poem to which it belongs.

BIBLIOGRAPHY

The following bibliography has no claim to completeness. It is a list of books which I have found useful for formulating my own ideas, and includes the works mentioned in the notes to the text.

I TEXT

GEOFFREY CHAUCER, *Works* ed. F. N. Robinson, 2nd. edition (Boston, 1957), (Oxford, 1974)

II. CRITICAL STUDIES

RALPH BALDWIN, *The Unity of the Canterbury Tales* (Copenhagen, 1955)

J. A. W. BENNETT, *The Parliament of Fowls* (Oxford, 1957) *Chaucer's Book of Fame* (Oxford, 1968)

MURIEL BOWDEN, *A Commentary on the General Prologue of the Canterbury Tales* (New York, 1948), (London, 1973)

B. H. BRONSON, *In Search of Chaucer* (Toronto, 1960)

W. CLEMEN, *Chaucer's Early Poetry* (London, 1963)

N. COGHILL, *The Poet Chaucer* (London, 1947)

T. W. CRAIK, *The Comic Tales of Chaucer* (London, 1964)

W. C. CURRY, *Chaucer and the Medieval Sciences* (London, 1960)

G. DEMPSTER, *Dramatic Irony in Chaucer* (Stanford, 1932)

E. TALBOT DONALDSON, *Speaking of Chaucer* (London, 1970)

T. M. F. GUNN, *The Mirror of Love: A Reinterpretation of the 'Romance of the Rose'* (Lubbock, Texas, 1952)

DONALD R. HOWARD, *The Idea of the Canterbury Tales* (London, 1976)

A. HUPPÉ, *A Reading of the Canterbury Tales* (New York, 1964)

A. HUPPÉ AND D. W. ROBERTSON, JR., *Fruyt and Chaf: Studies in Chaucer's Allegories* (Princeton, 1963)

R. M. JORDAN, *Chaucer and the Shape of Creation* (Cambridge, Mass. 1967)

P. M. KEAN, *Chaucer: Love Vision and Debate* (London, 1972) *Chaucer: The Art of Narrative* (London, 1972)

G. L. KITTREDGE, *Chaucer and his Poetry* (Cambridge, Mass., 1915)

JOHN LAWLOR, *Chaucer* (London, 1968)

C. S. LEWIS, *The Allegory of Love* (Oxford, 1936) *The Discarded Image* (Cambridge, 1964)

E. O. LOVEJOY, *The Great Chain of Being* (Cambridge, Mass., 1953)

G. L. LOWES, *Geoffrey Chaucer* (Boston, 1934)

R. M. LUMIANSKY, *Of Sondry Folk: The Dramatic Principle in the Art of the Canterbury Tales* (Austin, Texas, 1955)

K. MALONE, *Chapters on Chaucer* (Baltimore, 1951), (London, 1979)

C. MUSCATINE, *Chaucer and the French Tradition* (Berkeley, 1957)

C. A. OWEN, JR., *Pilgrimage and Story-Telling in the Canterbury Tales* (Oklahoma, 1977)

G. R. OWST, *Literature and Pulpit in Medieval England* (Oxford, 1962)

R. O. PAYNE, *The Key of Remembrance* (New Haven, 1963)

D. W. ROBERTSON, JR., *Preface to Chaucer* (Princeton, 1962)

IAN ROBINSON, *Chaucer and the English Tradition* (Cambridge, 1972)

P. G. RUGGIERS, *The Art of the Canterbury Tales* (Madison, 1965)

JEAN SEZNEC, *The Survival of the Pagan Gods* (New York, 1953)

J. SPEIRS, *Chaucer the Maker* (London, 1962)

J. S. T. TATLOCK, *The Mind and Art of Chaucer* (Syracuse, N.Y., 1950)

III   ESSAYS ON SPECIFIC ASPECTS OF THE TALES

JANET ADELMAN, 'That we may heere som wit' (Essay published in *Twentieth Century Interpretations of the Pardoner's Tale*, Englewood Cliffs, N.J, 1973)

ERICH AUERBACH, 'Figura' (Essay reprinted in *Scenes from the Drama of European Literature*, New York, 1959)

H. B. HINCKLEY, The Debate on Marriage in the Canterbury Tales (Reprinted in E. Wagenknecht's *Chaucer: Modern Essays in Criticism*, Oxford, 1959)

R. P. MILLER, Chaucer's Pardoner, the Scriptural Eunuch, and the Pardoner's Tale (*Speculum*, XXX. 1955)

CHARLES A. OWEN, JR., The development of the Canterbury Tales (*Journal of English and Germanic Philology*, LVII, 1958)

J. M. STEADMAN, Old Age and 'Contemptus Mundi' in the Pardoner's Tale (*Medium Aevum*, 33, 1964)

R. A. PRATT, The Development of the Wife of Bath (Essay published in *Studies in Medieval Literature*, ed. J. M. Leach, Philadelphia, 1961)

IV   COLLECTIONS OF INDIVIDUAL STUDIES

R. J. SHOEK AND J. TAYLOR, ed. *Chaucer Criticism*. 2 vols. (Notre Dame, 1960–61)

E. WAGENKNECHT, ed. *Chaucer: Modern Essays in Criticism* (Oxford, 1959)